RICHARD RUMELT is one of the world's most influential thinkers on strategy and management. *The Economist* profiled him as one of twenty-five living persons who have had the most influence on management concepts and corporate practice. *McKinsey Quarterly* described him as "strategy's strategist", and "a giant in the field of strategy". Rumelt has always challenged dominant thinking: in 1972, he was the first person to uncover a statistical link between corporate strategy and profitability. He received his doctoral degree from Harvard Business School and holds the Harry and Elsa Kunin Chair at the UCLA Anderson School of Management. He is a consultant to small firms such as the Samuel Goldwyn Company and giants such as Shell International, as well as to organisations in the educational and not-for-profit worlds. *Good Strategy/Bad Strategy* was shortlisted for the *FT* & Goldman Sachs Business Book Award 2011.

RICHARD RUMELT

GOOD STRATEGY BAD STRATEGY

The difference and why it matters

P

PROFILE BOOKS

This edition published in 2017

First published in Great Britain in 2011 by
PROFILE BOOKS LTD
3 Holford Yard
Bevin Way
London WC1X 9HD
www.profilebooks.com

First published in the United States of America in 2011 by
Crown Business, an imprint of the Crown Publishing Group,
a division of Random House, Inc., New York

9 10

Printed and bound in Great Britain by
CPI Group (UK) Ltd, Croydon, CR0 4YY

A CIP catalogue record for this book is available from the British Library.

ISBN 978 1 78125 617 6

eISBN 978 1 84765 746 6

For Ruthjane

CONTENTS

INTRODUCTION OVERWHELMING OBSTACLES 1

PART I GOOD AND BAD STRATEGY 9

CHAPTER 1 GOOD STRATEGY IS UNEXPECTED 11

How Steve Jobs saved Apple • Business 101 is surprising • General Schwarzkopf's strategy in Desert Storm • Why "Plan A" remains a surprise

CHAPTER 2 DISCOVERING POWER 21

David and Goliath is a basic strategy story • Discovering Wal-Mart's secret • Marshall and Roche's strategy for competing with the Soviet Union

CHAPTER 3 BAD STRATEGY 32

Is U.S. national security strategy just slogans? • How to recognize fluff • Why not facing the problem creates bad strategy • Chad Logan's 20/20 plan mistakes goals for strategy • What's wrong with a dog's dinner of objectives? • How blue-sky objectives miss the mark

CHAPTER 4 WHY SO MUCH BAD STRATEGY? 58

Strategy involves choice, and DEC's managers can't choose • The path from charisma to transformational leadership to fill-in-the-blanks template-style strategy • New Thought from Emerson to today and how it makes strategy seem superfluous

CHAPTER 5 THE KERNEL OF GOOD STRATEGY 77

The mixture of argument and action lying behind any good strategy • Diagnosing Starbucks, K–12 schools, the Soviet challenge, and IBM • Guiding policies at Wells Fargo, IBM, and Stephanie's market • The president of the European Business Group hesitates to act • Incoherent action at Ford • Centralization, decentralization, and Roosevelt's strategy in WWII

PART II SOURCES OF POWER 95

CHAPTER 6 USING LEVERAGE 97

Anticipation by Toyota and insurgents in Iraq • How Pierre Wack anticipated the oil crisis and oil prices • Pivot points at 7-Eleven and the Brandenburg Gate • Harold Williams uses concentration to make the Getty a world presence in art

CHAPTER 7 PROXIMATE OBJECTIVES 106

Why Kennedy's goal of landing on the moon was a proximate and strategic objective • Phyllis Buwalda resolves the ambiguity about the surface of the moon • A regional business school generates proximate objectives • A helicopter pilot explains hierarchies of skills • Why what is proximate for one organization is distant for another

CHAPTER 8 CHAIN-LINK SYSTEMS 116

Challenger's O-ring and chain-link systems • Stuck systems at GM and underdeveloped countries • Marco Tinelli explains how to get a chain-link system unstuck • IKEA shows how excellence is the flip side of being stuck

CHAPTER 9 USING DESIGN 124

Hannibal defeats the Roman army in 216 B.C. using anticipation and a coordinated design of action in time and space • How a design-type strategy is like a BMW • Designing the Voyager spacecraft at JPL • The trade-off between resources and tight configuration • How success leads to potent resources that, in turn, induce laxity and decline • Design shows itself as order imposed on chaos—the example of Paccar's heavy-truck business

CHAPTER 10 FOCUS 142

A class struggles to identify Crown Cork & Seal's strategy • Working back from policies to strategy • The particular pattern of policy and segmentation called "focus" • Why the strategy worked

CHAPTER 11 GROWTH 151

The all-out pursuit of size almost sinks Crown • A noxious adviser at Telecom Italia • Healthy growth

CHAPTER 12 USING ADVANTAGE 160

Advantage in Afghanistan and in business • Stewart and Lynda Resnick's serial entrepreneurship • What makes a business "interesting" • The puzzle of the silver machine • Why you cannot get richer by simply owning a competitive advantage • What bricklaying teaches us about deepening advantage • Broadening the Disney brand • The red tide of pomegranate juice • Oil fields, isolating mechanisms, and being a moving target

CHAPTER 13 USING DYNAMICS 178

Capturing the high ground by riding a wave of change • Jean-Bernard Lévy opens my eyes to tectonic shifts • The microprocessor changes everything • Why software is king and the rise of Cisco Systems • How Cisco rode three interlinked waves of change • Guideposts to strategy in transitions • Attractor states and the future of the New York Times

CHAPTER 14 INERTIA AND ENTROPY 202

The smothering effect of obsolete routine at Continental Airlines • Inertia at AT&T and the process of renewal • Inertia by proxy at PSFS and the DSL business • Applying hump charts to reveal entropy at Denton's • Entropy at GM

CHAPTER 15 PUTTING IT TOGETHER 223

Nvidia jumps from nowhere to dominance by riding a wave of change using a design-type strategy • How a game called Quake derailed the expected march of 3-D graphics • Nvidia's first product fails, and it devises a new strategy • How a faster release cycle made a difference • Why a powerful buyer like Dell can sometimes be an advantage • Intel fails twice in 3-D graphics and SGI goes bankrupt

PART III THINKING LIKE A STRATEGIST 239

CHAPTER 16 THE SCIENCE OF STRATEGY 241

Hughes engineers start to guess at strategies • Deduction is enough only if you already know everything worth knowing • Galileo heresy trial triggers the Enlightenment • Hypotheses, anomalies, and Italian espresso bars • Why Americans drank weak coffee • Howard Schultz as a scientist • Learning and vertical integration

CHAPTER 17 USING YOUR HEAD 257

A baffling comment is resolved fifteen years later • Frederick Taylor tells Andrew Carnegie to make a list • Being "strategic" largely means being less myopic than your undeliberative self • TiVo and quick closure • Thinking about thinking • Using mind tools: the kernel, problem-solution, create-destroy, and the panel of experts

CHAPTER 18 KEEPING YOUR HEAD 276

Can one be independent without being eccentric, doubting without being a curmudgeon? • Global Crossing builds a transatlantic cable • Build it for $1.5 and sell it for $8 • The worst industry structure imaginable • Kurt Gödel and stock prices • Why the 2008 financial crisis was almost certain to occur • The parallels among 2008, the Johnstown Flood, the Hindenburg, *the Hurricane Katrina aftermath, and the gulf oil spill • How the inside view and social herding blinded people to the coming financial storm • The common cause of the panics and depressions of 1819, 1837, 1873, 1893, and 2008*

NOTES 299

ACKNOWLEDGMENTS 311

INDEX 313

INTRODUCTION

OVERWHELMING OBSTACLES

In 1805, England had a problem. Napoléon had conquered big chunks of Europe and planned the invasion of England. But to cross the Channel, he needed to wrest control of the sea away from the English. Off the southwest coast of Spain, the French and Spanish combined fleet of thirty-three ships met the smaller British fleet of twenty-seven ships. The well-developed tactics of the day were for the two opposing fleets to each stay in line, firing broadsides at each other. But British admiral Lord Nelson had a strategic insight. He broke the British fleet into two columns and drove them at the Franco-Spanish fleet, hitting their line perpendicularly. The lead British ships took a great risk, but Nelson judged that the less-trained Franco-Spanish gunners would not be able to compensate for the heavy swell that day. At the end of the Battle of Trafalgar, the French and Spanish lost twenty-two ships, two-thirds of their fleet. The British lost none. Nelson was mortally wounded, becoming, in death, Britain's greatest naval hero. Britain's naval dominance was ensured and remained unsurpassed for a century and a half.

Nelson's challenge was that he was outnumbered. His strategy was to risk his lead ships in order to break the coherence of his enemy's fleet. With coherence lost, he judged, the more experienced English captains would come out on top in the ensuing melee. Good strategy almost always looks this simple and obvious and does not take a thick deck of PowerPoint slides to explain. It does not pop out of some "strategic management" tool, matrix, chart, triangle, or fill-in-the-blanks scheme. Instead, a talented leader identifies the one or two critical issues in the situation—the pivot points that can multiply the effectiveness of effort—and then focuses and concentrates action and resources on them.

Despite the roar of voices wanting to equate strategy with ambition, leadership, "vision," planning, or the economic logic of competition, strategy is none of these. The core of strategy work is always the same: discovering the critical factors in a situation and designing a way of coordinating and focusing actions to deal with those factors.

A leader's most important responsibility is identifying the biggest challenges to forward progress and devising a coherent approach to overcoming them. In contexts ranging from corporate direction to national security, strategy matters. Yet we have become so accustomed to strategy as exhortation that we hardly blink an eye when a leader spouts slogans and announces high-sounding goals, calling the mixture a "strategy." Here are four examples of this syndrome.

- The event was a "strategy retreat." The CEO had modeled it on a similar event at British Airways he had attended several years before. About two hundred upper-level managers from around the world gathered in a hotel ballroom where top management presented a vision for the future: to be the most respected and successful company in their field. There was a specially produced motion picture featuring the firm's products and services being used in colorful settings around the world. There was an address by the CEO accompanied by dramatic music to highlight the company's "strategic" goals: global leadership, growth, and high shareholder return. There were breakouts into smaller groups to allow discussion and buy-in. There was a colorful release of balloons. There was everything but strategy. As an invited guest, I was disappointed but not surprised.

- A specialist in bonds, Lehman Brothers had been a pioneer in the new wave of mortgage-backed securities that buoyed Wall Street in the 2002–6 period. By 2006, signs of strain were appearing: U.S. home sales had peaked in mid-2005, and home price appreciation had stopped. A small increase in the Fed's interest rate had triggered an increase in foreclosures. Lehman CEO Richard Fuld's response, formalized in 2006, was a "strategy" of continuing to gain market share by growing faster than the rest of the industry. In the language of Wall Street, Lehman would do this by increasing its "risk appetite." That is, it would take on the deals its competitors were rejecting. Operating with only 3 percent equity, and much of its debt supplied on a very short-term basis, this policy should have been accompanied by clever ways of mitigating the increased risk. A good strategy recognizes the nature of the challenge and offers a way of surmounting it. Simply being ambitious is not a strategy. In 2008, Lehman Brothers ended its 158 years as an investment bank with a crash that sent the global financial system into a tailspin. Here, the consequences of bad strategy were disastrous for Lehman, the United States, and the world.

- In 2003, President George W. Bush authorized the U.S. military to invade and conquer Iraq. The invasion went quickly. Once the army-to-army fighting stopped, administration leaders had expected to oversee a rapid transition to a democratic civil society in Iraq. Instead, as a violent insurgency gathered momentum, individual units of the U.S. military fell back on running "search and destroy" missions out of secure bases—the same approach that had failed so badly in Vietnam. There were numerous high-sounding goals—freedom, democracy, reconstruction, security—but no coherent strategy for dealing with the insurgency.

The change came in 2007. Having just written the *Army/Marine Corps Counterinsurgency Field Manual*, General David Petraeus was sent to Iraq, along with five additional brigades of troops. But more than the extra soldiers, Petraeus was armed with an actual strategy. His idea was that one could combat an insurgency as long as the large preponderance of civilians supported a legitimate government. The trick was to shift the military's focus from making patrols to protecting the populace. A populace that was not in fear of insurgent retaliation would provide the information necessary to isolate and combat the insurgent minority. This change, replacing amorphous goals with a true problem-solving strategy, made an enormous difference in the results achieved.

- In November 2006, I attended a short conference about Web 2.0 businesses. The term "Web 2.0" purportedly referred to a new approach to Web services, but none of the technologies involved were really new. The term was actually a code word for Google, MySpace, YouTube, Facebook, and various other new Web-based businesses that had suddenly become very valuable. At lunch, I found myself seated with seven other attendees at a round table. Someone asked me what I do. I briefly explained that I was a faculty member at UCLA where I taught and did research on strategy—and that I was a consultant on the subject to a variety of organizations.

  The CEO of a Web-services company was sitting directly across from me. He put down his fork and said, "Strategy is never quitting until you win." I could not have disagreed more, but I was not there to argue or lecture. "Winning is better than losing," I said, and the conversation turned to other matters.

The key insight driving this book is the hard-won lesson of a lifetime of experience at strategy work—as a consultant to organizations, as a personal adviser, as a teacher, and as a researcher. A good strategy does more than urge us forward toward a goal or vision. A good strategy honestly acknowledges the challenges being faced and provides an approach to overcoming them. And the greater the challenge, the more a good strategy focuses and coordinates efforts to achieve a powerful competitive punch or problem-solving effect.

Unfortunately, good strategy is the exception, not the rule. And the problem is growing. More and more organizational leaders say they have a strategy, but they do not. Instead, they espouse what I call *bad strategy*. Bad strategy tends to skip over pesky details such as problems. It ignores the power of choice and focus, trying instead to accommodate a multitude of conflicting demands and interests. Like a quarterback whose only advice to teammates is "Let's win," bad strategy covers up its failure to guide by embracing the language of broad goals, ambition, vision, and values. Each of these elements is, of course, an important part of human life. But, by themselves, they are not substitutes for the hard work of strategy.

■ ■ ■

The gap between good strategy and the jumble of things people label "strategy" has grown over the years. In 1966, when I first began to study business strategy, there were only three books on the subject and no articles. Today, my personal library shelves are fat with books about strategy. Consulting firms specialize in strategy, PhDs are granted in strategy, and there are countless articles on the subject. But this plentitude has not brought clarity. Rather, the concept has been stretched to a gauzy thinness as pundits attach it to everything from utopian visions to rules for matching your tie with your shirt. To make matters worse, for many people in business, education, and government, the word "strategy" has become a verbal tic. Business speech transformed marketing into "marketing strategy," data processing into "IT strategy," and making acquisitions into a "growth strategy." Cut some prices and an observer will say that you have a "low-price strategy."

Further confusion is created by equating strategy with success or with ambition. This was my problem with the Web-services CEO who claimed "Strategy is never quitting until you win." This sort of mishmash of pop culture, motivational slogans, and business buzz speak is, unfortunately, increasingly common. It short-circuits real inventiveness and fails to distinguish among different senior-level management tasks and virtues. Strategy cannot be a useful concept if it is a synonym for success. Nor can it be a useful tool if it is confused with ambition, determination, inspirational leadership, and innovation. Ambition is drive and zeal to excel. Determination is commitment and grit. Innovation is the discovery and engineering of new ways to do things. Inspirational leadership motivates people to sacrifice for their own and the common good.[1] And strategy, responsive to innovation and ambition, selects the path, identifying how, why, and where leadership and determination are to be applied.

A word that can mean anything has lost its bite. To give content to a concept one has to draw lines, marking off what it denotes and what it does not. To begin the journey toward clarity, it is helpful to recognize that the words "strategy" and "strategic" are often sloppily used to mark decisions made by the highest-level officials. For example, in business, most mergers and acquisitions, investments in expensive new facilities, negotiations with important suppliers and customers, and overall organizational design are normally considered to be "strategic." However, when you speak of "strategy," you should not be simply marking the pay grade of the decision maker. Rather, the term "strategy" should mean a cohesive response to an important challenge. Unlike a stand-alone decision or a goal, a strategy is a coherent set of analyses, concepts, policies, arguments, and actions that respond to a high-stakes challenge.

Many people assume that a strategy is a big-picture overall direction, divorced from any specific action. But defining strategy as broad concepts, thereby leaving out action, creates a wide chasm between "strategy" and "implementation." If you accept this chasm, most strategy work becomes wheel spinning. Indeed, this is the most common complaint about "strategy." Echoing many others, one top executive told me, "We have a sophisticated strategy process, but there is a huge problem of execution. We almost always fall short of the goals we set for ourselves." If you have followed my line of argument, you can see the reason for this complaint. A good strategy includes a set of coherent actions. They are not "implementation" details; they are the punch in the strategy. A strategy that fails to define a variety of plausible and feasible immediate actions is missing a critical component.

Executives who complain about "execution" problems have usually confused strategy with goal setting. When the "strategy" process is basically a game of setting performance goals—so much market share and so much profit, so many students graduating high school, so many visitors to the museum—then there remains a yawning gap between these ambitions and action. Strategy is about *how* an organization will move forward. Doing strategy is figuring out *how* to advance the organization's interests. Of course, a leader can set goals and delegate to others the job of figuring out what to do. But that is not strategy. If that is how the organization runs, let's skip the spin and be honest—call it goal setting.

■ ■ ■

The purpose of this book is to wake you up to the dramatic differences between good strategy and bad strategy and to give you a leg up toward crafting good strategies.

A good strategy has an essential logical structure that I call the *kernel*. The kernel of a strategy contains three elements: a diagnosis, a guiding policy, and coherent action. The guiding policy specifies the approach to dealing with the obstacles called out in the diagnosis. It is like a signpost, marking the direction forward but not defining the details of the trip. Coherent actions are feasible coordinated policies, resource commitments, and actions designed to carry out the guiding policy.

Once you gain a facility with the structure and fundamentals of a good strategy, you will develop the parallel ability to detect the presence of bad strategy. Just as you do not need to be a director to detect a bad movie, you do not need economics, finance, or any other abstruse special knowledge to distinguish between good and bad strategy. For example, looking at the U.S. government's "strategy" for dealing with the 2008 financial crisis, you will see that essential elements are missing. In particular, there was no official diagnosis of the underlying malady. So, there can be no focus of resources and actions on a cure. There has only been a shift of resources from the public to the banks. You do not need a PhD in macroeconomics to make this judgment—it follows from understanding the nature of good strategy itself.

Bad strategy is more than just the absence of good strategy. Bad strategy has a life and logic of its own, a false edifice built on mistaken foundations. Bad strategy may actively avoid analyzing obstacles because a leader believes that negative thoughts get in the way. Leaders may create bad strategy by mistakenly treating strategy work as an exercise in goal setting rather than problem solving. Or they may avoid hard choices because they do not wish to offend anyone—generating a bad strategy that tries to cover all the bases rather than focus resources and actions.

The creeping spread of bad strategy affects us all. Heavy with goals and slogans, the national government has become less and less able to solve problems. Corporate boards sign off on strategic plans that are little more than wishful thinking. Our education system is rich with targets and standards, but poor in comprehending and countering the sources of underperformance. The only remedy is for us to demand more from those who lead. More than charisma and vision, we must demand good strategy.

◆

PART I

GOOD AND BAD STRATEGY

The most basic idea of strategy is the application of strength against weakness. Or, if you prefer, strength applied to the most promising opportunity. The standard modern treatment of strategy has expanded this idea into a rich discussion of potential strengths, today called "advantages." There are advantages due to being a first mover: scale, scope, network effects, reputation, patents, brands, and hundreds more. None of these are logically wrong, and each can be important. Yet this whole midlevel framework misses two huge, incredibly important natural sources of strength:

1. *Having a coherent strategy—one that coordinates policies and actions.* A good strategy doesn't just draw on existing strength; it creates strength through the coherence of its design. Most organizations of any size don't do this. Rather, they pursue multiple objectives that are unconnected with one another or, worse, that conflict with one another.

2. *The creation of new strengths through subtle shifts in viewpoint.* An insightful reframing of a competitive situation can create whole new patterns of advantage and weakness. The most powerful strategies arise from such game-changing insights.

These two essential aspects of good strategy are explored in chapter 1, "Good Strategy Is Unexpected," and chapter 2, "Discovering Power."

The leader of an organization lacking a good strategy may simply believe that strategy is unnecessary. But more often the lack is due to the presence of bad strategy. Like weeds crowding out the grass, bad strategy crowds out good strategy. Leaders using bad strategies have not just chosen the wrong goals or made implementation errors. Rather, they have mistaken views about what strategy is and how it works. Chapter 3, "Bad Strategy," presents evidence for the existence of bad strategy and explains its hallmarks.

Having marked the nature of good and bad strategy, chapter 4 answers the obvious question: "Why So Much Bad Strategy?" Chapter 5, "The Kernel of Good Strategy," provides an analysis of the logical structure of a good strategy—a structure that acts as a guide on reasoning and a check against generating bad strategy.

◆

CHAPTER ONE

GOOD STRATEGY IS UNEXPECTED

The first natural advantage of good strategy arises because other organizations often don't have one. And because they don't expect you to have one, either. A good strategy has coherence, coordinating actions, policies, and resources so as to accomplish an important end. Many organizations, most of the time, don't have this. Instead, they have multiple goals and initiatives that symbolize progress, but no coherent approach to accomplishing that progress other than "spend more and try harder."

APPLE

After the 1995 release of Microsoft's Windows 95 multimedia operating system, Apple Inc. fell into a death spiral. On February 5, 1996, *BusinessWeek* put Apple's famous trademark on its cover to illustrate its lead story: "The Fall of an American Icon."

CEO Gil Amelio struggled to keep Apple alive in a world being rapidly dominated by Windows-Intel-based PCs. He cut staff. He reorganized the company's many products into four groups: Macintosh, information appliances, printers and peripherals, and "alternative platforms." A new Internet Services Group was added to the Operating Systems Group and the Advanced Technology Group.

Wired magazine carried an article titled "101 Ways to Save Apple." It included suggestions such as "Sell yourself to IBM or Motorola," "Invest heavily in Newton technology," and "Exploit your advantage in the K–12 education market." Wall Street analysts hoped for and urged a deal with Sony or Hewlett-Packard.

By September 1997, Apple was two months from bankruptcy. Steve Jobs, who had cofounded the company in 1976, agreed to return to serve on a reconstructed board of directors and to be interim CEO. Die-hard fans of the original Macintosh were overjoyed, but the general business world was not expecting much.

Within a year, things changed radically at Apple. Although many observers had expected Jobs to rev up the development of advanced products, or engineer a deal with Sun, he did neither. What he did was both obvious and, at the same time, unexpected. He shrunk Apple to a scale and scope suitable to the reality of its being a niche producer in the highly competitive personal computer business. He cut Apple back to a core that could survive.

Steve Jobs talked Microsoft into investing $150 million in Apple, exploiting Bill Gates's concerns about what a failed Apple would mean to Microsoft's struggle with the Department of Justice. Jobs cut all of the desktop models—there were fifteen—back to one. He cut all portable and handheld models back to one laptop. He completely cut out all the printers and other peripherals. He cut development engineers. He cut software development. He cut distributors and cut out five of the company's six national retailers. He cut out virtually all manufacturing, moving it offshore to Taiwan. With a simpler product line manufactured in Asia, he cut inventory by more than 80 percent. A new Web store sold Apple's products directly to consumers, cutting out distributors and dealers.

What is remarkable about Jobs's turnaround strategy for Apple is how much it was "Business 101" and yet how much of it was unanticipated. Of course you have to cut back and simplify to your core to climb out of a financial nosedive. Of course he needed up-to-date versions of Microsoft's Office software to work on Apple's computers. Of course Dell's model of Asian supply-chain manufacturing, short cycle times, and negative working capital was the state of the art in the industry and deserved emulation. Of course he stopped the development of new operating systems—he had just brought the industry's best operating system with him from NeXT.

The power of Jobs's strategy came from directly tackling the fundamental problem with a focused and coordinated set of actions. He did not announce ambitious revenue or profit goals; he did not indulge in messianic visions of the future. And he did not just cut in a blind ax-wielding frenzy—he redesigned the whole business logic around a simplified product line sold through a limited set of outlets.

In May 1998, while trying to help strike a deal between Apple and Telecom Italia, I had the chance to talk to Jobs about his approach to turning Apple around. He explained both the substance and coherence of his insight with a few sentences:

> The product lineup was too complicated and the company was bleeding cash. A friend of the family asked me which Apple computer she should buy. She couldn't figure out the differences among them and I couldn't give her clear guidance, either. I was appalled that there was no Apple consumer computer priced under $2,000. We are replacing all of those desktop computers with one, the Power Mac G3. We are dropping five of six national retailers—meeting their demand has meant too many models at too many price points and too much markup.

This kind of focused action is far from the norm in industry. Eighteen months earlier, I had been involved in a large-scale study, sponsored by Andersen Consulting, of strategies in the worldwide electronics industry. Working in Europe, I carried out interviews with twenty-six executives, all division managers or CEOs in the electronics and telecommunications sector. My interview plan was simple: I asked each executive to identify the leading competitor in their business. I asked how that company had become the leader—evoking their private theories about what works. And then I asked them what their own company's current strategy was.

These executives, by and large, had no trouble describing the strategy of the leader in their sectors. The standard story was that some change in demand or technology had appeared—a "window of opportunity" had opened—and the current leader had been the first one to leap through that window and take advantage of it. Not necessarily the first mover, but the first to get it right.

But when I asked about their own companies' strategies, there was a very different kind of response. Instead of pointing to the next window of opportunity, or even mentioning its possibility, I heard a lot of look-busy doorknob polishing. They were making alliances, they were doing 360-degree feedback, they were looking for foreign markets, they were setting challenging strategic goals, they were moving software into firmware, they were enabling Internet updates of firmware, and so on. They had each told me the formula for success in the 1990s electronics industry—take a good position quickly when a new window of opportunity opens—but none said that was their focus or even mentioned it as part of their strategy.

Given that background, I was interested in what Steve Jobs might say about the future of Apple. His survival strategy for Apple, for all its skill and drama, was not going to propel Apple into the future. At that moment in time, Apple had less than 4 percent of the personal computer market. The de facto standard was Windows-Intel and there seemed to be no way for Apple to do more than just hang on to a tiny niche.

In the summer of 1998, I got an opportunity to talk with Jobs again. I said, "Steve, this turnaround at Apple has been impressive. But everything we know about the PC business says that Apple cannot really push beyond a small niche position. The network effects are just too strong to upset the Wintel standard. So what are you trying to do in the longer term? What is the strategy?"

He did not attack my argument. He didn't agree with it, either. He just smiled and said, "I am going to wait for the next big thing."

Jobs did not enunciate some simple-minded growth or market share goal. He did not pretend that pushing on various levers would somehow magically restore Apple to market leadership in personal computers. Instead, he was actually focused on the sources of and barriers to success in his industry—recognizing the next window of opportunity, the next set of forces he could harness to his advantage, and then having the quickness and cleverness to pounce on it quickly like a perfect predator. There was no pretense that such windows opened every year or that one could force them open with incentives or management tricks. He knew how it worked. He had done it before with the Apple II and the Macintosh and then with Pixar. He had tried to force it with NeXT, and that had not gone well. It would be two years before he would make that leap again with the iPod and then online music. And, after that, with the iPhone.

Steve Jobs's answer that day—"to wait for the next big thing"—is not a general formula for success. But it was a wise approach to Apple's situation at that moment, in that industry, with so many new technologies seemingly just around the corner.

DESERT STORM

Another example of surprise at the existence of a strategy occurred at the end of the first Gulf War in 1991. People were surprised to discover that U.S. commanders actually had a focused strategy for defeating the entrenched Iraqi invaders.

On August 2, 1990, Iraq invaded Kuwait. Led by elite troops making airborne and amphibious landings, and four divisions of the Republican Guard, 150,000 Iraqi soldiers rolled into and occupied Kuwait. It is probable that Saddam Hussein's primary motive for the invasion was financial. The eight-year war he had started by invading Iran in 1980 had left his regime with massive debts to Kuwait and other Gulf states. By taking Kuwait and declaring it the nineteenth province of Iraq, Saddam would cancel his debts to that country and be able to use its massive oil income to repay his debts to other nations.

Five months later, a thirty-three-nation coalition organized by U.S. president George H. W. Bush was carrying out air strikes against Iraqi forces and rapidly building its ground forces. Iraq, in turn, had increased its force in Kuwait to more than five hundred thousand. It was hoped that air power alone might produce a resolution of the conflict, but if it did not, a ground offensive would be necessary to reverse Iraq's invasion and occupation of Kuwait.

There was no real doubt that the coalition had the ability to throw back the Iraqis. But how costly would it be? In October 1990, the French newspaper *L'Express* had estimated that retaking Kuwait would take about a week and cost twenty thousand U.S. casualties. As Iraqi forces swelled and built defensive positions, public discussion in the press, on television, and in the halls of Congress began to evoke images of World War I trench combat. In Congress, Senator Bob Graham (D-Florida) noted that "Iraq already has had five months to dig in and to fortify and they have done so in a major way. Kuwait has fortifications reminiscent of World War I." In the same vein, the *New York Times* described a battalion of the Sixteenth Infantry as "the men who expect to have the job of slogging it out in the trenches of Kuwait with their M-16 rifles and M-60 machine guns blazing." *Time* magazine described the Iraqi defenses this way:

> In an area about the size of West Virginia the Iraqis have poured 540,000 of their million-man army and 4,000 of their 6,000 tanks, along with thousands of other armored vehicles and artillery pieces. . . . Iraqi units are entrenched in their now traditional triangular forts, formed of packed sand, with an infantry company equipped with heavy machine guns holding each corner. Soldiers are protected by portable concrete shelters or dugouts of sheet metal and sand. Tanks are hull deep in the ground and bolstered with sandbags. Artillery pieces are deployed at the apex of each triangle, pre-aimed at "killing zones" created by flaming trenches and minefields.[1]

On the eve of the ground assault, the *Los Angeles Times* reminded its readers that "Iraqi troops along the front lines are well dug in, and assaulting such fortified positions is always a risky business. The debacles at Cold Harbor, the Somme and Gallipoli are grim reminders of the price of failure. Even success, as at Tarawa, Okinawa or Hamburger Hill, can come at a terrible price."[2]

What these commentators did not predict was that General Norman Schwarzkopf, commander in chief of U.S. Central Command, had a strategy for the ground war, a strategy he had developed back in early October.

The original plan generated by his staff, a direct attack into Kuwait, was estimated to cost 2,000 dead and 8,000 wounded. Schwarzkopf rejected this approach in favor of a two-pronged plan. Air attacks would be used to reduce the Iraqi capabilities by 50 percent. Then he planned a massive secret "left hook." While the world's attention was focused on CNN's 24/7 coverage of troops just south of Kuwait, the coalition would secretly shift a force of 250,000 soldiers well west of Kuwait and then have them move north into positions in the empty desert of southern Iraq. When the ground war began, this force would continue north and then turn east, completing the "left hook," and slamming into the flank of the Iraqi Republican Guard. Attacks aimed northward into Kuwait itself were to be minor. The U.S. Marines ground forces were ordered to move slowly northward into Kuwait, a ploy to entice the entrenched Iraqis southward and out of their fortifications, where they would be hit from the side by part of the massive left hook. The sea-based marines would not land, their floating presence being a diversion.

Schwarzkopf's combined-arms left-hook strategy was so successful that the intense ground war lasted only one hundred hours. A month of air bombardment had conditioned Iraqi troops to disperse and hide their tanks and artillery, stay out of their vehicles, and keep motors off. The swiftness and violence of the coalition ground assault, combining tanks, infantry, attack helicopters, and bombers, was decisive. Republican Guard units fought bravely but were unable to maneuver or call in reserves fast enough to respond to the speed and ferocity of the attack. Finally, and perhaps most important, Saddam Hussein had ordered his commanders not to use their chemical weapons. These artillery shells, used to halt Iranian attacks during the Iran-Iraq War, would have caused thousands of coalition casualties. Marine commanders had estimated they would lose 20 to 30 percent of their force if chemical weapons were used against them.[3] But Saddam was deterred—postwar intelligence gleaned from the Russians revealed that he feared a U.S. nuclear retaliation to such use.

Iraq fled Kuwait, much of its invading army destroyed.[4] Coalition casualties were light—on the first day there were eight dead and twenty-seven wounded. The coalition's success with the combined-arms left-hook strategy was so stark that pundits who were worried about trench warfare in February were, by March, opining that the coalition had amassed more forces than it needed and that the outcome had been a foregone conclusion.

Schwarzkopf revealed the ground-war strategy to the public in a widely viewed press briefing. Most people who saw this briefing and the map of the left hook were surprised and impressed. News commentators described the plan as "brilliant" and "secret." Few had anticipated this envelopment maneuver. But why hadn't they? The Department of the Army publishes field manuals fully describing its basic doctrines and methods. FM 100-5, published in 1986, was titled *Operations* and was described as "the Army's keystone warfighting manual." Part 2 of FM 100-5 was dedicated to "Offensive Operations," and on page 101 it described "envelopment" as the most important form of offensive maneuver—the U.S. Army's "Plan A." The manual said:

> Envelopment avoids the enemy's front, where its forces are most protected and his fires most easily concentrated. Instead, while fixing the defender's attention forward by supporting or diversionary attacks, the attacker maneuvers his main effort around or over the enemy's defenses to strike at his flanks and rear.

To illustrate this maneuver, FM 100-5 *Operations* offered a diagram reproduced on the facing page.

Given this vivid picture of a feint up the middle combined with a powerful "left hook," one must ask: *"How could Schwarzkopf's use of the primary offensive doctrine of the U.S. Army have been a surprise to anyone?"*

Some part of the answer lies in successful deception. Schwarzkopf intended to make it appear that the main attack would be launched into Kuwait from the sea and then overland directly into Iraqi defenses. This was supported by an early visible amphibious raid on the Kuwaiti coast and by actions to destroy Iraq's navy. The press unwittingly helped in this misdirection by reporting on the photogenic amphibious training, the build-up of troops just south of Kuwait, and then by anguishing over the prospect of World War I trench warfare.

But an essential element of the U.S. Army's "Plan A"—envelopment—

is the *illusion* of a direct attack coupled with a much more massive end run. And, since "Plan A" was available to anyone with twenty-five dollars to send to the U.S. Government Printing Office,[5] it remains puzzling as to why "Plan A" was a surprise—a surprise not only to Iraq but also to talking-head military commentators on television and to most of the U.S. Congress.

The best answer to this puzzle is that the real surprise was that such a pure and focused strategy was actually implemented. Most complex organizations spread rather than concentrate resources, acting to placate and pay off internal and external interests. Thus, we are surprised when a complex organization, such as Apple or the U.S. Army, actually focuses its actions. Not because of secrecy, but because good strategy itself is unexpected.

In the case of Desert Storm, the focus was much more than an intellectual step. Schwarzkopf had to suppress the ambitions and desires of the air force, marines, various army units, each coalition partner, and the political leadership in Washington. For example, the U.S. Army's best light infantry—the Eighty-Second Airborne—was tasked with pro-

ENVELOPMENT

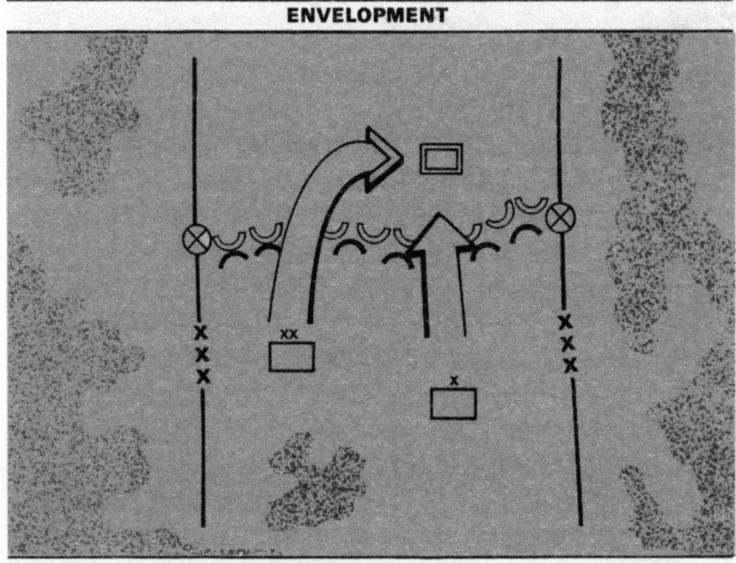

viding support to French armor and infantry, an assignment its leadership protested. Eight thousand U.S. Marines waited on ships to land on the beaches of Kuwait City, but did not. It was a diversion. Air force commanders wanted to demonstrate the value of strategic bombing—they believed that the war could be won by air attacks on Baghdad—and had to be forced against strenuous protest to divert their resources to fully support the land offensive. Secretary of Defense Dick Cheney wanted the mission accomplished with a smaller force and detailed an alternative plan of attack. Prince Khalid, commanding the Saudi forces in the coalition, insisted that King Fahd be involved in the planning, but Schwarzkopf convinced President Bush to ensure that U.S. Central Command retained control over strategy and planning.

■ ■ ■

Having conflicting goals, dedicating resources to unconnected targets, and accommodating incompatible interests are the luxuries of the rich and powerful, but they make for bad strategy. Despite this, most organizations will not create focused strategies. Instead, they will generate laundry lists of desirable outcomes and, at the same time, ignore the need for genuine competence in coordinating and focusing their resources. Good strategy requires leaders who are willing and able to say *no* to a wide variety of actions and interests. Strategy is at least as much about what an organization does not do as it is about what it does.

CHAPTER TWO

DISCOVERING POWER

The second natural advantage of many good strategies comes from insight into new sources of strength and weakness. Looking at things from a different or fresh perspective can reveal new realms of advantage and opportunity as well as weakness and threat.

A SLUNG STONE

In about 1030 B.C., David the shepherd boy defeated the warrior Goliath. When Goliath stepped from the ranks of the Philistines and shouted a challenge, the army of King Saul cringed in terror. Goliath was over nine feet tall, his spear like a weaver's beam. His bronze helmet and body armor shone in the sunlight. David was not old enough to soldier like his brothers, yet nonetheless wanted to face the giant. Saul advised David that he was too young and the giant a skilled veteran, but relented and gave him armor. The armor was heavy and David discarded it, rushing to combat in shepherd's garb. Moving toward Goliath, he took a stone and launched it with his sling. Struck in the forehead, Goliath fell dead on the spot. David moved forward and took the fallen champion's head. The Philistines fled.

It is said that strategy brings relative strength to bear against relative weakness. Let's follow the advice of countless articles and textbooks and make a list of David's and Goliath's apparent strengths and weaknesses:

	Strengths	Weaknesses
David	Very brave	Small, inexperienced
Goliath	Huge, strong, experienced, and brave	?

This mismatch must have been Saul's concern as he tried to hold David back, then relented and gave him armor. In the story, it is only after the stone is slung that the listener's viewpoint shifts and one realizes that the boy's experience with a shepherd's sling is a strength, as is his youthful quickness. Then the listener realizes that David discarded the armor because it would only slow him down; had he come close enough to receive a blow from the giant, bronze armor would not have saved him. Finally, when the stone strikes Goliath's forehead, the listener suddenly discovers a critical weakness—Goliath's armor didn't cover this vital area. David's weapon delivered force with precision over a distance, neutering Goliath's supposed advantages of size and strength. The story teaches us that our preconceived ideas of strength and weakness may be unsound.

It is the victory of apparent weakness over apparent strength that gives this tale its bite. More than the deft wielding of power, the listener experiences the actual *discovery* of power in a situation—the creation or revelation of a decisive asymmetry. How someone can see what others have not, or what they have ignored, and thereby discover a pivotal objective and create an advantage, lies at the very edge of our understanding, something glimpsed only out of the corner of our minds. Not every good strategy draws on this kind of insight, but those that do generate the extra kick that separates "ordinary excellence" from the extraordinary.

WAL-MART

Much of my work with MBA students and companies involves helping them uncover the hidden power in situations. As part of this process I often teach a case about Wal-Mart's founding and rise, ending in 1986 with Sam Walton as the richest person in the United States.[1] In a subsequent session I will follow up by discussing the modern Wal-Mart, pushing into urban areas, stretching out to Europe, and becoming the largest corporation on the planet in terms of revenue. But the older case portrays a simpler, leaner Wal-Mart—a youthful challenger rather than the behemoth it has become. Hard as it is to believe today, Wal-Mart was once David, not Goliath.

Before beginning the discussion, I copy a phrase from the case onto the whiteboard and draw a box around it:

CONVENTIONAL WISDOM:
A full-line discount store needs a population base of at least 100,000.

The question for the group is simple: Why has Wal-Mart been so successful? To start, I call on Bill, who had some experience in sales during the earlier part of his career. He begins with the ritual invocation of founder Sam Walton's leadership. Neither agreeing nor disagreeing, I write "Sam Walton" on the board and press him further. "What did Walton do that made a difference?"

Bill looks at my labeled box on the board and says, "Walton broke the conventional wisdom. He put big stores in small towns. Wal-Mart had everyday low prices. Wal-Mart ran a computerized warehousing and trucking system to manage the movement of stock into stores. It was nonunion. It had low administrative expenses."

It takes about thirty minutes for six other participants to flesh out this list. They are willing to throw anything into the bin, and I don't stop them. I prod for detail and context, asking, "How big were the stores?" "How small were the towns?" "How did the computerized logistics system work?" And "What did Wal-Mart do to keep its administrative expenses so low?"

As the responses flood in, three diagrams take shape on the whiteboard. A circle appears, representing a small town of ten thousand persons. A large box drawn in the circle represents a forty-five-thousand-square-foot Wal-Mart store. A second diagram of the logistical system emerges. A square box represents a regional distribution center. From the box, a line marks the path of a truck, swooping out to pass by some of the 150 stores served by the distribution center. On the return path, the line passes vendors, picking up pallets of goods. The line plunges back to the square, where an "X" denotes cross-docking to an outgoing truck. Lines of a different color depict the data flows, from the store to a central computer, and then out to vendors and the distribution center. Finally, as we discuss the management system, I draw the paths of the regional managers as they follow a weekly circuit: Fly out from Bentonville, Arkansas, on Monday, visit stores, pick up and distribute information, and return to Bentonville on Thursday for group meetings on Friday and Saturday. The last two diagrams are eerily similar—both revealing the hub structure of efficient distribution.

The discussion slows. We have gotten most of the facts out. I look around the room, trying to include them all, and say, "If the policies you have listed are the reasons for Wal-Mart's success, and if this case was published—let's see—in 1986, then why was the company able to run rampant over Kmart for the next decade? Wasn't the formula obvious? Where was the competition?"

Silence. This question breaks the pleasant give-and-take of reciting case facts. The case actually says almost nothing about competition, referring broadly to the discounting industry. But surely executives and MBA students would have thought about this in preparing for this discussion. Yet it is totally predictable that they will not. Because the case does not focus on competition, neither do they. I *know* it will turn out this way—it always does. Half of what alert participants learn in a strategy exercise is to consider the competition even when no one tells you to do it in advance.

Looking just at the actions of a winning firm, you see only part of the picture. Whenever an organization succeeds greatly, there is also, at the same time, either blocked or failed competition. Sometimes competition is blocked because an innovator holds a patent or some other legal claim to a temporary monopoly. But there may also be a natural reason imitation is difficult or very costly. Wal-Mart's advantage must stem from something that competitors cannot easily copy, or do not copy because of inertia and incompetence. In the case of Wal-Mart, the principal competitive failure was Kmart. Originally named the S. S. Kresge Corporation, Kmart was once the leader in low-cost variety retailing. It spent much of the 1970s and 1980s expanding internationally and ignoring Wal-Mart's innovations in logistics and its growing dominance of small-town discounting. It filed for bankruptcy in 2002.

After some moments I ask a more pointed question: "Both Wal-Mart and Kmart began to install bar-code scanners at cash registers in the early 1980s. Why did Wal-Mart seem to benefit from this more than Kmart?"

First used in grocery supermarkets, bar-code scanners at retail checkout stations are now ubiquitous. Mass merchandisers began to use them in the early 1980s. Most retailers saw the bar-code scanner as a way of eliminating the cost of constantly changing the price stickers on items. But Wal-Mart went further, developing its own satellite-based information systems. Then it used this data to manage its inbound logistics system and traded it with suppliers in return for discounts.

Susan, a human resources executive, suddenly perks up. Isolating one small policy has triggered a thought. I gave a talk the day before on "complementary" policies and she sees the connection. "By itself," she says, "it doesn't help that much. Kmart would have to move the data to distribution centers and suppliers. It would have to operate an integrated inbound logistics system."

"Good," I say, and point out to everyone that Wal-Mart's policies fit together—the bar codes, the integrated logistics, the frequent just-in-time deliveries, the large stores with low inventory—they are complements to one another, forming an integrated design. This whole design—structure, policies, and actions—is coherent. Each part of the design is shaped and specialized to the others. The pieces are not interchangeable parts. Many competitors do not have much of a design, shaping each of their elements around some imagined "best practice" form. Others will have more coherence but will have aimed their designs at different purposes. In either case, such competitors will have difficulty in dealing with Wal-Mart. Copying elements of its strategy piecemeal, there will be little benefit. A competitor would have to adopt the whole design, not just a part of it.

There is much more to be discussed: first-mover advantages, quantifying its cost advantage, the issue of competence and learning developed over time, the function of leadership, and whether this design can work in cities. We proceed.

With fifteen minutes to go, I let the discussion wind down. They have done a good job analyzing Wal-Mart's business, and I say so. But, I tell them, there is one more thing. Something I barely understand but that seems important. It has to do with the "conventional wisdom"—the phrase from the case I put on the whiteboard at the beginning of the class: "A full-line discount store needs a population base of at least 100,000."

I turn to Bill and say: "You started us out by arguing that Walton *broke* the conventional wisdom. But the conventional wisdom was based on the straightforward logic of fixed and variable cost. It takes a lot of customers to spread the overhead and keep costs and prices low. Exactly how did Walton break the iron logic of cost?"

I push ahead, putting Bill into a role: "I want you to imagine that you are a Wal-Mart store manager. It's 1985 and you are unhappy with the whole company. You feel that they don't understand your town. You complain to your dad, and he says, 'Why don't we just buy them out? We can run the store ourselves.' Assuming Dad has the resources, what do you think of his proposal?"

Bill blinks, surprised at being put on the spot for a second time. He thinks a bit, then says, "No, it's not a good idea. We couldn't make a go of it alone. The Wal-Mart store needs to be part of the network."

I turn back the whiteboard and stand right next to the boxed principle: "A full-line discount store needs a population base of at least 100,000." I repeat his phrase, "The Wal-Mart store needs to be part of the network," while drawing a circle around the word "store." Then I wait.

With luck, someone will get it. As one student tries to articulate the discovery, others get it, and I sense a small avalanche of "ahas," like a pot of corn kernels suddenly popping. It isn't the store; it is the *net-*

work of 150 stores. And the data flows and the management flows and a distribution hub. The network replaced the store. A regional network of 150 stores serves a population of millions! *Walton didn't break the conventional wisdom; he broke the old definition of a store*. If no one gets it right away, I drop hints until they do.

When you understand that Walton redefined the notion of "store," your view of how Wal-Mart's policies fit together undergoes a subtle shift. You begin to see the interdependencies among location decisions. Store locations express the economics of the network, not just the pull of demand. You also see the balance of power at Wal-Mart. The individual store has little negotiating power—its options are limited. Most crucially, the network, not the store, became Wal-Mart's basic unit of management.

In making an integrated network into the operating unit of the company, instead of the individual store, Walton broke with an even deeper conventional wisdom of his era: the doctrine of decentralization, that each kettle should sit on its own bottom. Kmart had long adhered to this doctrine, giving each store manager authority to choose product lines, pick vendors, and set prices. After all, we are told that decentralization is a good thing. But the oft-forgotten cost of decentralization is lost coordination across units. Stores that do not choose the same vendors or negotiate the same terms cannot benefit from an integrated network of data and transport. Stores that do not share detailed information about what works and what does not cannot benefit from one another's learning.

If your competitors also operate this kind of decentralized system, little may be lost. But once Walton's insights made the decentralized structure a disadvantage, Kmart had a severe problem. A large organization may balk at adopting a new technique, but such change is manageable. But breaking with doctrine—with one's basic philosophy—is rare absent a near-death experience.

The hidden power of Wal-Mart's strategy came from a shift in perspective. Lacking that perspective, Kmart saw Wal-Mart like Goliath saw David—smaller and less experienced in the big leagues. But Wal-Mart's advantages were not inherent in its history or size. They grew out of a subtle shift in how to think about discount retailing. Tradition saw discounting as tied to urban densities, whereas Sam Walton saw a way to build efficiency by embedding each store in a network of computing and logistics. Today we call this supply-chain management, but in 1984 it was as an unexpected shift in viewpoint. And it had the impact of David's slung stone.

ANDY MARSHALL

I first met Andy Marshall in mid-1990. He is the director of net assessment for the Defense Department, and his normal habitat is a small suite of offices in the Pentagon, just down the hall from the secretary of defense. Since the Office of Net Assessment was created in 1973, there has been only one director: Andrew Marshall. His challenging job is to think broadly about the security situation of the United States.

Andy Marshall and I were both interested in how the process of planning shapes strategic outcomes. He explained to me how during the Cold War the traditional budget cycle of the military and the Congress had created a reactive mindset.

"Our defense planning," he said, "had become driven by the annual budgeting process." Each year, he explained, the Joint Chiefs developed an assessment of the Soviet threat, which was essentially an estimate of their present and planned weapons inventory. The Pentagon then developed a response to the threat that amounted to a shopping list. Congress would appropriate some fraction of what was requested, and the cycle would begin again.

"This process of justifying expenditures as counters to Soviet expenditures conditioned U.S. actions on Soviet strengths, expressed as threats, not on Soviet weaknesses and constraints. We had a war strategy—a catastrophic spasm—but no plan about how to compete with the Soviet Union over the long term."

Soft-spoken, Marshall watched my eyes, checking that I understood the implications of his statements. He took out a document, a thin sheaf of paper, and began to explain its meaning: "This document reflects thoughts about how to actually use U.S. strengths to exploit Soviet weaknesses, a very different approach."

Titled "Strategy for Competing with the Soviets in the Military Sector of the Continuing Political-Military Competition,"[2] it had been written in 1976, near the end of the Ford administration, and bore marginal notations by President Carter's secretary of defense, Harold Brown. It had evidently received attention. (Its authors were Andy Marshall and James Roche, who was, at that time, his assistant director.)*

This fascinating analysis of the situation worked to redefine "defense" in new terms—a subtle shift in point of view. It argued that "in dealing effectively with the other side, a nation seeks opportunities to use one or more distinctive competences in such a way as to develop *competitive advantage*—both in specific areas and overall." It then went on to explain that the crucial area of competition was technology because the United States had more resources and better capabilities in that area. And, most important, it argued that having a true *competitive* strategy meant engaging in actions that imposed exorbitant costs on the other side. In particular, it recommended investing in technologies that were expensive to counter and where the counters did not add to Soviet offensive capabilities. For instance, increasing the accuracy of missiles or the quietness of submarines forced the Soviet Union to spend scarce resources on counters without increasing the threat to the United States. Investments in systems that made Soviet systems obsolete would also force them to spend, as would selectively advertising dramatic new technologies.

Marshall and Roche's idea was a break with the budget-driven balance-of-forces logic of 1976. It was simple. The United States should actually compete with the Soviet Union, using its strengths to good effect and exploiting the Soviets' weaknesses. There were no complex charts or graphs, no abstruse formulas, no acronym-jammed buzz speak: just an idea and some pointers to how it might be used—the terrible simplicity of the discovery of hidden power in a situation.

As Andy Marshall and I spoke about this fourteen-year-old document in 1990, the Soviet Union was faltering. A year earlier the Berlin Wall had fallen. It would be another sixteen months before the USSR dis-

* James Roche went on to hold senior executive positions at Northrup Grumman and served as secretary of the air force (2001–5).

solved. But in 1990, when we discussed policy processes, before revisionists of all stripes started to rewrite history, it was clear that the Soviet Union was faltering because it was overextended. It was going broke economically, politically, and militarily. The United States' more accurate missiles, the rise of integrated circuits and the yawning technology gap, forward missile placements in Europe, Ronald Reagan's Strategic Defense Initiative, and investments in underwater surveillance had all put an unbearable pressure on the USSR to invest. But at the same time, its resources were limited: Saudi Arabia and the United Kingdom (with its new North Sea production) worked to keep oil prices down, denying the Soviet Union extra foreign exchange and making Europeans less anxious to buy Russian gas. The USSR's closed system and status prevented easy access to Western technology. The Soviets' war in Afghanistan had sapped money and internal political support. Behind almost all of these forces and events lay the indirect competitive logic that Marshall and Roche expressed in 1976: *use your relative advantages to impose out-of-proportion costs on the opposition and complicate his problem of competing with you*.

All my life, the Soviet Union had dominated discussions of politics, war, and peace. I had grown up diving beneath my third-grade desk until the all-clear sounded, and worrying about Sputnik. During my undergraduate years at the University of California, Berkeley, professors had me read Karl Marx, Lenin, John Reed's vivid account of the Russian Revolution (*Ten Days That Shook the World*), and articles on worker-peasant self-management during the revolution. Today, we know that during the five years I heard lectures on the wonders of revolution at Berkeley (1960–65), about 1.5 million people were killed in the Soviet gulag. During the whole post-WWII period, the Soviet Union murdered upward of 20 million people, its own citizens and others under its control, a grisly improvement over the 40 million executed, purposefully starved, and worked to death in the 1917–48 period. As that strange and deadly empire collapsed, how much of the implosion was due to internal contradictions, and how much to the costs imposed on it by U.S. policy? As in any complex event, there were many causes. If Marshall and Roche's strategy was one of them, and I believe it was, then it compels our attention. Their insight was framed in the language of business strategy: identify your strengths and weaknesses, assess the opportunities and risks (your opponent's strengths and weaknesses), and build on your strengths. But the power of that strategy derived from their discovery of a different way of viewing competitive advantage—a shift from thinking about pure military capability to one of looking for ways to impose asymmetric costs on an opponent.

■ ■ ■

Marshall and Roche's analysis included a list of U.S. and Soviet strengths and weaknesses. Such lists were not new, and the traditional response to them would have been to invest more to tip the "balance" in one's favor. But Marshall and Roche, like Sam Walton, had an insight that, when acted upon, provided a much more effective way to compete—the discovery of hidden power in the situation.

CHAPTER 3

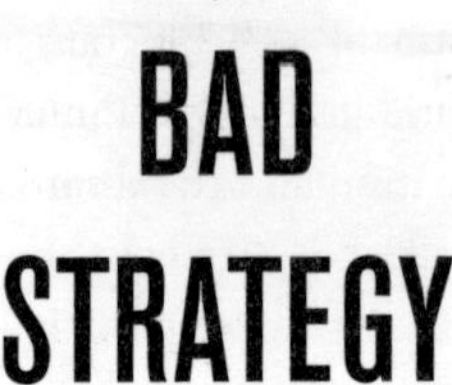

BAD STRATEGY

Bad strategy is not simply the absence of good strategy. It grows out of specific misconceptions and leadership dysfunctions. Once you develop the ability to detect bad strategy, you will dramatically improve your effectiveness at judging, influencing, and creating strategy. To detect a bad strategy, look for one or more of its four major hallmarks:

- *Fluff.* Fluff is a form of gibberish masquerading as strategic concepts or arguments. It uses "Sunday" words (words that are inflated and unnecessarily abstruse) and apparently esoteric concepts to create the illusion of high-level thinking.

- *Failure to face the challenge.* Bad strategy fails to recognize or define the challenge. When you cannot define the challenge, you cannot evaluate a strategy or improve it.

- *Mistaking goals for strategy.* Many bad strategies are just statements of desire rather than plans for overcoming obstacles.

- *Bad strategic objectives.* A strategic objective is set by a leader as a means to an end. Strategic objectives are "bad" when they fail to address critical issues or when they are impracticable.

THE ORIGIN OF THE "BAD STRATEGY" CONCEPT

I coined the term "bad strategy" in 2007 at a short Washington, D.C., seminar on national security strategy. To understand the concept, it is helpful to understand the nature of the disorder it describes.

Organized by the Center for Strategic and Budgetary Assessments (CSBA), the 2007 seminar had nine participants, including major figures such as James R. Schlesinger, former secretary of defense, secretary of energy, and director of the CIA; and Fred C. Iklé, member of the Council on Foreign Relations, former undersecretary of defense for policy, director of the U.S. Arms Control and Disarmament Agency, and chairman of the bipartisan Commission on Integrated Long-Term Strategy.[1] We did not come together to examine any particular strategy but, rather, to understand the reasons for what all agreed was a decline in the quality of strategy work at the national level.

There was no disagreement about the facts. During and after World War II, especially with the advent of nuclear weapons, U.S. national leadership took national security strategy very seriously. But after 1989, as the threat of a major offensive attack by another large power faded, the need for a new integrated strategic review of U.S. national security strategy became apparent. A new post–Cold War strategy was needed, one that would deal with issues such as nuclear proliferation, infrastructure protection, the use of space, energy use and supply, global financial markets, the information revolution, advances in biotechnology, the future of NATO, ethnic conflicts and failing states, and difficulties with Russia and China.

This need for a dramatic redesign of the United States' security-oriented institutional structures and processes became even more important following the September 11, 2001, attacks. One analysis, the Princeton Project on National Security, succinctly described the situation: "While the Bush administration's 2002 National Security Strategy did articulate a set of U.S. national goals and objectives, it was not the product of a serious attempt at strategic planning. . . . The articulation of a national vision that describes America's purpose in the post–

September 11th world is useful—indeed, it is vital—but describing a destination is no substitute for developing a comprehensive roadmap for how the country will achieve its stated goals."[2]

Despite the obvious need, very little had been done. The central question on the table was "Why not?" Was it a problem of leadership, institutional structure, or shortened time horizons? The seminar was guided by a fascinating paper arguing that there had been a general decline in competence at understanding and formulating strategy.[3] It contended, "All too much of what is put forward as strategy is not. The basic problem is confusion between strategy and strategic goals." With regard to the recent editions of the national security strategy, it said "when you look closely at either the 2002 or 2006 documents, all you find are lists of goals and sub-goals, not strategies."

Reading the documents referenced, I had to agree.[4] They presented a plethora of broad goals and affirmations of values such as democracy and economic well-being. But there was little guidance as to how to actually deal with the national security situation.

At the center of these documents lay President George W. Bush's dramatic new doctrine of responding to the threat of weapons of mass destruction with preventive war, if necessary. Yet there were no indications that this doctrine had been turned into a coherent strategy. That is, the conditions of its actual use to dissuade, deter, and intervene were not explored. Further, the problems created by this policy, and the competitive reactions to it, were not thought through. For instance, to avoid debacles as happened in the 2003 Iraq hunt for weapons of mass destruction, a policy of preemption should be backed up with much stronger intelligence.

To initiate a preemptive war, it is reasonable to expect that one would move far beyond secondhand intelligence and demand actual hands-on hard evidence obtained by U.S. forces. Preparing the capability for such a major evidence-producing prestrike operation would have to be a critical objective, yet it was not. Nor was there any evidence that the policy makers had thought through the problem, evident in both the Bosnian and Iraqi interventions, of the United States being fed false or exaggerated intelligence information in order to induce military action to the benefit of an external constituency. Finally, a policy of preemption encourages adversaries to use extreme secrecy, cover parties, and cutouts, and to use, rather than hold, weapons. Policies that anticipated these predictable patterns in others' behavior were lacking.

Looking at another section of the national security strategy, I found that the United States will "work with others to defuse regional conflicts." This is an amazingly superficial political slogan. After all, are there really any other alternatives for dealing with regional conflicts? It seems unlikely that the United States could act alone all over the world to defuse regional conflicts, and it seems equally unlikely that we would completely ignore regional conflicts. Stating this slogan provided no useful guidance to anyone. Even worse, it relegated to the status of an annoying detail the fact that this approach was less and less effective. NATO had failed to deliver most of its promised military and development support in Afghanistan, and the United Nations appeared incapable of solving the problems in the Sudan, Uganda, and Nepal, and it appeared to actually foster Israeli-Palestinian conflict.

One supposes that the slogan might have been code for "We give up on the United Nations and will work with whoever can help defuse regional conflicts." But a general willingness to work with interested others can hardly be elevated to the status of a "strategy." A strategy would have to explain why regional conflicts, which have been a constant in human activity for millennia, are suddenly a major security problem. And it would have to explain which instruments of U.S. power and influence might be used to convince others to work with the United States on such crusades. It would also have to address the criteria for working with nations that violated the national security strategy's other goals of "human dignity," "free trade," "democracy," and "freedom."

As another example of slogans substituted for strategy, consider this keystone goal of the national security strategy: "to prevent our enemies from threatening us, our allies, and our friends, with weapons of mass destruction." Importantly, the 2006 document explained the objective this way: "We aim to convince our adversaries that they cannot achieve their goals with WMD, and thus deter and dissuade them from attempting to use or even acquire these weapons in the first place."

It is difficult to understand what the author of this passage had in mind. What would "convince" enemies of the United States that *threats* based on WMDs would not advance their goals? America's own Cold War strategy had been based on threats to use WMD, which should be convincing evidence that such threats work quite well. It is clear, for instance, that had Saddam Hussein possessed nuclear weapons and the will to use them against allied military forces encamped in Saudi Arabia in 1991, or in Kuwait in 2003, his country would not have been invaded. His threat to kill our soldiers would have been credible, whereas a reciprocal threat to mass murder Iraqi civilians would have been less credible. Russian intelligence officers reported that he understood this logic very well in 1991 and was frustrated that his then-secret nuclear project was not further along. Since the 2006 National Security Strategy does not explain how the deadly effectiveness of nuclear threat is to be mitigated, this particular "goal" appears to be wishful thinking.

A logical reaction to these documents' weaknesses might be that they were public—that the real strategies were concealed. I had to reject this explanation. Other analysts with access to privileged information had also called out the lack of substance and coherence in U.S. national strategy. Furthermore, the participants at the CSBA conference were insiders, people who had shaped national policy at the highest levels, and among them there was no disagreement with the assessment that recent attempts at national security strategy had produced a plentitude of vague aspirations and new funding for existing institutions, but no policies or programs that could reasonably be expected to make a difference.

My role at the seminar was to provide a business and corporate strategy perspective on these issues. My impression was that the participants anticipated that I would say that business and corporate strategy was done seriously and with growing competence.

Using words and slides, I told the group that many businesses did have powerful, effective strategies. But in my personal experiences with corporate practice, both as a consultant and as a field researcher, I saw a growing profusion of what I termed "bad strategy."

Bad strategy, I explained, is not the same thing as no strategy or strategy that fails rather than succeeds. Rather, it is an identifiable way of thinking and writing about strategy that has, unfortunately, been gaining ground. Bad strategy is long on goals and short on policy or action. It assumes that goals are all you need. It puts forward strategic objectives that are incoherent and, sometimes, totally impracticable. It uses high-sounding words and phrases to hide these failings.

In the several years since that seminar, I have had the opportunity to discuss the bad strategy concept with a number of senior executives. In the process, I have condensed my list of its key hallmarks to the four listed in the beginning of this chapter: fluff, the failure to face the challenge, mistaking goals for strategy, and bad strategic objectives.

FLUFF

Fluff is superficial restatement of the obvious combined with a generous sprinkling of buzzwords. Fluff masquerades as expertise, thought, and analysis. As a simple example of fluff in strategy work, here is a quote from a major retail bank's internal strategy memoranda: "Our fundamental strategy is one of customer-centric intermediation." The Sunday word "intermediation" means that the company accepts deposits and then lends them to others. In other words, it is a bank. The buzz phrase "customer-centric" could mean that the bank competes by offering depositors and lenders better terms or better service. But an examination of its policies and products does not reveal any distinction in this regard. The phrase "customer-centric intermediation" is pure fluff. Pull off the fluffy covering and you have the superficial statement "Our bank's fundamental strategy is being a bank."

Fluff has its origins in the academic world and, more recently, in the information technology industry. There, for example, a recent EU report defines "cloud computing" as "an elastic execution environment of resources involving multiple stakeholders and providing a metered service at multiple granularities for a specified level of quality-of-service."[5] A less fluffy explanation is that when you do a Google search, or send data to an Internet backup service, you do not know or care which physical computer, data server, or software system is being used—there is a "cloud" of machines and networks, and it is up to the external service provider to work out how the job is performed and how you will be charged.

I saw an example of prime fluff in a summer 2000 presentation by the now-defunct Arthur Andersen. At that moment Enron was a darling of Wall Street, and Arthur Andersen, its auditor, was busy trying to attract new clients based on its knowledge of Enron's business strategy. (This was a presentation by a unit of the Arthur Andersen accounting firm, not by the firm's true consulting arm, Andersen Consulting.) The session was titled "Strategies of the Movers and Shakers."[6]

The presenter made it clear that the key "mover and shaker" was Enron, and the excitement was about its recent announcement that it would create a market for trading bandwidth. In the words of the speaker, "Nine months ago, when Enron first announced its bandwidth trading strategy, its market value jumped by $9 billion. Today, the market is valuing the bandwidth trading business at about $30 billion."

Deregulation in gas and electricity had created price volatility in these markets. Public utilities, however, preferred stable prices for their inputs. Enron's strategy in the gas and electricity businesses had been to own some physical assets and engage in "basis trading." That is, it would sell a utility a contract for future delivery of gas or electricity at a fixed price and then try to cover that commitment with a mixture of its own supplies and futures contracts. It used a barrage of contracts with speculators and other traders to hedge weather, price, and other risks. By being the dominant player in both gas and electricity trading, it was able to capture information about supplies, demand, and congestion that gave it an edge in its trading activities.

The question that should have been on everyone's mind was whether Enron could actually replicate this way of doing business in bandwidth trading. There was no spot price in bandwidth to use for basis trading. There was no standard of quality to help define the deliverable. There was no way to ship bandwidth around to balance supply and demand across geographies. Enron wanted every trader to deal directly with it—the company would not be a middleman—yet its own network node in New York City was some distance from the node used by almost everyone else. And, unlike gas and electricity, the incremental cost of a unit of bandwidth was zero. That meant as long as capacity exceeded demand, the spot price in such a market would be close to zero. Furthermore, by the summer of 2000, it was becoming clear that installed fiber-optic capacity greatly exceeded demand. Finally, in gas and electricity, Enron traded the deliverable, not capacity. But bandwidth was capacity, not the content being delivered. Enron did not have a position in supplying content—online movies and other bandwidth-intensive content were hardly commodities.

The argument given at the presentation was that commodity markets "evolve" in the same way, so the same business strategies apply to all. This theory was summarized with the following diagram, a page taken from the PowerPoint handouts at this presentation. This diagram seemed to be describing some sort of "evolution" in these markets from physical delivery toward a "knowledge space" and "exotics." There was the implication that derivative securities (bets on prices) were a means of "sophisticated value extraction."

Rather than address the real challenges of establishing a market for bandwidth, this diagram and the accompanying verbal presentation were pure fluff. There was the surface appearance of being analytical and summing up a great deal of information. But a closer examination revealed that it was a stew of half-truths, complex drawings, and buzzwords.

IN TODAY'S BANDWIDTH MARKETS, CONNECTIVITY IS KEY

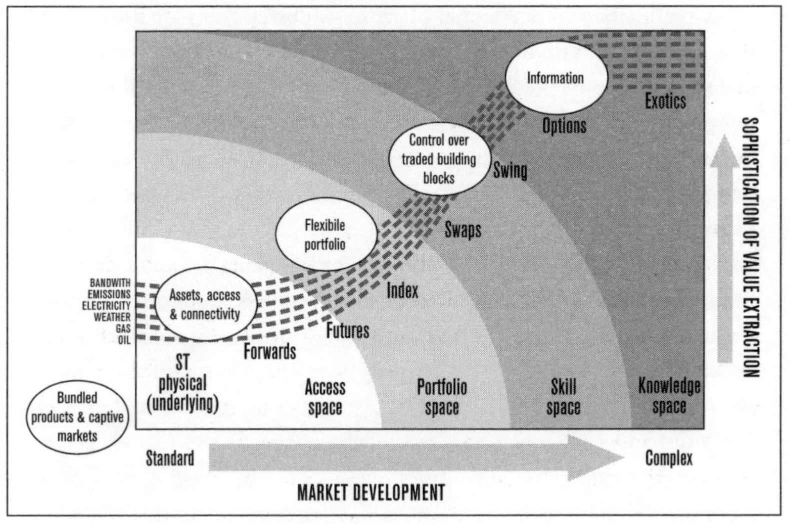

Markets do not necessarily evolve from "simple" to "complex"—it often goes the other way around. Yes, you need a basis to create futures and options, but a basis does not have to be a commodity or even a price. Traders, for example, write futures contracts on the Chicago Board Options Exchange Volatility Index (VIX), which is a created measure of price volatility. Yes, Enron's gas and electricity trading were developed out of the ownership of physical assets, but that might be a temporary phenomenon. The oil and agriculture industries had long supported futures contracts and options without heavy participation by producers.

Waiting for answers to my questions, I was disappointed. The "meat" in the presentation was the above fluffy diagram and a listing of the new "strategies of the market enablers." The "strategies" mentioned were having an electronic trading platform, being an over-the-counter broker, and being an information provider. These were not strategies—they were just names, like butcher, baker, and candlestick maker. If you accept that the phrase "information provider" describes a business strategy, then you are a prime customer for this sort of fluff.

Fourteen months later, it became evident that Enron was failing. With the company's mountain of debt, falling profit margins, failed major projects in the United Kingdom and Brazil, and huge losses in bandwidth trading, outsiders began to doubt its ability to fulfill its side of its contracts. No one wants to write a futures contract with a firm that may fail—which ensures that the firm will fail. As it went bankrupt in December 2001, evidence accumulated about fraudulent accounting practices. The scandal took its auditor, Arthur Andersen, down as well. (The accountant's consulting arm, Andersen Consulting, was renamed Accenture.) A systematic market for trading bandwidth has yet to develop.

A hallmark of true expertise and insight is making a complex subject understandable. A hallmark of mediocrity and bad strategy is unnecessary complexity—a flurry of fluff masking an absence of substance.

FAILURE TO FACE THE PROBLEM

A strategy is a way through a difficulty, an approach to overcoming an obstacle, a response to a challenge. If the challenge is not defined, it is difficult or impossible to assess the quality of the strategy. And if you cannot assess a strategy's quality, you cannot reject a bad strategy or improve a good one.

International Harvester was once the fourth largest corporation in the United States. Its roots lay in Cyrus McCormick's reaper, a machine that, together with the railroad, had developed the American plains. In 1977, Harvester's board brought in a new CEO, Archie McCardell, who had been president of Xerox. The board gave him a mandate to turn around the sleepy company.

McCardell's administration was the culmination of a decade of modernization. The consulting firm Booz Allen Hamilton had redesigned the organization; Hay Associates had put in modern managerial job descriptions and incentives. McCardell brought with him a new cadre of financial and strategic planners. In July 1979, they produced a thick sheaf of paper titled "Corporate Strategic Plan." It was classic bad strategy.

Harvester's corporate strategic plan was an amalgam of five separate strategic plans, each created by one of the operating divisions—agricultural equipment ($3 billion), truck making ($4 billion), industrial equipment ($1 billion), gas turbines ($0.3 billion), and components ($1 billion). The overall "strategy" was to increase the company's market share in each market, cut costs in each business, and thereby ramp up revenue and profit. A summary page from that confidential plan is reproduced on the next page. The graph showing past and forecast profit forms an almost perfect "hockey stick," with an immediate recovery from decline followed by a steady rise.

The strategic plan did not lack for texture and detail. Looking within the agricultural equipment group, for example, there is information and discussion about each segment. The overall intent was to strengthen the dealer/distributor network and to reduce manufacturing costs. Market share in agricultural equipment was projected to increase from

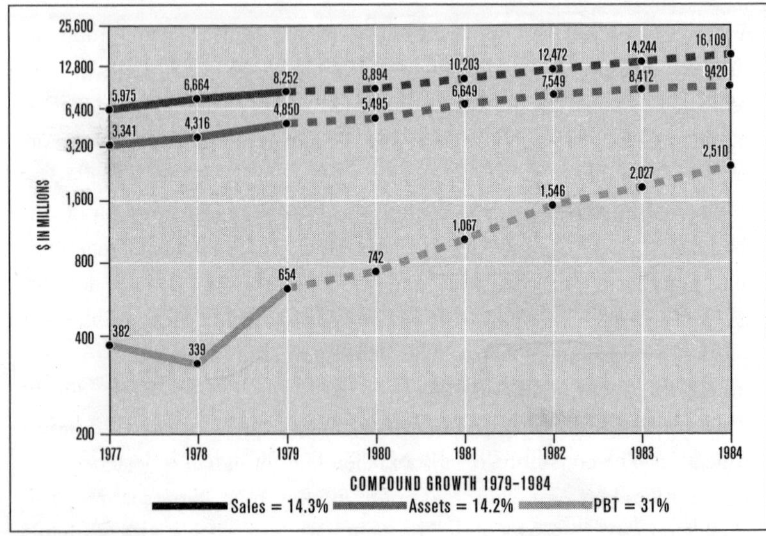

16 percent to 20 percent against competitors John Deere, Ford, Massey Ferguson, and J. I. Case.

The problem with all this was that it ignored the elephant in the elevator. You can't discern the elephant by studying the plan because the plan doesn't mention it. The elephant was Harvester's grossly inefficient work organization, a problem that would not be solved by investing in new equipment or by pressing managers to grow market share. Work rules at Harvester plants, for instance, allowed those with seniority to transfer jobs at will, each transfer setting in motion a cascade of other transfers. As a result, Harvester's profit margin had been about one-half of its competitors' for a long time. In addition, Harvester had the *worst* labor relations in American industry. It had been the nexus of some of the earliest labor disputes in the United States, especially the 1886 Haymarket riot in Chicago, when an anarchist's bomb killed police and workers at a rally.

If you fail to identify and analyze the obstacles, you don't have a strategy.

Instead, you have either a stretch goal, a budget, or a list of things you wish would happen.

McCardell did improve Harvester's reported profits for a year or two by cutting administrative overhead. But he then forced the company to endure a six-month strike in an attempt to obtain a better union contract. He failed to gain any significant concessions and, after the strike ended, the company quickly began to collapse. During the whole 1979–85 period, it lost more than $3 billion, closed thirty-five of its forty-two plants, and shed eighty-five thousand workers, leaving only fifteen thousand in employment. The company sold off its various businesses, the agricultural equipment going to Tenneco, to merge with its J. I. Case division. The truck division was renamed Navistar and has survived. It is, today, a leading maker of heavy trucks and engines.

Today, Harvester's 1979-style strategic planning is out of fashion. Instead of long tables of numbers and bubble charts, we have a different type of ritualized formalism for producing "strategic plans." The current fill-in-the-blanks template starts with a statement of "vision," then a "mission statement" or a list of "core values," then a list of "strategic goals," then for each goal a list of "strategies," and then, finally, a list of "initiatives." (Template-style strategy is explored further in chapter 4, "Why So Much Bad Strategy?")

Despite the fact that they are adorned with modern phrases and slogans, most of these strategic plans are as bad as International Harvester's. Like Harvester's, they do not identify and come to grips with the fundamental obstacles and problems that stand in the organization's way. Looking at most of this product, or listening to the managers who have produced it, you will find an almost total lack of strategic thinking. Instead, you will find high-sounding sentiments together with plans to spend more and somehow "get better."

■ ■ ■

The Defense Advanced Research Projects Agency (DARPA) works to achieve radical technological innovation to support national security. As a counterpoint to Harvester, DARPA's strategy is based on a clear-sighted recognition of the nature of the challenge. Here is DARPA's own statement of a fundamental problem its strategy addresses:

> A basic challenge for any military research organization is matching military problems with technological opportunities, including the new operational concepts those technologies make possible. Parts of this challenge are extremely difficult because: (1) some military problems have no easy or obvious technical solutions; and (2) some emerging technologies may have far-reaching military consequences that are still unclear. DARPA focuses its investments on this "DARPA-hard" niche—a set of technical challenges that, if solved, will be of enormous benefit to U.S. national security, even if the risk of technical failure is high.[7]

To attack this challenge, DARPA focuses on projects the military services see as too risky or too removed from their current missions. It tries to imagine what commanders will want in the future rather than what they are calling for today, but it restricts its work to that conducted by very talented people with very good ideas. Some of DARPA's successes include ballistic missile defense, stealth technology, GPS, speech recognition, the Internet, unmanned land and air vehicles, and nanotechnology.

DARPA's strategy is more than a general direction. It includes specific policies that guide its everyday actions. For example, it retains program managers for only four to six years to limit empire building and to bring in fresh talent. The expectation is that a new program manager will be willing to challenge the ideas and work of predecessors. In addition, DARPA has a very limited investment in overhead and physical facilities in order to prevent entrenched interests from thwarting progress in new directions. These policies are based on a realistic appraisal of the obstacles to innovation. They are a far cry from vague aspirations such as "retain the best talent" and "maintain a culture of innovation."

DARPA's surprising strategy has a shape and structure common to all good strategy. It follows from a careful definition of the challenge. It anticipates the real-world difficulties to be overcome. It eschews fluff. It creates policies that concentrate resources and actions on surmounting those difficulties.

MISTAKING GOALS FOR STRATEGY

Chad Logan, the CEO of a graphics arts company, introduced himself to me after hearing a talk I gave on self-control and commitment. He asked me to work with his management team on "strategic thinking."

With offices in a downtown commercial building, Logan's company provided custom graphics services to magazines, book publishers, advertisers, and corporations. Logan was a college sports hero turned graphics artist who had moved into sales. He was also the nephew of the founder; when the founder died two years before, Logan became the company's principal owner.

The edge-of-town offices and work spaces were utilitarian; the CEO's conference room was paneled in teak. Brightly lighted examples of the company's work hung on the walls and reflected from the surface of the polished conference table.

The business was organized into a large design group and three sales departments: Media sold to magazines and newspapers, Corporate sold to corporations for catalogs and brochures, and Digital sold mainly to Web-based customers.

Logan explained that his overall goal was simple—he called it the "20/20" plan. Revenues were to grow at 20 percent per year and the profit margin was to be 20 percent or higher. "Our overall strategy is set," he said. "We are going to grow, and grow profitably. My problem is getting everyone aligned for this push. What I need is some coaching for my top people. I want them to be totally up to speed on strategic thinking. I want skills they can use tomorrow in a meeting with a client."

I asked Logan if he had worked out any elements of his strategy other than the growth and margin goals. He slid a document across the tabletop. It was titled "2005 Strategic Plan." Mostly, it was a set of projections: revenues, costs, gross profit, and so on. The projections went out four years. In the previous four or five years, the company had held its market share and its after-tax profit margin had been about 12 percent, which is typical for this industry. The projections were based on a 20 percent profit margin and 20 percent per year revenue growth. The first page of the document was labeled "Our Key Strategies:"

OUR KEY STRATEGIES

- We will be the graphics arts services firm of choice.
- We will delight our customers with unique and creative solutions to their problems.
- We will grow revenue by at least 20% each year.
- We will maintain a profit margin of at least 20%.
- We will have a culture of commitment. Corporate goals are commitments we all work to keep.
- We will foster an honest and open work environment.
- We will work to support the broader community in which we operate.

"We spent about three weeks, going around to everyone, to develop these key strategies," said Logan. "I believe in them. I believe that we can have a company that we are each proud to be part of and that is worth the effort it takes to win. There is very good buy-in on these key strategies."

"This 20/20 plan is a very aggressive financial goal," I said. "What has to happen for it to be realized?"

Logan tapped the plan with a blunt forefinger. "The thing I learned as a football player is that winning requires strength and skill, but more than anything it requires the will to win—the drive to succeed. The managers and staff in this company have worked hard, and the transition to digital technologies was handled well. But there is a difference between working hard and having your eye on the prize and the will to win. Sure, 20/20 is a stretch, but the secret of success is setting your sights high. We are going to get moving and keep pushing until we get there."

When I asked Logan "What has to happen?" I was looking for some point of leverage, some reason to believe this fairly quiet company could explode with growth and profit. A strategy is like a lever that magnifies force. Yes, you might be able to drag a giant block of rock across the ground with muscles, ropes, and motivation. But it is wiser to build levers and wheels and then move the rock. I tried again: "Chad, when a company makes the kind of jump in performance your plan envisions, there is usually a key strength you are building on or a change in the industry that opens up new opportunities. Can you clarify what the point of leverage might be here, in your company?"

Logan frowned and pressed his lips together, expressing frustration that I didn't understand his meaning. He pulled a sheet of paper out of his briefcase and ran a finger under the highlighted text. "This is what Jack Welch says," he told me. The text read: "We have found that by reaching for what appears to be the impossible, we often actually do the impossible."

"That's what we are going to do here," said Logan.

I didn't think that Logan's concept of his 20/20 goal was a useful way to proceed. Strategic objectives should address a specific process or accomplishment, such as halving the time it takes to respond to a customer, or getting work from several Fortune 500 corporations. However, arguing with him at that juncture wouldn't have been productive. A client has to first agree to engage in a dialogue before a tough back-and-forth can be productive. "All right," I said. "I see where you are coming from. Give me some time to look over these numbers."

In truth, I didn't really need to study the numbers. What I needed was some time to think about my own approach to helping Logan. Although he was well-intentioned, his plan, to me, was all results and no action. In his own mind, he believed in courage, boldness, motivation, and push. His reference to "pushing until we get there" triggered, in my mind, an association with the great pushes of 1915–17 during World War I, especially at Passchendaele.

■ ■ ■

When war broke out in 1914, jubilant crowds jammed the streets of cities, and young men hurled hats in the air as they marched off to prove themselves. The philosophy of the age, most fervently adopted by the French, was that willpower, spirit, morale, élan, and aggressiveness were the keys to success. For three years, generals flung highly motivated men at fortified machine-gun emplacements, only to see tens of thousands, then hundreds of thousands, shredded to mincemeat to gain a mile of useless ground.

In 1917, around the village of Passchendaele in Flanders, British general Douglas Haig planned an assault. He wanted to break through the Germans' fortified lines and open up a path to the sea, dividing the German army. He had been advised that shelling the German fortified positions would destroy the dikes and flood the below-sea-level fields. He shelled the German fortifications anyway. The shelling broke the dikes and churned the rich soil to sticky yellow clay, a quagmire that men sank into up to their knees and bellies. It drowned tanks, horses, and the wounded.

Haig, stung by the death of 100,000 British troops at the Somme a year earlier, had promised to call off the advance if it did not go well. It didn't, yet the doctrine of motivation and "one last push" continued for three months, despite appalling losses. In a final ten-day assault, Canadian troops pressed directly into the machine-gun fire, floundering in the mud and body parts of comrades; they suffered 16,000 casualties to take a small hill. Over the three months of battle, five miles of ground were gained and more than 70,000 Allied soldiers died in the muck. Another 250,000 were wounded. Winston Churchill described Passchendaele as "a forlorn expenditure of valour and life without equal in futility."

At the Somme and Passchendaele, Haig led an entire generation of British and Dominion youth to their deaths—as Joseph Joffre did for the French at the Somme, and Erich von Falkenhayn did for the Germans at Verdun.

In Europe, motivational speakers are not the staple on the management lecture circuit that they are in the United States, where the doctrine of leadership as motivation is alive and well. Here, for example, is H. Ross Perot: "Most people give up just when they're about to achieve success. They quit on the one-yard line. They give up at the last minute of the game, one foot from a winning touchdown."

Hearing this, many Americans nod in agreement. Many Europeans, by contrast, hear the echo of the "one last push" at Passchendaele. There, the slaughtered troops did not suffer from a lack of motivation. They suffered from a lack of competent strategic leadership. Motivation is an essential part of life and success, and a leader may justly ask for "one last push," but the leader's job is more than that. The job of the leader is also to create the conditions that will make that push effective, to have a strategy worthy of the effort called upon.

■ ■ ■

I met with Chad Logan a few days after our first get-together. I told him that I would explain my point of view and then let him decide whether he wanted to work with me on strategy. I said:

> I think you have a lot of ambition, but you don't have a strategy. I don't think it would be useful, right now, to work with your managers on strategies for meeting the 20/20 goal.
>
> What I would advise is that you first work to discover the very most promising opportunities for the business. Those opportunities may be internal, fixing bottlenecks and constraints in the way people work, or external. To do this, you should probably pull together a small team of people and take a month to do a review of who your buyers are, who you compete with, and what opportunities exist. It's normally a good idea to look very closely at what is changing in your business, where you might get a jump on the competition. You should open things up so there are as many useful bits of information on the table as possible. If you want, I can help you structure some of this process and, maybe, help you ask some of the right questions. The end result will be a strategy that is aimed at channeling energy into what seem to be one or two of the most attractive opportunities, where it looks like you can make major inroads or breakthroughs.
>
> I can't tell you in advance how large such opportunities are, or where they may be. I can't tell you in advance how fast revenues will grow. Perhaps you will want to add new services, or cut back on doing certain things that don't make a profit. Perhaps you will find it more promising to focus on grabbing the graphics work that currently goes in-house, rather than to competitors. But, in the

> end, you should have a very short list of the most important things for the company to do. Then you will have a basis for moving forward. That is what I would do were I in your shoes.
>
> If you continue down the road you are on you will be counting on motivation to move the company forward. I cannot honestly recommend that as a way forward because business competition is not just a battle of strength and wills; it is also a competition over insights and competencies. My judgment is that motivation, by itself, will not give this company enough of an edge to achieve your goals.

Chad Logan thanked me and, a week later, retained someone else to help him. The new consultant took Logan and his department managers through an exercise he called "Visioning." The gist of it was the question "How big do you think this company can be?" In the morning they stretched their aspirations from "bigger" to "very much bigger." Then, in the afternoon, the facilitator challenged them to an even grander vision: "Think twice as big as that," he pressed. Logan was pleased. I was pleased to be elsewhere engaged.

■ ■ ■

Chad Logan's "key strategies" had little to do with strategy. They were simply performance goals. This same problem affects many corporate "strategy plans."

Business leaders know their organizations should have a strategy. Yet many express frustration with the whole process of strategic planning. The reason for this dissatisfaction is that most corporate strategic plans are simply three-year or five-year rolling budgets combined with market share projections. Calling a rolling budget of this type a "strategic plan" gives people false expectations that the exercise will somehow result in a coherent strategy.

There is nothing wrong with planning. It is an essential part of management. Take, for example, a rapidly growing retail chain. It needs a plan to guide property acquisition, construction, training, and so on. This is what a resource plan does—it makes sure resources arrive when they are needed and helps management detect surprises. Similarly, a multinational engineering company needs a plan to guide and fit together its human resource activities, the opening and expansion of offices in various regions, and its financing policies.

You can call these annual exercises "strategic planning" if you like, but they are not strategy. They cannot deliver what senior managers want: a pathway to substantially higher performance. To obtain higher performance, leaders must identify the critical obstacles to forward progress and then develop a coherent approach to overcoming them. This may require product innovation, or new approaches to distribution, or a change in organizational structure. Or it may exploit insights into the implications of changes in the environment—in technology, consumer tastes, laws, resource prices, or competitive behavior. The leader's responsibility is to decide which of these pathways will be the most fruitful and design a way to marshal the organization's knowledge, resources, and energy to that end. Importantly, opportunities, challenges, and changes don't come along in nice annual packages. The need for true strategy work is episodic, not necessarily annual.

BAD STRATEGIC OBJECTIVES

If you are a midlevel manager, your boss sets your goals. Or, if you work in an enlightened company, you and your boss negotiate over your goals. In either setting, it is natural to think of strategies as actions designed to accomplish specific goals. However, taking this way of thinking into a top-level position is a mistake.

Being a general manager, CEO, president, or other top-level leader means having more power and being less constrained. Effective senior leaders don't chase arbitrary goals. Rather, they *decide* which general goals should be pursued. And they design the subgoals that various pieces of the organization work toward. Indeed, the cutting edge of any strategy is the set of strategic objectives (subgoals) it lays out. One of the challenges of being a leader is mastering this shift from having others define your goals to being the architect of the organization's purposes and objectives.

To help clarify this distinction it is helpful to use the word "goal" to express overall values and desires and to use the word "objective" to denote specific operational targets. Thus, the United States may have "goals" of freedom, justice, peace, security, and happiness. It is *strategy* which transforms these vague overall goals into a coherent set of actionable objectives—defeat the Taliban and rebuild a decaying infrastructure. A leader's most important job is creating and constantly adjusting this strategic bridge between goals and objectives.

For example, Chen Brothers was a rapidly growing regional distributor of specialty foods. Its overall goals included growing profit, being a good place to work, and being seen as the go-to distributor for organic foods. These were all worthy goals. None of them, however, implied a particular strategy or action, although they can be seen as constraints (that is, these sorts of broad "goals" work like the rules of football in that they rule out a great many actions without specifying what the team should actually do).

Chen Brothers' strategy had been to target local specialty retailers that would pay a price premium to carry distinctive products not available at the large chain stores. Top management had divided its customers and potential customers into three tiers and set strategic objectives for each tier. The most important objectives were shelf-space dominance in the top tier, promotional parity or better in the middle tier, and growing penetration in the lowest tier.

The recent rapid growth of Whole Foods was putting increasing pressure on the local specialty shops that had been Chen Brothers' target market. Accordingly, management was formulating a new strategy of linking together small local food producers under a common brand that could be sold through Whole Foods. This change in strategy had no impact on the company's overall goals, but clearly meant a radical restructuring of its current strategic objectives. Instead of penetration objectives for different classes of retailers, Chen Brothers put together a "Whole Foods" team that combined production, marketing, advertising, distribution, and financial expertise. The team was entirely focused on the objective of making Chen Brothers' most distinctive new product a national account at Whole Foods. Once that was accomplished, further objectives concerning other products, shelf space, and market share would be set.

Chen Brothers did not fall into the trap of believing that strategy is a grand vision or a set of financial goals. Instead, management had skillfully designed a "way forward" that concentrated corporate attention on one or two important objectives. Once accomplished, new opportunities would open up and more ambitious objectives could be set.

Dog's Dinner Objectives

Good strategy works by focusing energy and resources on one, or a very few, pivotal objectives whose accomplishment will lead to a cascade of favorable outcomes. One form of bad strategic objectives occurs when there is a scrambled mess of things to accomplish—a "dog's dinner" of strategic objectives.

A long list of "things to do," often mislabeled as "strategies" or "objectives," is not a strategy. It is just a list of things to do. Such lists usually grow out of planning meetings in which a wide variety of stakeholders make suggestions as to things they would like to see done. Rather than focus on a few important items, the group sweeps the whole day's collection into the "strategic plan." Then, in recognition that it is a dog's dinner, the label "long-term" is added so that none of them need be done today.

As a vivid example, I recently had the chance to discuss strategy with the mayor of a small city in the Pacific Northwest. His planning committee's strategic plan contained 47 "strategies" and 178 action items. Action item number 122 was to "create a strategic plan." As another example, the Los Angeles Unified School District's strategic plan for "high-priority schools" (discussed on the next page) contained 7 "strategies," 26 "tactics," and 234 "action steps," a true dog's dinner of things to do. This pattern is all too common in city, school district, and non-profit strategy work, as well as in some business firms.

Blue-Sky Objectives

The second form of bad strategic objectives is one that is "blue sky." A good strategy defines a critical challenge. What is more, it builds a bridge between that challenge and action, between desire and immediate objectives that lie within grasp. Thus, the objectives a good strategy sets should stand a good chance of being accomplished, given existing resources and competence. (See the discussion of proximate objectives in chapter 7.) By contrast, a blue-sky objective is usually a simple restatement of the desired state of affairs or of the challenge. It skips over the annoying fact that no one has a clue as to how to get there.

A leader may successfully identify the key challenge and propose an overall approach to dealing with the challenge. But if the consequent strategic objectives are blue sky, not much has been achieved. The purpose of good strategy is to offer a potentially achievable way of surmounting a key challenge. If the leader's strategic objectives are just as difficult to accomplish as the original challenge, there has been little value added by the strategy.

■ ■ ■

In 2006, David Brewer, a former admiral in the U.S. Navy, took the job of superintendent of the giant Los Angeles Unified School District (LAUSD). His daunting assignment was to make a difference in the nation's largest school district.

In California, schools are measured in terms of a statewide aggregate test score—the Academic Performance Index, or API. Of Los Angeles's 991 schools, many did well on these tests. Still, 309 did not meet the U.S. Department of Education's No Child Left Behind goals. Soon after reviewing the situation, Brewer defined the challenge as making a significant improvement in the test performance scores at the district's 34 weakest schools: 17 middle and 17 high schools he termed "high priority." His idea was to work on improving these 34 weakest schools first, but to then build on success by expanding efforts to the rest of the system.

Brewer deserves credit for creating a strategy with a focus—the thirty-four high-priority schools that had been the consistently worst performing on the API tests. By focusing on the lowest performing 34 of 991 schools, there was the opportunity to break with the past and with the many-layered system of regulation, union control, and grossly oversized central administration. Indeed, it might have been reasonable to decide that this challenge, by itself, was worth being the single keystone of the strategy. By zeroing in on this one critical issue something might have been accomplished.

Still, it is worth noting that this definition of "performance" was itself "strategic" in an unpleasant way. Using API test scores sidestepped LAUSD's horrendous dropout rate, especially among black and Hispanic students who together form the overwhelming majority of students in Los Angeles (13 and 70 percent respectively). Of black students entering LAUSD high schools, 33 percent dropped out. Of Hispanics, 28 percent dropped out. The terrible truth was that one way to increase a school's API score was to encourage the weakest students to drop out—the API measured only active students.

When a leader characterizes the challenge as underperformance, it sets the stage for bad strategy. Underperformance is a result. The true challenges are the reasons for the underperformance. Unless leadership offers a theory of why things haven't worked in the past, or why the challenge is difficult, it is hard to generate good strategy.

For example, one of Brewer's seven key strategies was to "build school and District leadership teams that share common beliefs, values, and high expectations for all adults and students and that support a cycle of continuous improvement to ensure high-quality instruction in their schools." This would be accomplished by building the "capacity of administrative and other school leaders. . . . Transformational leaders need a strongly focused program to define, sharpen and apply critical skill sets in their everyday work."

This strategy/objective is "bad" in several respects. First, there is no diagnosis of the reasons that leadership is weak and expectations are low. A serious look at this issue would reveal that the high-priority schools had been failing for decades. A system spending $25,000 per student per year[8] and that cannot guarantee that eighth-graders read, write, and do sums is broken. While many teachers and principals are dedicated, many are also incompetent. More important, the top-heavy bureaucratic system has had decades to remedy the system and has not.

Second, it is an absurdly blue-sky objective to ask for "transformational leadership" when (1) the text of the plan explains that many administrators and leaders have limited ability to meet their daily problems, (2) no one knows how to create "transformational" leaders even in the best of conditions, and (3) these schools remain embedded in a giant all-controlling bureaucracy and union system. The so-called transformational leaders cannot change the color of the paper they use without permission from higher-ups, and it is virtually impossible to remove a principal, even if he or she fails to be transformational. The proposed solutions—lots of coordination up and down the hierarchy, time off, and in-house training—are woefully inadequate and illustrate the system's wasteful self-serving sclerosis.

An interesting aspect of this language is the idea that leadership teams must share common beliefs and values. This is now a frequent demand in education circles. One would hope that the experience of North Korea would have cured people of the idea that forcing everyone to believe in and value the same things is the road to high performance. Yet, within politically correct edu-speak, this impossible state of affairs is continually sought as the path to "transformational change."

Another "strategy" was to "build at each school a community of informed and empowered parents, teachers, staff, and community partners who work collaboratively to support high-quality teaching and learning." In particular, the plan called for the creation of a "community liaison" position, mandating monthly meetings, twice-a-year parent conferences, and a parent volunteer program.

A high rate of community involvement might be a very desirable state of affairs. But it is hardly a strategy. It is a blue-sky objective. Much of the underperformance in these thirty-four schools appears at kindergarten and deepens as students grow older. A principal cause of this underperformance is the poverty-stricken chaotic communities these schools serve. In the LAUSD, many students are illegal immigrants or the children of illegal immigrants. Names and addresses are often fictitious, and parents may be unwilling to sign up for school programs. Many students are the children of teen mothers who never finished their own educations, don't read books themselves, and have little free time or energy, spending hours each day commuting to and from low-paying jobs. These are the kinds of true challenges a good strategy would have to recognize.

■ ■ ■

As we have seen through the examples of U.S. national security strategy, Arthur Andersen's presentation, International Harvester, Chad Logan, and the LAUSD, bad strategy is vacuous and superficial, has internal contradictions, and doesn't define or address the problem. Bad strategy generates a feeling of dull annoyance when you have to listen to it or read it. The next chapter examines why so much bad strategy exists.

CHAPTER FOUR

WHY SO MUCH BAD STRATEGY?

Given the almost universal recognition of the importance of strategy, it is natural to ask "Why is bad strategy so common?" To begin, bad strategy is not miscalculation. I am intimately familiar with the myriad mistakes and errors that can be made in assessing the competition, one's own resources, the lessons of the past, and the opportunities and problems presented by change and innovation.

However, after years of working with companies and teaching strategy to executives and MBA students, I have found that more training in these fundamental areas barely puts a dent in the proclivity to create bad strategy. Bad strategy flourishes because it floats above analysis, logic, and choice, held aloft by the hot hope that one can avoid dealing with these tricky fundamentals and the difficulties of mastering them.

Not miscalculation, bad strategy is the active avoidance of the hard work of crafting a good strategy. One common reason for choosing avoidance is the pain or difficulty of choice. When leaders are unwilling or unable to make choices among competing values and parties, bad strategy is the consequence. A second pathway to bad strategy is the siren song of template-style strategy—filling in the blanks with vision, mission, values, and strategies. This path offers a one-size-fits-all substitute for the hard work of analysis and coordinated action. A third pathway to bad strategy is New Thought—the belief that all you need to succeed is a positive mental attitude. There are other pathways to bad strategy, but these three are the most common. Understanding how and why they are taken should help you guide your footsteps elsewhere.

THE UNWILLINGNESS OR INABILITY TO CHOOSE

Strategy involves focus and, therefore, choice. And choice means setting aside some goals in favor of others. When this hard work is not done, weak amorphous strategy is the result.

In early 1992, I sat in on a strategy discussion among senior executives at the Digital Equipment Corporation (DEC) that concerned the future direction of the company. A leader of the minicomputer revolution of the 1960s and '70s and an innovator of user-friendly operating systems, DEC was rapidly losing ground to the newer 32-bit personal computers. There were serious doubts that the company could survive without dramatic changes.

While there were several key people at this meeting, I will simplify matters by summarizing the positions of those attending through the voices of only three executives: "Alec," "Beverly," and "Craig," each of whom argued in favor of a different direction for the company.

Alec held that DEC was and always had been a computer company, integrating hardware and software into usable systems.

Beverly derisively named Alec's preference as the "Boxes" strategy. She felt that "Boxes" had become a commodity and that the only real resource DEC had to build on was its customer relationships. Hence, she argued in favor of a strategy that solved customer problems, a strategy the others named "Solutions."

Craig disagreed with both Alec and Beverly, holding that the heart of the computer industry was semiconductor technology, and that the company should focus its resources on designing and building better "Chips." DEC had no distinctive competence, Craig argued, in finding Solutions to customer problems. "We are having enough trouble solving our own problems," he said. Alec and Beverly disagreed with the Chips strategy, believing that DEC would not be able to catch up to companies such as IBM and Intel in the chip business.

Why not forgo the arguments and do all three? There were two reasons. First, if one has a policy of resolving conflict by adopting all the options on the table, there will be no incentive for anyone to develop and sharpen their arguments in the first place. Only the prospect of choice inspires peoples' best arguments about the pluses of their own proposals and the negatives of others'. As in the law, disciplined conflict calls forth stronger evidence and reasoning. Second, both Chips and Solutions represented dramatic transformations of the firm, and each would require developing wholly new skills and work practices. One wouldn't choose either risky alternative unless the status quo Boxes strategy was failing. And one wouldn't choose to do both Chips and Solutions at the same time because there was little common ground between them. It is not feasible to do two separate deep transformations of a company's core at once.

■ ■ ■

Here are Alec, Beverly, and Craig's rank-order preferences for the three alternatives facing DEC:

	Alec	Beverly	Craig
Boxes	1	2	3
Chips	2	3	1
Solutions	3	1	2

Their rankings create what is known as Condorcet's paradox.[1] The paradox arises if the three vote on the strategies in paired comparisons. In a first contest between Boxes and Chips, Alec and Beverly both prefer Boxes, so Boxes wins. Now, compare the winner of that vote (Boxes) to Solutions. In this second vote, Beverly and Craig both prefer Solutions, so Solutions wins. Thus, Solutions beat Boxes, which beat Chips. Given these outcomes, one would think that the group would prefer the two-round winner (Solutions) to the first-round loser (Chips). But, alas, in a contest between Solutions and Chips, Alec and Craig both prefer

Chips, so Chips beats Solutions. This cycling of results, with no ending point, is Condorcet's paradox.

You might imagine resolving this problem with a cleverer voting scheme. Perhaps the three could weight their preferences and one could somehow combine these weights. Economist Kenneth Arrow received a Nobel Prize in 1972 for proving that such attempts are fruitless.[2] This sort of group irrationality is a central property of democratic voting, a fact not covered in high school civics.

The DEC group did not carry out a formal vote in its meetings. However, the effect of the Condorcet paradox was felt in the group's inability to form a stable majority coalition. Staying with the simplification of three people, when any two tried to agree on an outcome, forming a majority, one of them was then tempted to defect and join forces with the third, forming a different majority that was closer to their desire. Suppose, for example, that Beverly and Craig formed a coalition to support Solutions. Because this policy was Craig's second-best choice, he would be tempted to defect and join with Alec in a majority supporting Chips. But that coalition was also unstable as Alec would then be tempted to defect and team up with Beverly to support Boxes, and so on.

■ ■ ■

With equally powerful executives arguing for three conflicting strategies, the meeting was intense. The opinions expressed were not grounded in self-centered motives, but expressed differing beliefs about what was good for the company.

DEC's chief executive, Ken Olsen, had made the mistake of asking the group to reach a consensus. The group was unable to do that because there was no basis in logic or hierarchy to reject a subgroup's passionately held positions. Instead, the group compromised on a statement like this: "DEC is committed to providing high-quality products and services and being a leader in data processing."

This fluffy, amorphous statement was, of course, not a strategy. It was a political outcome reached by individuals who, forced to reach a consensus, could not agree on which interests and concepts to forgo. So they avoided the hard work of choice, set nothing aside, hurt no interest groups or individual egos, but crippled the whole.

CEO Ken Olsen was replaced in June 1992 by Robert Palmer, who had headed semiconductor engineering. In short order, Palmer made it clear that the strategy would be Chips. He stopped the losses for a while but could not stem the tide of ever more powerful personal computers that were overtaking the firm. DEC was acquired by Compaq in 1998, which, in turn, was acquired by Hewlett-Packard three years later.

Serious strategy work in an already successful organization may not take place until the wolf is at the door—or even until the wolf's claws actually scratch on the floor—because good strategy is very hard work. At DEC, the wolf was at the door in 1988, but still the hard work of combining the knowledge and judgments of people with different backgrounds and talents was sidestepped. When the wolf finally broke into the house itself, one point of view won and pressed aside the others. By then, it was five years too late to matter.

■ ■ ■

There has been a lot of ink spilled on the inner logic of competitive strategy and on the mechanics of advantage. But the essential difficulty in creating strategy is not logical; it is choice itself. Strategy does not eliminate scarcity and its consequence—the necessity of choice. Strategy is scarcity's child and to have a strategy, rather than vague aspirations, is to choose one path and eschew others. There is difficult psychological, political, and organizational work in saying "no" to whole worlds of hopes, dreams, and aspirations.

When a strategy works, we tend to remember what was accomplished, not the possibilities that were painfully set aside. For instance, one of President Eisenhower's campaign promises made during the presidential election of 1952 was to roll back the Soviet Union from Eastern Europe. He won the election in a landslide. But after the election he initiated a study (Project Solarium) of national policy with regard to the Soviet Union, a project that remains the gold standard for how security strategy should be made. Having studied the problem and the alternatives he then made the hard choice—he put aside his campaign promises and chose not to challenge the USSR's conquests in Eastern Europe.[3] We would deter the Soviet Union from military attacks on Western Europe, but there would be no rollback. There would be Radio Free Europe and spies, but the countries dominated by the Soviet Union at the end of the World War II would be left under its control.

Any coherent strategy pushes resources toward some ends and away from others. These are the inevitable consequences of scarcity and change. Yet this channeling of resources away from traditional uses is fraught with pain and difficulty. Intel CEO Andy Grove vividly relates the intellectual, emotional, and political difficulties in moving the company from producing dynamic random access memory (DRAM) to one focused on microprocessors.

Intel was known as a memory company and had developed much of the complex technology required to design and manufacture chips. But by 1984 it was clear that Intel could not match the prices of its Japanese rivals in DRAM. Losing money, Grove recalls, "We persevered because we could afford to." Losing more and more money, senior management engaged in endless debates about what to do. Grove recalls the turning point in 1985 when he gloomily asked Intel's chairman, Gordon Moore, "If we got kicked out and the board brought in a new CEO, what do you think he would do?" Moore immediately replied, "He would get us out of memories." Grove recalls that he went numb and then finally said, "Why shouldn't you and I walk out the door, come back and do it ourselves?"[4]

Even after forming that conviction, it took over a year to make the change. The memory business had been the engine that drove research, production, careers, and pride at Intel. Salespeople worried about customer response, and researchers resisted the cancellation of memory-based projects. Grove pushed through the exit from the memory business and refocused the company on microprocessors. The success of the new 32-bit 386 chips propelled Intel into being the world's largest semiconductor company by 1992. (This generation of chips was, interestingly, the undoing of DEC, discussed earlier.)

Strategies focus resources, energy, and attention on some objectives rather than others. Unless collective ruin is imminent, a change in strategy will make some people worse off. Hence, there will be powerful forces opposed to almost any change in strategy. This is the fate of many strategy initiatives in large organizations. There may be talk about focusing on this or pushing on that, but at the end of the day no one wants to change what they are doing very much. When organizations are unable to make new strategies—when people evade the work of choosing among different paths into the future—then you get vague mom-and-apple-pie goals that everyone can agree on. Such goals are direct evidence of leadership's insufficient will or political power to make or enforce hard choices. Put differently, universal buy-in usually signals the absence of choice.

In organizations and politics, the longer a pattern of activity is maintained, the more it becomes entrenched and the more its supporting resource allocations are taken to be entitlements. Compare, for example, the inertia in today's national security apparatus with that experienced by Presidents Truman and Eisenhower. During Eisenhower's administration, the Defense Department, an independent air force, the CIA, the National Security Council, and NATO were *all* newly created. Because new structures are more malleable, President Eisenhower had enough power to reshape their missions and induce some coordination with the Department of State. But today, after more than half a century, the power required to reshape and compel coordination among these organizations is many times greater than Eisenhower ever used. It would take enormous political will and the exercise of great centralized power to overcome the present levels of institutional resistance to change. Such power is, of course, possible, but it would take a crisis of epic proportions to engender it.

TEMPLATE-STYLE STRATEGY

Oddly enough, the study of charisma has led to a common type of bad strategy. The path starts with the recognition that truly inspirational leaders—ranging from Moses to Churchill to Gandhi to Martin Luther King Jr.—occupy a different space than leaders who draw authority from birth or organizational rank. The path then passes through the dry baked clay of academic sociology before cutting through the shifting sand dunes of management consulting.

The idea of charismatic leadership dates back to Max Weber (1864–1920), the father of sociology. Describing leaders, he found it necessary to distinguish between formal leaders and those who led by personal charisma. The latter, he wrote, seemed "endowed with supernatural, superhuman, or at least specifically exceptional powers or qualities . . . not accessible to the ordinary person."[5]

Traditionally, charisma was associated with religious and political leaders, not CEOs or school principals. This began to change in the mid-1980s. The tipping point was the appearance of two books in 1985: Warren Bennis and Bert Nanus's *Leaders: The Strategies for Taking Charge* and Bernard Bass's influential *Transformational Leadership: Industrial, Military, and Educational Impact*. These authors broke with tradition and argued that charismatic (now "transformational") leadership can be learned and practiced in settings ranging from schools to corporations to art museums. The transformational leader, they argued, unlocks human energy by creating a vision of a different reality and connecting that vision to people's values and needs. These works were followed by a raft of books and articles in a similar vein: *The Leadership Challenge: How to Get Extraordinary Things Done in Organizations* (1987), *The Transformational Leader: The Key to Global Competitiveness* (1990), and *Executive Charisma: Six Steps to Mastering the Art of Leadership* (2003).

Not everyone was drawn to this formulation. Peter Drucker, one of the foremost thinkers about management, said, "Effective leadership doesn't depend on charisma. Dwight Eisenhower, George Marshall, and Harry Truman were singularly effective leaders, yet none possessed any more charisma than a dead mackerel. . . . Charisma does not by itself guarantee effectiveness as a leader."

The key innovation in this growing stream has been the reduction of charismatic leadership to a formula. The general outline goes like this: the transformational leader (1) develops or has a vision, (2) inspires people to sacrifice (change) for the good of the organization, and (3) empowers people to accomplish the vision. Some experts place more emphasis on the moral qualities of the leader, others on commitment, and others on the leader being intellectually stimulating.

This conceptual scheme has been hugely popular with college-educated people who have to manage other college-educated people. It satisfies their sense that organizations should somehow be forced to change and improve while also satisfying their contradictory sense that it is awkward to tell other people what to do.

Whatever you think about this definition of leadership, a problem arises when it is confused with strategy. Leadership and strategy may be joined in the same person, but they are not the same thing. Leadership inspires and motivates self-sacrifice. Change, for example, requires painful adjustments, and good leadership helps people feel more positively about making those adjustments. Strategy is the craft of figuring out which purposes are both worth pursuing and capable of being accomplished.

■ ■ ■

As an example of charismatic leadership without the craft of strategy, consider the famous Children's Crusade. It began in 1212 when young Stephen, a French shepherd boy, had a vision of a band of children traveling to Jerusalem to throw out the Muslims. In his vision, the sea parted before them as it had for Moses. Those who heard him speak of this vision and his purpose were impressed with his passion and eloquence. Word of Stephen's vision traveled to Germany, where another young man, Nicholas, organized his own crusade, his vision being the conversion of the Muslims rather than their conquest. Both youthful charismatic leaders gathered followers and began their arduous journeys.

Stephen's large band walked for months, finally arriving at Marseilles, on the Mediterranean coast. There they managed to embark on seven ships. Two wrecked, killing all aboard. The other five were captured by Muslim raiders, and all aboard were sold into slavery.

Nicholas, starting his trek south with twenty thousand German children, reached Rome with a much smaller number. There, most were convinced to return home. Only a few made it back. The parents of the dead children hanged Nicholas's father.

There is no denying the power of charismatic vision to move people.

It is a potent way to overcome inertia and motivate both action and self-sacrifice. But in 1212, as in many other times, thousands sacrificed to no end.

To achieve great ends, charisma and visionary leadership must almost always be joined with a careful attention to obstacles and action, as Gandhi was able to do in India. There, his carefully orchestrated demonstrations, marches, publicity, and times in jail built his base and eroded the British rulers' self-image of fairness and morality. His charisma and vision, coupled with a good strategy, gave India both independence and a proud heritage.

■ ■ ■

By the early 2000s, the juxtaposition of vision-led leadership and strategy work had produced a template-style system of "strategic planning." (Google "vision mission strategy" to find thousands of examples of this template for sale and in use.) The template generally looks like this:

The Vision: Fill in your unique vision of what the school/business/nation will be like in the future. Currently popular unique visions are to be "the best" or "the leading" or "the best known." For example, Dow Chemical's vision is "To be the most profitable and respected science-driven chemical company in the world."[6] Enron's vision was "to become the world's leading energy company."

The Mission: Fill in a high-sounding politically correct statement of the purpose of the school/business/nation. Dow's mission is "To passionately innovate what is essential to human progress by providing sustainable solutions to our customers."

The Values: Fill in a statement describing the company's values. Make sure they are noncontroversial. Dow's values are "Integrity, Respect for People, and Protecting

Our Planet." Enron's were "Respect, Integrity, Communication and Excellence."

The Strategies: Fill in some aspirations/goals but call them strategies. For example, Dow's corporate strategies are "Preferentially invest in a portfolio of technology-integrated, market-driven performance businesses that create value for our shareholders and growth for our customers. Manage a portfolio of asset-integrated building block businesses to generate value for our downstream portfolio."

This template-style planning has been enthusiastically adopted by corporations, school boards, university presidents, and government agencies. Scan through these documents and you will find pious statements of the obvious presented as if they were decisive insights.

There is a large industry of consultants and book writers who are willing to provide instruction on the delicate differences between missions, visions, strategies, initiatives, and priorities. From small boutiques to the large IT-based firms trying to break into strategy work, consultants have found that template-style strategy frees them from the onerous work of analyzing the true challenges and opportunities faced by the client. Plus, by couching strategy in terms of positives—vision, mission, and values—no feelings are hurt.

To get a flavor of this genre, it is useful to examine a number of specific visions and missions:

- The mission of the Department of Defense is to "deter conflict—but should deterrence fail, to fight and win the nation's wars." It would be hard to find anyone who would argue with this, but it would also be equally hard to find anyone informed by it. A waste of print.

- Cornell University's mission is to be a "learning community that seeks to serve society by educating the leaders of tomorrow and extending the frontiers of knowledge." In other words, Cornell University is a university. This is hardly surprising and is certainly not informative. It provides absolutely no guidance to further planning or policy making. It is embarrassing for an intelligent adult to be associated with this sort of bloviating.

- California State University, Sacramento (CSUS), announces that its vision is to "be known throughout and increasingly beyond the Sacramento Region for its excellent and comprehensive academic and co-curricular student programs. We will be a key partner in developing the highly diverse 'New California.'"[7] As in many other official visions, the standard of excellence set is the *People* magazine measure of success: "being known."

  The CSUS plan goes on to establish several "strategic priorities." The first is "a strategically focused, campus-wide effort to improve recruitment, retention, and graduation rates." The fine print informs the alert reader that this is a key priority because state funding is linked to enrollment. In other words, if students drop out or flunk out, the school loses revenue. One of the "strategies" for improving retention is to have a "culture where retention, graduation, and student success in all its forms are embraced and pursued." It is difficult to see any actionable element in this fluffy admonition. By contrast, the more specific "strategy" to (somehow) push the graduation rate up from 57 to 62 percent is clearly achievable. However, there is no discussion of the obvious conflict between a vision of educational excellence and an objective of increasing state funding by lowering the dropout rate.

  The bottom line is that the increased monies gained from a lower dropout rate will be used to raise faculty salaries and build a new library.

- The vision of the Central Intelligence Agency is "One Agency. One Community. An Agency unmatched in its core capabilities, functioning as one team, fully integrated into the Intelligence Community."[8] Digging slightly deeper, the CIA's publically stated priorities all have to do with better teamwork and more investment in capabilities. Nowhere did it say that finding and killing Osama bin Laden was a top priority. Of course, one does not expect to see the strategies of the CIA on a public website. But if that is the case, why publish this fluff?

- I recently attended a strategy presentation in Tokyo by a senior executive of NEC Corporation. NEC's *vision* for the next decade is to "be a leading global company leveraging the power of innovation to realize an information society friendly to humans and the earth." Over the next hour, I also learned that the company aims to help develop a "sustainable ubiquitous networking society that uses a knowledge-based ICT [information and communications technology] mega-platform." Now, NEC is a computer and telecom equipment maker that has a reasonable share of the local Japanese business but has not succeeded abroad. This equipment market is increasingly competitive with low margins for most players. NEC is earning less than 2 percent on equity, and its operating profit is an astoundingly low 1.5 percent of revenue. It certainly cannot afford the R & D to which it aspires. It needs a strategy, not a set of slogans.

This class of verbiage is a mutant offspring of the concept of charismatic, then transformational, leadership. In reality, these are the flat-footed attempts of organization men to turn the magic of personal charisma into a bureaucratic product—charisma-in-a-can.

One might conclude that if the audience for this verbiage is happy, why care? The enormous problem all this creates is that someone who actually wishes to conceive and implement an effective strategy is surrounded by empty rhetoric and bad examples. And the general public is either led astray or puts all such pronouncements into the same mental bin as late-night TV advertising.

NEW THOUGHT

Earlier I described how Chad Logan wished to run his graphics art company by emulating Jack Welch, pointing out that Welch recommended "reaching for the impossible." Logan's desire to emulate Welch was understandable. At that moment, Jack Welch was viewed as one of the most successful managers in history. He had written, spoken, and been interviewed extensively on leadership, strategy, and management. However, like dipping into the Bible, you could find whatever you wanted in his body of work. Yes, Welch thought formal strategic planning was a waste of time, but he also said, "The first step of making strategy real is figuring out the big 'aha' to gain sustainable competitive advantage—in other words, a significant, meaningful insight about how to win." Yes, Welch believed in stretch, but he also said "If you don't have a competitive advantage, don't compete." Welch didn't ask people to "stretch" in home appliances, or coal, or semiconductors. He dropped those businesses entirely, focusing GE on businesses where he believed it was possible to make a difference. He didn't ask those divisions to buy in to the vision of their being dropped. If you want to manage like Jack Welch, pay attention to what he did, not to what he, or his ghost writers, say he did.

The Jack Welch quote about "reaching for what appears to be the impossible" is fairly standard motivational fare, available from literally hundreds of motivational speakers, books, calendars, memo pads, and websites. This fascination with positive thinking, and its deep connections to inspirational and spiritual thought, was invented about 150 years ago in New England as a mutation of Protestant Christian individualism.

The Protestant Reformation was founded on the principle that people did not need the Catholic Church to stand between them and the deity. In the 1800s, starting with Ralph Waldo Emerson's "transcendentalism," American theology began to develop the idea that each person's individual communication with God was possible because everyone has a spark of the divine within themselves, experienced as certain states of mind.

The next stage in the development of this idea was Mary Baker Eddy's Christian Science, which held that a mind holding the correct thoughts and beliefs could draw on divine power to eliminate disease. By 1890, this stream of religious philosophy had morphed into a set of mystical beliefs in the power of thought to affect the material world beyond the self. Called the *New Thought* movement, it combined religious sentiment with recommendations for worldly success. The theory was that thinking about success leads to success. And that thinking about failure leads to failure.

Prentice Mulford was a comic and a gold miner in California before he turned to inspirational writing. His book *Thoughts Are Things*, published in 1889, was a founding epistle of New Thought movement. Here is his theme:

> When we form a plan for any business, any invention, any undertaking, we are making something of that unseen element, our thought, as real, though unseen, as any machine of iron or wood. That plan or thought begins, as soon as made, to draw to itself, in more unseen elements, power to carry itself out, power to materialize itself in physical or visible substance. When we dread a misfortune, or live in fear of any ill, or expect ill luck, we make also a construction of unseen element, thought,—which, by the same *law of attraction*, draws to it destructive, and to you damaging, forces or elements.[9]

In the first two decades of the twentieth century, hundreds of volumes and articles on the mind and success were published. Perhaps the most influential was Wallace Wattles's *The Science of Getting Rich* (1910). His theme was that each person has godlike powers, but he stripped out any direct references to religion, creating a series of quasi-religious incantations:

> There is a thinking stuff from which all things are made, and which, in its original state, permeates, penetrates, and fills the interspaces of the universe. A thought, in this substance, produces the thing that is imaged by the thought. Man can form things in

> his thought, and, by impressing his thought upon formless substance, can cause the thing he thinks about to be created. . . . To think health when surrounded by the appearances of disease, or to think riches when in the midst of appearances of poverty, requires power; but he who acquires this power becomes a MASTER MIND. He can conquer fate; he can have what he wants.[10]

Ernest Holmes was the founder of the Religious Science movement. Influenced by Christian Science, he felt limited by its narrow focus on health. His book, *Creative Mind and Success*, published in 1919, took New Thought ideas to a wide public and helped establish a church that remains active today. Notice that Holmes insists that the successful person must banish any thoughts of failure:

> Thought is not only power; it is also the form of all things. The conditions that we attract will correspond exactly to our mental pictures. It is quite necessary, then, that the successful business man should keep his mind on thoughts of happiness, which should produce cheerfulness instead of depression; he should radiate joy, and should be filled with faith, hope and expectancy. . . . Put every negative thought out of your mind once and for all. Declare your freedom. Know no matter what others may say, think or do, you are a success, now, and nothing can hinder you from accomplishing your goal.[11]

As a social and religious movement, New Thought reached its peak in the early 1920s, when it again morphed, leaving behind the local societies, faith healers, and churches. By the 1930s it had transformed into a stream of motivational and positive-thinking books and speakers. In this vein are the still popular *Think and Grow Rich* (Napoleon Hill, 1937), *The Power of Positive Thinking* (Norman Vincent Peale, 1952), *Success Through a Positive Mental Attitude* (Clement Stone, 1960), *The Dynamic Laws of Prosperity: Forces That Bring Riches to You* (Catherine Ponder, 1962), *Awaken the Giant Within* (Anthony Robbins, 1991), and *The Seven Spiritual Laws of Success* (Deepak Chopra, 1995). The most recent major writer in this stream is Rhonda Byrne, an unabashed admirer of Wattles. Her 2007 book, *The Secret,* was a smash best-seller, has been turned into a film, and was touted by Oprah. Byrne's "secret" is identical with Mulford's original principle that you get what you think about. Today, these ideas are called "New Age," despite the fact that they are almost verbatim repetitions of books published a century ago.

Elements of New Thought have recently seeped into strategic thinking through literature on leadership and vision. Much of the work in this area provides a healthy counterweight to bureaucratic and rational-action views of management and organization. But recently it has taken on a flavor reminiscent of Mulford's 1889 *Thoughts Are Things*. The analogy fostering this displacement is between an individual *thought* and *shared vision* within an organization.

To see this displacement, consider Peter Senge's enormously successful book *The Fifth Discipline,* published in 1990. One of Senge's most influential ideas was the vital importance of "shared vision": "It is impossible to imagine the accomplishments of building AT&T, Ford, or Apple in the absence of shared vision. . . . What is most important is that these individual's visions became genuinely shared among people throughout all levels of their companies—focusing the energies of thousands and creating a common identity among enormously diverse people."[12]

This statement is very appealing to many people and, at the same time, is quite obviously untrue. Ascribing the success of Ford and Apple to a vision, *shared at all levels,* rather than pockets of outstanding competence mixed with luck, is a radical distortion of history. Apple did not invent the personal computer—the technology was in the air and hundreds of entrepreneurs sought to design and build "computers for everyman." Apple's success derived, in large measure, from Steve Wozniak's ability to cleverly trick the Motorola microprocessor at the center of the Apple II into directly driving the video and a floppy disk—using straight outputs from the CPU—rather than building expensive controllers. And, from the advent of VisiCalc, which gave people other than hobbyists a reason to buy an Apple II.[13]

Similarly, Ford's "cars for everyman" vision was hardly unique and not necessarily shared by the five-dollar-a-day assembly line workers.

Detroit was the "Silicon Valley" of 1907 and there were hundreds, even thousands, of engineers and tinkerers working on ways to make and sell automobiles. Ford's special genius was in materials, industrial engineering, and promotion.

Interestingly, Senge urges leaders to "personal mastery," which is a spiritual inward journey. In this regard, he quotes Ford's mystical belief that "the smallest indivisible reality is, to my mind, intelligent and is waiting there to be used by human spirits if we reach out and call them in." Ford was indeed a mystic, believed in reincarnation, and attributed much of his success to reading New Thought writer Ralph Waldo Trine's *In Tune with the Infinite,* a book containing the standard advice to avoid negative thoughts and form a clear picture in your mind of what you want. Of course, Senge's respect for Ford's philosophical musings does not extend to the point of urging readers to also study Ford's rabid anti-Jewish ranting.[14]

Just as New Thought writers advised people to never let negative thoughts enter their heads, the shared-vision school places a premium on commitment—the unwavering belief that the vision is right. In *Guiding Growth: How Vision Keeps Companies on Course,* Mark Lipton writes:

> Yet another disorienting factor in the process is a requirement that those involved in developing the growth vision suspend disbelief. After all, executives have spent years of education and experience learning to be realistic and pragmatic. But suspending disbelief is necessary to enable the executive to think, from the start, that what he or she has envisioned can and will be achieved. While it represents the antithesis of practicality, it is nonetheless a necessary competency of executive leadership. Not only must there be a belief in the dream but also a belief in one's ability to make that dream come true.[15]

In Senge's newest work, *Presence* (coauthored with C. Otto Scharmer, Joseph Jaworski, and Betty Sue Flowers), he admiringly quotes Srikumar S. Rao, a contributing editor to *Forbes* and head of the marketing department at Long Island University. Rao says:

> If you form and hold your intent long enough, it becomes true. . . . You become extremely clear about what it is you want to do. . . . This process of refinement—thinking about your intention many, many times—is, in a sense, a broadcast of intention. When you broadcast such an intention, there's very little else you have to do. The broadcast of intention goes out and makes it happen. Your role is to remain keenly aware, patiently expectant, and open to all possibilities.[16]

The amazing thing about New Thought is that it is always presented as if it were new! And no matter how many times the same ideas are repeated, they are received by many listeners with fresh nods of affirmation. These ritual recitations obviously tap into a deep human capacity to believe that intensely focused desire is magically rewarded.

I do not know whether meditation and other inward journeys perfect the human soul. But I do know that believing that rays come out of your head and change the physical world, and that by thinking only of success you can become a success, are forms of psychosis and cannot be recommended as approaches to management or strategy. All analysis starts with the consideration of what may happen, including unwelcome events. I would not care to fly in an aircraft designed by people who focused only on an image of a flying airplane and never considered modes of failure. Nevertheless, the doctrine that one can impose one's visions and desires on the world by the force of thought alone retains a powerful appeal to many people. Its acceptance displaces critical thinking and good strategy.

CHAPTER FIVE

THE KERNEL OF GOOD STRATEGY

Good strategy is coherent action backed up by an argument, an effective mixture of thought and action with a basic underlying structure I call the *kernel*. A good strategy may consist of more than the kernel, but if the kernel is absent or misshapen, then there is a serious problem. Once you apprehend this kernel, it is much easier to create, describe, and evaluate a strategy. The kernel is not based on any one concept of advantage. It does not require one to sort through legalistic gibberish about the differences between visions, missions, goals, strategies, objectives, and tactics. It does not split strategies into corporate, business, and product levels. It is very straightforward.

The kernel of a strategy contains three elements:

1. A *diagnosis* that defines or explains the nature of the challenge. A good diagnosis simplifies the often overwhelming complexity of reality by identifying certain aspects of the situation as critical.

2. A *guiding policy* for dealing with the challenge. This is an overall approach chosen to cope with or overcome the obstacles identified in the diagnosis.

3. A set of *coherent actions* that are designed to carry out the guiding policy. These are steps that are coordinated with one another to work together in accomplishing the guiding policy.

Here are some examples:

- For a doctor, the challenge appears as a set of signs and symptoms together with a history. The doctor makes a clinical diagnosis, naming a disease or pathology. The therapeutic approach chosen is the doctor's guiding policy. The doctor's specific prescriptions for diet, therapy, and medication are the set of coherent actions to be taken.

- In foreign policy, challenging situations are usually diagnosed in terms of analogies with past situations. The guiding policy adopted is usually an approach deemed successful in some past situation. Thus, if the diagnosis is that Iran's president, Mahmoud Ahmadinejad, is "another Hitler," war might be the logical implication. However, if he is "another Moammar Gadhafi," then strong pressure coupled with behind-the-scenes negotiation might be the chosen guiding policy. In foreign policy, the set of coherent actions are normally a mix of economic, diplomatic, and military maneuvers.

- In business, the challenge is usually dealing with change and competition. The first step toward effective strategy is diagnosing the specific structure of the challenge rather than simply naming performance goals. The second step is choosing an overall guiding policy for dealing with the situation that builds on or creates some type of leverage or advantage. The third step is the design of a configuration of actions and resource allocations that implement the chosen guiding policy.

- In many large organizations, the challenge is often diagnosed as internal. That is, the organization's competitive problems may be much lighter than the obstacles imposed by its own outdated routines, bureaucracy, pools of entrenched interests, lack of cooperation across units, and plain-old bad management. Thus, the guiding policy lies in the realm of reorganization and renewal. And the set of coherent actions are changes in people, power, and procedures. In other cases the challenge may be building or deepening competitive advantage by pushing the frontiers of organizational capability.

I call this combination of three elements the *kernel* to emphasize that it is the bare-bones center of a strategy—the hard nut at the core of the concept. It leaves out visions, hierarchies of goals and objectives, references to time span or scope, and ideas about adaptation and change. All of these are supporting players. They represent ways of thinking about strategy, stimulating the creation of strategies, energizing groups of people, denoting specific sources of advantage, communicating, summarizing, and analyzing strategies, and so on. The core content of a strategy is a *diagnosis* of the situation at hand, the creation or identification of a *guiding policy* for dealing with the critical difficulties, and a set of *coherent actions*. I will explore the three elements of the kernel one by one.

THE DIAGNOSIS

After my colleague John Mamer stepped down as dean of the UCLA Anderson School of Management, he wanted to take a stab at teaching strategy. To acquaint himself with the subject, he sat in on ten of my class sessions. Somewhere around class number seven we were chatting about pedagogy and I noted that many of the lessons learned in a strategy course come in the form of the questions asked as study assignments and asked in class. These questions distill decades of experience about useful things to think about in exploring complex situations. John gave me a sidelong look and said, "It looks to me as if there is really only one question you are asking in each case. That question is 'What's going on here?'"

John's comment was something I had never heard said explicitly, but it was instantly and obviously correct. A great deal of strategy work is trying to figure out what is going on. Not just deciding what to do, but the more fundamental problem of comprehending the situation.

At a minimum, a diagnosis names or classifies the situation, linking facts into patterns and suggesting that more attention be paid to some issues and less to others. An especially insightful diagnosis can transform one's view of the situation, bringing a radically different perspective to bear. When a diagnosis classifies the situation as a certain type, it opens access to knowledge about how analogous situations were handled in the past. An explicit diagnosis permits one to evaluate the rest of the strategy. Additionally, making the diagnosis an explicit element of the strategy allows the rest of the strategy to be revisited and changed as circumstances change.

Consider Starbucks, which grew from a single restaurant to an American icon. In 2008, Starbucks was experiencing flat or declining same-store traffic growth and lower profit margins, its return on assets having fallen from a generous 14 percent to about 5.5 percent. An immediate question arose: How serious was this situation? Any rapidly growing company must, sooner or later, saturate its market and have to clamp down on its expansion momentum. Slowing growth is a problem for Wall Street but is a natural stage in the development of any noncancerous entity. Although the U.S. market may have been saturated, were there still opportunities for expansion abroad? Deutsche Bank opined that Starbucks faced a great deal of competition oversees, noting in particular that its 23 remaining restaurants in Australia competed with 764 McDonald's outlets selling McCafe-branded coffee, lattes, cappuccinos, and smoothies.[1] By contrast, Oppenheimer opined, "We would expect that these markets [Europe] are still under-penetrated enough to maintain growth."[2] Was the foreign market saturated?

Or were there more serious problems? Was overbuilding outlets a sign of poor management? Were consumers' tastes changing once again? As competitors improved their coffee offerings, was Starbucks' differentiation vanishing? In fact, how important for Starbucks was the coffee-shop setting it provided versus the coffee itself? Was Starbucks a coffee restaurant, or was it actually an urban oasis? Could its brand be stretched to other types of products and even other types of restaurants?

At Starbucks, one executive might diagnose this challenging situation as "a problem in managing expectations." Another might diagnose it as "a search for new growth platforms." A third might diagnose it as "an eroding competitive advantage." None of these viewpoints is, by itself, an action, but each suggests a range of things that might be done and sets aside other classes of action as less relevant to the challenge.

Importantly, none of these diagnoses can be *proven* to be correct—each is a judgment about which issue is preeminent. Hence, diagnosis is a judgment about the meanings of facts.

The challenge facing Starbucks was *ill-structured*. By that I mean that no one could be sure how to define the problem, there was no obvious list of good approaches or actions, and the connections between most actions and outcomes were unclear. Because the challenge was ill-structured, a real-world strategy could not be logically deduced from the observed facts. Rather, a diagnosis had to be an educated guess as to what was going on in the situation, especially about what was critically important.

The diagnosis for the situation should replace the overwhelming complexity of reality with a simpler story, a story that calls attention to its crucial aspects. This simplified model of reality allows one to make sense of the situation and engage in further problem solving.

Furthermore, a good strategic diagnosis does more than explain a situation—it also defines a domain of action. Whereas a social scientist seeks a diagnosis that best predicts outcomes, good strategy tends to be based on the diagnosis promising leverage over outcomes. For instance, we know from research that K–12 student performance is better explained by social class and culture than by expenditures per student or class size, but that knowledge does not lead to many useful policy prescriptions. A very different strategic diagnosis has been provided by my UCLA colleague Bill Ouchi. His book *Making Schools Work* diagnoses the challenge of school performance as one of *organization* rather than as one of class, culture, funding, or curriculum design.[3] Decentralized schools, he argues, perform better. Now, whether the organization of a school system explains *most* of the variations in school performance is not actually critical. What is critical, and what makes his diagnosis useful to policy makers, is that organization explains some part of school performance and that, unlike culture or social class, organization is something that can be addressed with policy.

A diagnosis is generally denoted by metaphor, analogy, or reference to a diagnosis or framework that has already gained acceptance. For example, every student of U.S. national strategy knows about the diagnosis associated with the Cold War guiding policy of containment.

This concept originated with George Kennan's famous "long telegram" of 1946. Having served as an American diplomat in the USSR for more than a decade, and having seen Soviet terror and politics at close hand, he carefully analyzed the nature of Soviet ideology and power. Kennan started with the observation that the Soviet Union was not an ordinary nation-state. Its leaders defined their mission as opposition to capitalism and as spreading the gospel of revolutionary communism by whatever means necessary. He stressed that antagonism between communism and capitalist societies was a central foundation of Stalin's political regime, preventing any sincere accommodation or honest international agreements. However, he also pointed out that the Soviet leaders were realists about power. Therefore, he recommended a guiding policy of vigilant counterforce:

> In the light of the above, it will be clearly seen that the Soviet pressure against the free institutions of the western world is something that can be contained by the adroit and vigilant application of counter-force at a series of constantly shifting geographical and political points, corresponding to the shifts and maneuvers of Soviet policy, but which cannot be charmed or talked out of existence. The Russians look forward to a duel of infinite duration, and they see that already they have scored great successes.[4]

Kennan's diagnosis for the situation—a long-term struggle without the possibility of a negotiated settlement—was widely adopted within policy-making circles in the United States. His guiding policy of containment was especially attractive as it specified a broad domain of action—the USSR was, metaphorically speaking, infected by a virus. The United States would have to keep the virus from spreading until it finally died out. Kennan's policy is sometimes called a strategy, but it lacked the element of action. All presidents from Truman through George H. W. Bush struggled with the problem of turning this guiding policy into actionable objectives. Over time, the guiding policy of containment led to NATO and SEATO, the Berlin Airlift, the Korean War, placing missiles in Europe, the Vietnam War, and other Cold War actions.

The power of Kennan's diagnosis can be seen by considering how history might have been different if the situation had been framed another way in 1947. Perhaps the Soviet Union could have been enticed into the world community through a policy of engagement by including it in the Marshall Plan. Or perhaps it wasn't an American problem at all, but an issue for the United Nations. Or perhaps the Soviet Union was a tyranny rivaling Nazi Germany, and the United States should have sought to actively oppose it, undermine it, and liberate its population.

In business, most deep strategic changes are brought about by a change in diagnosis—a change in the definition of the company's situation. For example, when Lou Gerstner took over the helm at IBM in 1993, the company was in serious decline. Its historically successful strategy had been organized around offering complete, integrated, turnkey end-to-end computing solutions to corporations and government agencies. However, the advent of the microprocessor changed all that. The computer industry began to fragment, with separate firms offering chips, memory, hard disks, keyboards, software, monitors, operating systems, and so on. (The vertical disintegration of the computer industry is analyzed in chapter 13, "Using Dynamics.") As computing moved to the desktop, and as IBM's desktop offering became commoditized by clone competitors and the Windows-Intel standard, what should the company do? The dominant view at the company and among Wall Street analysts was that IBM was too integrated. The new industry structure was fragmented and, it was argued, IBM should be broken up and fragmented to match. As Gerstner arrived, preparations were under way for separate stock offerings for various pieces of IBM.

After studying the situation, Gerstner changed the diagnosis. He believed that in an increasingly fragmented industry, IBM was the one company that had expertise in all areas. Its problem was not that it was integrated but that it was failing to use the integrated skills it possessed. IBM, he declared, needed to become more integrated—but this time around customer solutions rather than hardware platforms. The primary obstacle was the lack of internal coordination and agility. Given this new diagnosis, the guiding policy became to exploit the fact that IBM was different, in fact, unique. IBM would offer customers tailored solutions to their information-processing problems, leveraging its brand name and broad expertise, but willing to use outside hardware and software as required. Put simply, its primary value-added activity would shift from systems engineering to IT consulting, from hardware to software. Neither the "integration is obsolete" nor the "knowing all aspects of IT is our unique ability" viewpoints are, by themselves, strategies. But these diagnoses take the leader, and all who follow, in very different directions.

THE GUIDING POLICY

The guiding policy outlines an overall approach for overcoming the obstacles highlighted by the diagnosis. It is "guiding" because it channels action in certain directions without defining exactly what shall be done. Kennan's containment and Gerstner's drawing on all of IBM's resources to solve customers' problems are examples of guiding policies. Like the guardrails on a highway, the guiding policy directs and constrains action without fully defining its content.

Good guiding policies are not goals or visions or images of desirable end states. Rather, they define a *method* of grappling with the situation and ruling out a vast array of possible actions. For example, Wells Fargo's corporate vision is this: "We want to satisfy all of our customers' financial needs, help them succeed financially, be the premier provider of financial services in every one of our markets, and be known as one of America's great companies."[5]

This "vision" communicates an ambition, but it is not a strategy or a guiding policy because there is no information about *how* this ambition will be accomplished. Wells Fargo chairman emeritus and former CEO Richard Kovacevich knew this and distinguished between this vision and his company's guiding policy of using the network effects of cross-selling. That is, Kovacevich believed that the more different financial products Wells Fargo could sell to a customer, the more the company would know about that customer and about its whole network of customers. That information would, in turn, help it create and sell more financial products. This guiding policy, in contrast to Wells Fargo's vision, calls out a way of competing—a way of trying to use the company's large scale to advantage.

You may correctly observe that many other people use the term "strategy" for what I am calling the "guiding policy." I have found that defining a strategy as just a broad guiding policy is a mistake. Without a diagnosis, one cannot evaluate alternative guiding policies. Without working through to at least the first round of action one cannot be sure that the guiding policy can be implemented. Good strategy is not just "what" you are trying to do. It is also "why" and "how" you are doing it.

A good guiding policy tackles the obstacles identified in the diagnosis by creating or drawing upon sources of *advantage*. Indeed, the heart of the matter in strategy is usually advantage. Just as a lever uses mechanical advantage to multiply force, strategic advantage multiplies the effectiveness of resources and/or actions. Importantly, not all advantage is competitive. In nonprofit and public policy situations, good strategy creates advantage by magnifying the effects of resources and actions.

In most modern treatments of competitive strategy, it is now common to launch immediately into detailed descriptions of specific sources of competitive advantage. Having lower costs, a better brand, a faster product-development cycle, more experience, more information about customers, and so on, can all be sources of advantage. This is all true, but it is important to take a broader perspective. A good guiding policy itself can be a source of advantage.

A guiding policy creates advantage by *anticipating* the actions and reactions of others, by *reducing the complexity and ambiguity* in the situation, by exploiting the *leverage* inherent in concentrating effort on a pivotal or decisive aspect of the situation, and by creating policies and actions that are *coherent*, each building on the other rather than canceling one another out. (These sources of advantage are discussed in detail in chapter 6, "Using Leverage.")

For example, Gerstner's "provide customer solutions" policy certainly counted on the advantages implicit in IBM's world-class technological depth and expertise in almost all areas of data processing. But the policy itself also created advantage by resolving the uncertainty about what to do, about how to compete, and about how to organize. It also began the process of coordinating and concentrating IBM's vast resources on a specific set of challenges.

To look more closely at how a guiding policy works, follow the thinking of Stephanie, a friend who owns a corner grocery store. She does the accounts, manages personnel, sometimes runs the cash register, and makes all the decisions. Several years ago, Stephanie told me about some of the issues she was facing. She was considering whether she should keep prices down or offer more expensive, fresh organic produce. Should she begin to stock more Asian staples for the many Asian students who lived in the area? Should the store be open longer hours? How important was it to have a helpful, friendly staff that gets to know the regulars? Would adding a second checkout stand pay off? What about parking in the alley? Should she advertise in the local college newspaper? Should she paint the ceiling green or white? Should she put some items on sale each week? Which ones?

An economist would tell her that she should take actions that maximize profit, a technically correct but useless piece of advice. In the economics textbook it is simple: choose the rate of output *Q* that provides the biggest gap between revenue and cost. In the real world, however, "maximize profit" is not a helpful prescription, because the challenge of making, or maximizing, profit is an ill-structured problem. Even in a corner grocery store, there are hundreds or thousands of possible adjustments one can make, and millions in a business of any size—the complexity of the situation can be overwhelming.

Thinking about her store, Stephanie diagnosed her challenge to be competition with the local supermarket. She needed to draw customers away from a store that was open 24/7 and had lower prices. Seeking a way forward, she believed that most of her customers were people who walked by the store almost every day. They worked or lived nearby. Scanning her list of questions and alternatives, she determined that there was a choice between serving the more price-conscious students or the more time-sensitive professionals. Transcending thousands of individual choices and instead framing the problem in terms of choosing among a few customer groups provided a dramatic reduction in complexity.

Of course, if both of these customer segments could be served with the same policies and actions, then the dichotomy would have been useless and should be cast aside. In Stephanie's case, the difference seemed significant. More of her customers were students, but the professionals who stopped in made much larger purchases. Pushing further along, Stephanie began to explore the guiding policy of "serve the busy professional." After some more tinkering, Stephanie sharpened the guiding policy a bit more, deciding to target "the busy professional who has little time to cook."

There was no way to establish that this particular guiding policy was the only good one, or the best one. But, absent a good guiding policy, there is no principle of action to follow. Without a guiding policy, Stephanie's actions and resource allocations would probably be inconsistent and incoherent, fighting with one another and canceling one another out. Importantly, adopting this guiding policy helped reveal and organize the interactions among the many possible actions. Considering the needs of the busy professional with little time to cook, she could see that the second checkout stand would help handle the burst of traffic at 5 p.m. So would more parking in the alley. In addition, she felt she could take space currently used for selling munchies to students and offer prepared high-quality take-home foods instead. Professionals, unlike students, would not come shopping at midnight, so there was no need for very late hours. The busy professionals would appreciate adequate staffing after work and, perhaps, at lunchtime. Having a guiding policy helped create actions that were coordinated and concentrated, focusing her efforts.

COHERENT ACTION

Many people call the guiding policy "the strategy" and stop there. This is a mistake. Strategy is about action, about doing something. The kernel of a strategy must contain *action*. It does not need to point to all the actions that will be taken as events unfold, but there must be enough clarity about action to bring concepts down to earth. To have punch, actions should coordinate and build upon one another, focusing organizational energy.

Moving to Action

INSEAD, a global business school located in France, was the brainchild of Harvard professor General Georges F. Doriot. The INSEAD library holds a bronze statue of Doriot inscribed with his observation "Without action, the world would still be an idea."

In many situations, the main impediment to action is the forlorn hope that certain painful choices or actions can be avoided—that the whole long list of hoped-for "priorities" can all be achieved. It is the hard craft of strategy to decide which priority shall take precedence. Only then can action be taken. And, interestingly, there is no greater tool for sharpening strategic ideas than the necessity to act.

■ ■ ■

The president of the European Business Group had a discrete private office in a classic London town home, just west of St. James' Park. I was there to discuss progress on the company's "Pan-European" initiative.

A consumer goods producer, the company had a typically complex international organization. There were country-based marketing organizations; globally run manufacturing operations; and four product development centers, one in North America, one in Japan, one in Germany, and one in the United Kingdom. Product managers were responsible for coordinating activities but had no direct authority. Products tended to be tailored to country or regional differences, partly as a result of some local acquisitions and partly due to perceptions of local differences in tastes.

Senior management believed that the company's European business was too fragmented. They wanted most of the products offered in Europe to be Pan-European, exploiting greater economies of scale in both production and marketing. Management had spent time and effort communicating the message about a Pan-European product line and had created some mechanisms to bring it about. The heads of the country-based organizations were placed on a Pan-Europe Executive Committee, which met once a quarter. Developers from Germany and the United Kingdom were rotated between the two locations. A New

Products group had been created to consult with all departments on opportunities for Pan-European concepts and brands. Part of each executive's evaluation for promotion was based on his or her contribution to the Pan-European initiative. Despite these measures, nothing much had happened. The German and British developers each claimed that their initiatives were unsupported by the other. The one British-German joint initiative had not been picked up by the rest of the organization.

As we discussed the situation, my client's frustration was evident. I stopped taking notes, and we both got up and walked over to the window, looking down on the mews houses below. "Suppose," I said, "that this was really important, really top-priority critical. Suppose you absolutely had to get some Pan-European products developed and marketed in the next eighteen months or everything would collapse. What would you do then?"

"For one thing," he said, throwing his arms up in mock surrender, "I would close one of the development groups. They spend more time bickering than developing."

Then he thought for a moment and said, "I just might close both and start over in the Netherlands. There is a market-test office there we could use as a seed. We could take some of the best people from the UK and Germany and start fresh. Still, that doesn't solve the problem of getting the country managers on board."

"And the country managers' lack of enthusiasm is because . . . ?" I asked.

"Well, each country manager has spent years understanding the special conditions in a country, tailoring products and marketing programs to that country's local conditions. They don't trust the Pan-European idea. The French don't want to waste marketing efforts on products they see as 'too British' or 'too German.' And there really has not yet been a compelling Pan-European product that all could get behind. If it were already a success in three or four countries, the rest would get behind it. But everyone has their current portfolio of products to worry about."

"Right," I said. "Their jobs are running the present country-based system. And you want new Pan-European initiatives. Now, you can use a shoe to hammer a nail, but it will take a long time. Don't you need a different tool for this task? If it were really important to get this done, I think you know how you would do it."

"Of course," he said. "We could have a single group develop, roll out, and market Pan-European products and take full profit responsibility."

"At the same time," I added, "you would have to intervene in the country-based system with special budget overrides for this initiative, promotions for people who help it along, and career problems for people who don't."

We moved back to the center of the office, and he sat at his desk, a position of authority. He looked at me and said, "That would be a very painful road. Many noses would get out of joint. It would be better to win people over to this point of view rather than force them over."

"Right," I said. "You would only take all those painful steps if it were really important to get action on this concept. Only if it were really important."

It took another nine months for him to decide that the Pan-European initiative was indeed important and move to reorganize European operations. There was no magical solution to his problem of wanting strong country-based marketing, Pan-European initiatives, and no noses out of joint, all at the same time. As long as strategy remained at the level of intent and concept, the conflicts among various values and between the organization and the initiative remained tolerable. It was the imperative of action that forced a decision about which issue was actually the most important.

This executive's problem was primarily organizational rather than rooted in product-market competition. Yet the kernel of strategy—a diagnosis, a guiding policy, and coherent action—applies to any complex setting. Here, as in so many situations, the required actions were not mysterious. The impediment was the hope that the pain of those actions could, somehow, be avoided. Indeed, we always hope that a brilliant insight or very clever design will allow us to accomplish several apparently conflicting objectives with a single stroke, and occasionally we are vouchsafed this kind of deliverance. Nevertheless, strategy is primarily about deciding what is truly important and focusing resources and action on that objective. It is a hard discipline because focusing on one thing slights another.

Coherence

The actions within the kernel of strategy should be coherent. That is, the resource deployments, policies, and maneuvers that are undertaken should be consistent and coordinated. The coordination of action provides the most basic source of leverage or advantage available in strategy.

In a fight, the simplest strategy is a feint to the left and then punch from the right, a coordination of movement in time and space. The simplest business strategy is to use knowledge gleaned by sales and marketing specialists to affect capacity expansion or product design decisions—coordination across functions and knowledge bases. Even when an organization has an apparently simple and basic source of advantage, such as being a low-cost producer, a close examination will always reveal a raft of interrelated mutually supporting policies that, in this case, keep costs low. Furthermore, it will be found that these costs are lower only for a certain type of products delivered under certain conditions. *Using* such a cost advantage to good effect will require the alignment of many actions and policies.

Strategic actions that are not coherent are either in conflict with one another or taken in pursuit of unrelated challenges. Consider Ford Motor Company. When Jacques Nasser was the CEO of Ford Europe and vice president of Ford product development, he told me, "Brand is the key to profits in the automobile industry."[6] Moving into the corporate CEO spot in 1999, Nasser quickly acted to acquire Volvo, Jaguar, Land Rover, and Aston Martin. However, at the same time, the company's original guiding policy of "economies of scale" was fully alive and kicking. A senior Ford executive told me in 2000: "You cannot be competitive in the automobile industry unless you produce at least one million units per year on a platform." Thus, the actions of buying Volvo and Jaguar were conjoined with actions designed to put both brands on a common platform. Putting Jaguar and Volvo on the same platform dilutes the brand equity of both marques and annoys the most passionate customers, dealers, and service shops. Volvo buyers don't want a "safe Jaguar"; they want a car that is uniquely safe. And Jaguar buyers want something more distinctive than a "sporty Volvo." These two sets of concepts and actions were in conflict rather than being coherent.

What about a list of nonconflicting but uncoordinated actions? In 2003, I worked with a company whose initial "strategy" was to (1) close a plant in Akron and open a new plant in Mexico, (2) spend more on advertising, and (3) initiate a 360-degree feedback program. Now these actions may all have been good ideas, but they did not complement one another. They are "strategic" only in the sense that each probably requires the approval of top management. My view is that doing these things might be sound operational management, but it did not constitute a strategy. A strategy coordinates action to address a specific challenge. It is not defined by the pay grade of the person authorizing the action.

The idea that coordination, by itself, can be a source of advantage is a very deep principle. It is often underappreciated because people tend to think of coordination in terms of continuing mutual adjustments among agents. Strategic coordination, or coherence, is not ad hoc mutual adjustment. It is coherence imposed on a system by policy and design. More specifically, design is the engineering of fit among parts, specifying how actions and resources will be combined. (This approach to coherence is the subject of chapter 9, "Using Design.")

Another powerful way to coordinate actions is by the specification of a proximate objective. By "proximate," I mean a state of affairs close enough at hand to be feasible. If an objective is clear and feasible, it can help coordinate both problem solving and direct action. (You will find more about this important tool in chapter 7, "Proximate Objectives.")

Strategy is visible as coordinated action *imposed* on a system. When I say strategy is "imposed," I mean just that. It is an exercise in centralized power, used to overcome the natural workings of a system. This coordination is unnatural in the sense that it would not occur without the hand of strategy.

The idea of centralized direction may set off warning bells in a modern educated person. Why does it make sense to exercise centralized power when we know that many decisions are efficiently made on a decentralized basis? One of the great lessons of the twentieth century—the most dramatic controlled experiment in human history—was that centrally controlled economies are grossly inefficient. More people starved to death in Stalin's and Mao Tse-tung's centrally planned regimes than were killed in World War II. People continue to starve to death in North Korea today. In modern economies, trillions of decentralized choices are made each year, and this process can do a pretty good job of allocating certain kinds of scarce resources. Thus, when the price of gasoline rises, people start buying more fuel-efficient cars without any central planning. After a hurricane, when there is much to rebuild, wages rise, attracting more workers to the stricken area.

But decentralized decision making cannot do everything. In particular, it may fail when either the costs or benefits of actions are not borne by the decentralized actors. The split between the costs and benefits may occur across organizational units or between the present and the future. And decentralized coordination is difficult when benefits accrue only if decisions are properly coordinated. Of course, centrally designed policies can also fail if the decision makers are foolish, in the pay of special interest groups, or simply choose incorrectly.

As a simple example, salespeople love to please customers with rush orders, and manufacturing people prefer long uninterrupted production runs. But you cannot have long production runs and handle unexpected rush orders all at the same time. It takes policies devised to benefit the whole to sort out this conflict.

On a larger canvas, in World War II, President Franklin D. Roosevelt coordinated political, economic, and military power to defeat Nazi Germany, using the United States' productive capacity to support the Soviet Union, thus allowing it to survive and degrade the Nazi war machine before Americans landed in Normandy. Another element of his strategy, one with great consequences, was to focus the bulk of American resources to first winning in Europe before fully taking on Japan, a complex coordination of forces over time. Neither of these crucial policies would have emerged out of decentralized decision making among the Departments of State and War, the various war production boards, and multiple military commands.

On the other hand, the potential gains to coordination do not mean that more centrally directed coordination is always a good thing. Coordination is costly, because it fights against the gains to specialization, the most basic economies in organized activity. To specialize in something is, roughly speaking, to be left alone to do just that thing and not be bothered with other tasks, interruptions, and other agents' agendas. As is clear to anyone who has belonged to a coordinating committee, coordination interrupts and de-specializes people.

Thus, we should seek coordinated policies only when the gains are very large. There will be costs to demanding coordination, because it will ride roughshod over economies of specialization and more nuanced local responses. The brilliance of good organization is not in making sure that everything is connected to everything else. Down that road lies a frozen maladaptive stasis. Good strategy and good organization lie in specializing on the right activities and imposing only the essential amount of coordination.

◆

PART II
SOURCES OF POWER

In very general terms, a good strategy works by harnessing power and applying it where it will have the greatest effect. In the short term, this may mean attacking a problem or rival with adroit combinations of policy, actions, and resources. In the longer term, it may involve cleverly using policies and resource commitments to develop capabilities that will be of value in future contests. In either case, a "good strategy" is an approach that magnifies the effectiveness of actions by finding and using sources of power.

This section of the book explores a number of fundamental sources of power used in good strategies: leverage, proximate objectives, chain-link systems, design, focus, growth, advantage, dynamics, inertia, and entropy. Obviously, this set is not exhaustive. There is more to know about strategy than any one volume can possibly treat. The sources of power (and trouble) highlighted here were chosen for both their generality and freshness. Most extend beyond a business context and apply to government, security, and nonprofit situations as well. Plus, they explore particular issues that I believe are fundamental but that have not been given as much attention as they deserve.

The last piece in this section, chapter 15, "Putting It Together," uses the example of Nvidia's strategy in the 3-D graphics market to illustrate almost every source of power treated here. Some readers may prefer to start there and then return to chapters 6–14 for more depth on each issue.

◆

CHAPTER SIX

USING LEVERAGE

A good strategy draws power from focusing minds, energy, and action. That focus, channeled at the right moment onto a pivotal objective, can produce a cascade of favorable outcomes. I call this source of power *leverage*.*

Archimedes, one of the smartest people who ever lived, said, "Give me a lever long enough, a fulcrum strong enough, and I'll move the world." What he no doubt knew, but did not say, was that to move the earth, his lever would have to be billions of miles long.[1] With this enormous lever, a swing of Archimedes' arm might move the earth by the diameter of one atom. Given the amount of trouble involved, he would be wise to apply his lever to a spot where this tiny movement would make a large difference. Finding such crucial pivot points and concentrating force on them is the secret of strategic leverage.

Knock loose a keystone, and a giant arch will fall. Seize the moment, as James Madison did in 1787, turning colleague Edmund Randolph's ideas about three branches of government with a bicameral legislature into the first draft of the Constitution, and you just might found a great nation. When the largest computer company in the world comes knocking at your door in 1980, asking if you can provide an operating system

* More technically, leverage is a type of advantage that is context free, not being rooted in the particular mechanics of a business, industry, or situation.

for a new personal computer, say, "Yes, we can!" And be sure to insist, as Bill Gates did in 1980, that, after they pay you for the software, the contract still permits you to sell it to third parties. You just might become the richest person in the world.

In general, strategic leverage arises from a mixture of anticipation, insight into what is most *pivotal* or critical in a situation, and making a *concentrated* application of effort.

ANTICIPATION

The strategist may have insight into predictable aspects of others' behavior that can be turned to advantage. At the simplest level, a strategy of investing in Manhattan real estate is based on the anticipation that other people's future demand for this real estate will raise its value. In competitive strategy, the key anticipations are often of buyer demand and competitive reactions.

As an example of anticipation, while the SUV craze was booming in the United States, Toyota invested more than $1 billion in developing hybrid gasoline-electric technologies: an electronically controlled continuously-variable-speed transmission and its own chips and software to control the system. There were two anticipations guiding this investment. First, management believed that fuel economy pressures would, over time, make hybrid vehicles a major product category. Second, management believed that, once presented with the chance to license Toyota's technology, other automakers would do so and not invest in developing possibly superior systems. Thus far, both anticipations have proven reasonably accurate.

The most critical anticipations are about the behavior of others, especially rivals. It is now clear that U.S. military plans for the invasion of Iraq in the spring of 2003 failed to anticipate the rise of a vigorous insurgency. As the army's own assessment states: "The difficulty in Iraq in April and May 2003 for the Army, and the other Services, was that the transition to a new campaign was not well thought out, planned for, and prepared for before it began. Additionally, the assumptions about the nature of post-Saddam Iraq on which the transition was planned proved to be largely incorrect."[2]

At the same time, the Iraqi insurgency was, at least in part, initiated by Iraqi ex-military officers who anticipated that media coverage of U.S. casualties would tilt U.S. public opinion in favor of withdrawal, as it had in Vietnam and, more recently, in Mogadishu. Indeed, according to Bob Woodward, "Saddam had commissioned an Arabic translation of *Black Hawk Down* and issued copies to his senior officers."[3] So, in a deeper sense, U.S. planners failed to anticipate the Iraqis' anticipations.

Most strategic anticipation draws on the predictable "downstream" results of events that have already happened, from trends already at work, from predictable economic or social dynamics, or from the routines other agents follow that make aspects of their behavior predictable.

Some of the most striking anticipations made in any modern business were created by Pierre Wack and Ted Newland of Group Planning at Shell International. I got to know Pierre Wack in 1980. He told me that "certain aspects of future events are predetermined: If there is a storm in the Himalayas, you can confidently predict that tomorrow, or the next day, there will be flooding in the Ganges plain." The flood Wack and Newland had predicted back in 1970 was the rise of OPEC and the ensuing energy crisis. The storm creating this flood had been discerned in the pattern of incomes and populations of key oil-producing countries. In particular, Iran, Iraq, and Venezuela all had high oil reserves, large growing populations, and ambitious development goals. Wack and Newland predicted that such countries would be strongly motivated to seek price increases. They saw that price increases would, in turn, make countries such as Saudi Arabia and Kuwait realize that oil in the ground might appreciate faster than the dollars it bought once it was pumped and sold.[4]

In 1981, I was fortunate enough to spend a week with Pierre Wack at a Shell Group Planning retreat in Runnymede, England. Talking about scenarios, he told me:

> If you do standard "scenario" forecasting, you wind up with a graph with three lines labeled "high," "medium," and "low." Everyone

> looks at it and believes that they have paid attention to the uncertainty. Then, of course, they plan on "medium"! But they are missing the risk. The risk is not that the price of oil may be high or may be low. The risk is that it will go high, suckering you into a major investment, and then turn and dive to low, leaving you with useless assets.

The sucker bet Pierre Wack was worried about in 1981 would play out over the next decade as the price of oil stopped its upward trend at about thirty-six dollars per barrel, then turned and sank to twenty dollars a barrel. As he foresaw, the sharply higher oil prices of the late 1970s spurred renewed drilling and exploration. But when the new finds in the North Sea and Alaska came on line, the increased supply forced the price of oil down. People without Wack's insight, such as American oilman George W. Bush, who had invested heavily in offshore drilling, saw their businesses collapse.

■ ■ ■

Anticipation does not require psychic powers. In many circumstances, anticipation simply means considering the habits, preferences, and policies of others, as well as various inertias and constraints on change. Thus, I do not expect California to balance its budget anytime soon, but I do anticipate a continued exodus of talent from the state. I expect another serious terrorist attack on the United States, but I do not anticipate that the stultifying iron curtain between the CIA and the FBI will be removed short of all-out war. I expect that Google will continue to develop office-oriented applications that can be used online through a browser, but I do not anticipate effective responses from Microsoft, who will be loath to cannibalize its PC-based Microsoft Office business. I anticipate a rapidly growing use of smart phones, but I also anticipate that this will overtax the cell phone infrastructure, leading to some industry consolidation and a usage-based fee structure.

PIVOT POINTS

To achieve leverage, the strategist must have insight into a pivot point that will magnify the effects of focused energy and resources. As an example of a pivotal objective, in 2008 I was in Tokyo, discussing competitive strategy with Noritoshi Murata, the president and chief operating officer of Seven & i Holdings. This company owns all of the 7-Eleven convenience stores in the United States and Asia, as well as grocery superstores and department stores in Japan and other ventures. Focusing on Japan, Murata explained that the company had come to the conclusion that Japanese customers were extremely sensitive to variations in local tastes and fond of both newness and variety. "In Japan," he told me, "consumers are easily bored. In soft drinks, for example, there are more than two hundred soft-drink brands and lots of new ones each week! A 7-Eleven displays fifty varieties with a turnover of seventy percent each year. The same holds true in many food categories."

To create leverage around this pattern, 7-Eleven Japan has developed a method of collecting information from store managers and employees about local tastes and forming quick-response merchandising teams to develop new product offerings. To further leverage this information and team skills, the company has developed relationships with a number of second- and third-tier food manufacturers and found ways to quickly bring new offerings to market under its own private-label brand, at low prices, using the food manufacturers' excess capacity.

At the same time, 7-Eleven was expanding its operations in China. There, Murata explained, their outstanding advantage was cleanliness and service. The Chinese consumers were used to being supplicants at a retail outlet, and 7-Eleven Japan's tradition of spotless interiors and white-gloved service personnel who greeted customers with bows and smiles, as well as its good-tasting lunches, were producing twice as many sales per square foot than any competitor obtained.

Murata's strategy focused organizational energy on decisive aspects of the situation. It was not a profit plan or a set of financial goals. It was an entrepreneurial insight into the situation that had the potential to actually create and extend advantage.

■ ■ ■

A pivot point magnifies the effect of effort. It is a natural or created imbalance in a situation, a place where a relatively small adjustment can unleash much larger pent-up forces. The business strategist senses such imbalances in pent-up demand that has yet to be fulfilled or in a robust competence developed in one context that can be applied to good effect in another.

In direct rivalry, the pivot point may be an imbalance between a rival's position or disposition of forces and their underlying capabilities, or between pretension and reality. On June 12, 1987, President Reagan stood at the Brandenburg Gate in West Berlin and said: "General Secretary Gorbachev, if you seek peace, if you seek prosperity for the Soviet Union and Eastern Europe, if you seek liberalization: Come here to this gate! Mr. Gorbachev, open this gate! Mr. Gorbachev, tear down this wall!"

Of course, Reagan did not expect Gorbachev to do any such thing. The speech was directed to Western Europeans, and its purpose was to highlight, and thereby exploit, the imbalance between a system that allowed the free movement of people with one that had to restrain its citizens with barbed wire and concrete. That imbalance had existed for decades. Had Reagan given a similar challenge to Yuri Andropov in 1983, it would have had little effect. It became a pivot point because of the extra imbalance between Mikhail Gorbachev's claim that the Soviet Union was liberalizing and the facts on the ground.

CONCENTRATION

Returns to concentration arise when focusing efforts on fewer, or more limited, objectives generates larger payoffs. These gains flow from combinations of constraints and threshold effects. If resources were not limited, there would be no need to select one objective over another. If rivals could easily see our moves and quickly mobilize responses, we would gain little from concentrating on temporary weaknesses. If senior leadership did not have limited cognition, they would gain nothing from concentrating their attention on a few priorities.

A "threshold effect" exists when there is a critical level of effort necessary to affect the system. Levels of effort below this threshold have little payoff. When there are threshold effects, it is prudent to limit objectives to those that can be affected by the resources at the strategist's disposal.

For example, there seems to be a threshold effect in advertising. That is, a very small amount of advertising will produce no result at all. One has to get over this hump, or threshold, to start getting a response to advertising efforts.[5] This means it may pay companies to pulse their advertising, concentrating it into relatively short periods of time, rather than spreading it evenly. It may also make sense for a company to roll out a new product region by region, concentrating its advertising where the product is new so as to spur adoption.

Due to similar forces, business strategists will often prefer to dominate a small market segment over having an equal number of customers who represent only a sliver of a larger market. Politicians will often prefer a plan that delivers a clear benefit to a recognizable group over one that provides larger benefits spread more thinly across the population.

Within organizations, some of the factors giving rise to concentration are the substantial threshold effects in effecting change and the cognitive and attention limits of the senior management group. Just as an individual cannot solve five problems at once, most organizations concentrate on a few critical issues at any one time.

From a psychological perspective, there can be returns to focus or concentration when people ignore signals below a certain threshold (called a "salience effect" in psychology) or when they believe in momentum—that success leads to success. In either case, the strategist can increase the perceived effectiveness of action by focusing effort on targets that will catch attention and sway opinion. It may, for example, have more impact on public opinion to completely turn around two schools than to make a 2 percent improvement in two hundred schools. In turn, peoples' perceptions of efficacy affect their willingness to support and take part in further actions.

An example of concentrating on an effective objective was Harold

William's strategy for the Getty Trust. When oil billionaire J. Paul Getty died in 1976, he left $700 million in trust for the museum he had built and run in Malibu, California. Williams, who had been dean of the UCLA management school, had gone on to chair the Securities and Exchange Commission. Then, in 1983, he got the world's best job—chairman of the Getty Trust. By then, the trust had grown to $1.4 billion and was required by law to spend 4.5 percent of its principle, about $65 million, each year.

During Williams's tenure, the Getty Foundation grew from a small elite collection to a major force in the art world. In a conversation I had with him in 2000, three years after he retired, Williams explained his strategy:

> The Getty Trust was a very large amount of money, and we had to spend a considerable amount each year. Our mandate was art, but I had to decide how to actually spend the funds. We could have simply built a great collection—that would have been the obvious thing to do. Buy art. But I wasn't comfortable with that as a direction. All we would really accomplish would be to drive up the price of art and move some of it from New York and Paris to Los Angeles.
>
> It took some time, but I began to develop the idea that art could be, indeed, should be, a more serious subject than it was. Art is not just pretty objects; it is a vital part of human activity. In a university, people spend a great deal of effort studying languages and histories. We know all about marriage contracts in remote tribes and the histories of many peoples. But art has been treated as a sideshow. I decided that the Getty could change this. *Instead of spending our income on buying art, we could transform the subject.* The Getty would begin to build a complete digital catalog of all art, including dance, song, and textiles. It would develop programs to educate art teachers and host advanced research on art and society. The Getty would host the best conservation talent in the world and develop new methods of conserving and restoration. In this way, I decided, we would have an impact far beyond simply putting art on display.

With $65 million to spend each year, Williams could have simply bought art or given money to schools and universities for their arts programs. But by aiming to transform the study of art, Williams designed an objective that was novel and nicely scaled to the resources at his disposal. Put simply, he invested where his resources would make a large and more visible difference. That is the power of concentration—of choosing an objective that can be decisively affected by the resources at hand. There is no way to know whether Williams's strategy created greater good than a simpler strategy of giving away money, but it did make a bigger bang and, thereby, attracted more energy and support from employees and outside organizations.

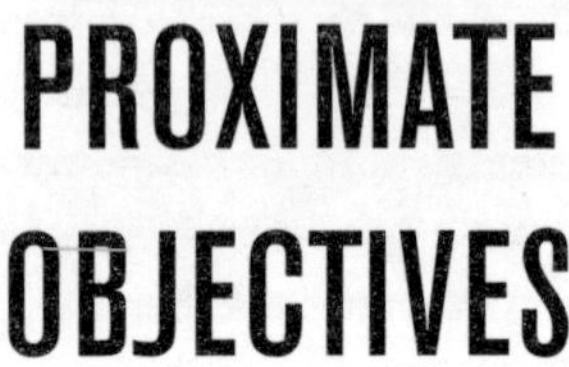

CHAPTER SEVEN

PROXIMATE OBJECTIVES

Folly is the direct pursuit of happiness and beauty.
—George Bernard Shaw

One of a leader's most powerful tools is the creation of a good proximate objective—one that is close enough at hand to be feasible. A proximate objective names a target that the organization can reasonably be expected to hit, even overwhelm.

For example, President Kennedy's call for the United States to place a man on the moon by the end of the 1960s is often held out as a bold push into the unknown. Along with Martin Luther King Jr.'s "I Have a Dream" speech, it has become almost a required reference in any of today's "how to be a charismatic leader" manuals extolling the magical virtues of vision and audacious goals. Actually, however, landing on the moon was a carefully chosen *proximate* strategic objective.

Kennedy's 1961 speech on this issue remains a model of clarity. Look it up on the Web and read it. You will be startled at how political speech has changed since then. Kennedy spoke as a decision maker talking to adults, not as a preacher addressing children.

In his speech, Kennedy diagnosed the problem as world opinion. He said, "The dramatic achievements in space which occurred in recent weeks should have made clear to us all, as did the Sputnik in 1957, the impact of this adventure on the minds of men everywhere." He argued that the Soviet Union's strategy of focusing its much poorer technological resources on space was leveraging, to its advantage, the world's natural interest in these out-of-this-world accomplishments. He argued that being first to land people on the moon would be a dramatic affirmation of American leadership. The United States had, ultimately, much greater resources to draw upon; it was a matter of allocating and coordinating them.

Importantly, the moon mission had been judged feasible. Kennedy did much more than simply point at the objectives; he laid out the steps along the way—unmanned exploration, larger booster rockets, parallel development of liquid and solid fuel rockets, and the construction of a landing vehicle.

This objective was feasible because engineers knew how to design and build rockets and spacecraft. Much of the technology had already been developed as part of the ballistic missile program. And this objective was intensely strategic. It grew directly out of Kennedy's question "How can we beat the Russians in space?" In response to this question, rocket scientist Werner von Braun wrote an insightful memorandum to Vice President Lyndon Johnson. Von Braun noted that the Soviet Union had a big lead in heavy-lift rockets. That meant they could win in a race to put up a manned orbiting laboratory or to put an unmanned vehicle on the moon. But, von Braun argued:

> We have a sporting chance of sending a 3-man crew *around the moon* ahead of the Soviets (1965–66) . . . [and] we have an excellent chance of beating the Soviets to the *first landing of a crew on the moon* (including return capability, of course). The reason is that a performance jump by a factor of 10 over their present rockets is necessary to accomplish this feat.[1]

Whereas the Soviet Union's large launch vehicles put the United States at a disadvantage in achieving a number of near-term space spectaculars, the moon landing would require much larger rockets than either nation possessed, giving the United States an advantage because of its larger base of resources. Thus, von Braun recommended a preemptive announcement of the more ambitious objective because the United

States had a good chance of beating the Russians to its accomplishment. Kennedy's speech was delivered one month after von Braun's memorandum arrived.

The objective Kennedy set, seemingly audacious to the layman, was quite proximate. It was a matter of marshaling the resources and political will. Today, for instance, placing an American on Mars by 2020 is a tough but proximate objective—there would be problems to be solved, but no reason not to expect their resolution. Unfortunately, since Kennedy's time, there has been an increased penchant for defining goals that no one really knows how to achieve and pretending that they are feasible. Take, for example, the War on Drugs. No matter how desirable it might be to stop the use of illegal drugs, it is not a proximate objective because it is not feasible within the present legal and law-enforcement framework. Indeed, the enormous efforts directed at this objective may only drive out the small-time smuggler, raise the street price, and make it even more profitable for the sophisticated drug cartels. Another example is the continuing call for energy independence, an objective that remains infeasible absent the political courage to raise gasoline prices and commit to the development of nuclear power.

RESOLVING AMBIGUITY

Two years after Kennedy committed the United States to landing a person on the moon, I was working as an engineer at NASA's Jet Propulsion Laboratory (JPL). There I learned that a good proximate objective's feasibility does wonders for organizational energy and focus.

One of the main projects at JPL was Surveyor, an unmanned machine that would soft-land on the moon, take measurements and photographs, and, in later missions, deploy a small roving vehicle. The most vexing problem for the Surveyor design team had been that no one knew what the moon's surface was like.[2] Scientists had worked up three or four theories about how the moon was formed. The lunar surface might be soft, the powdery residue of eons of meteoric bombardment. It might be a nest of needle-sharp crystals. It might be a jumble of large boulders, like a glacial moraine. Would a vehicle sink into powder? Would it be speared on needlelike crystals? Would it wedge between giant boulders? Given this ambiguity about the lunar surface, engineers had a difficult time creating designs for Surveyor. It wasn't that you couldn't design a vehicle; it was that you couldn't defend any one design against someone else's story about the possible horrors of the lunar surface.

At that time, I worked for Phyllis Buwalda, who directed Future Mission Studies at JPL. Homeschooled on a ranch in Colorado, Phyllis had a tough, practical intellect that could see to the root of a problem. She was best known for her work on a model of the lunar surface.[3] With this specification in place, JPL engineers and subcontractors were able to stop guessing and get to work.

The lunar surface Phyllis described was hard and grainy, with slopes of no more than about fifteen degrees, scattered small stones, and boulders no larger than about two feet across spaced here and there. Looking at this specification for the first time, I was amazed. "Phyllis," I said, "this looks a lot like the Southwestern desert."

"Yes, doesn't it?" she said with a smile.

"But," I complained, "*you* really don't know what the moon is like. Why write a spec saying it is like the local desert?"

"This is what the smoother parts of the earth are like, so it is probably a pretty good guess as to what we'll find on the moon if we stay away from the mountains."

"But, you really have no idea what the surface of the moon is like! It could be powder, or jagged needles. . . ."

"Look," she said, "the engineers can't work without a specification. If it turns out to be a lot more difficult than this, we aren't going to be spending much time on the moon anyway."

Her lunar specification wasn't the truth—the truth was that we didn't know. It was a strategically chosen proximate objective—one the engineers knew how to tackle, so it helped speed the project along. And it was sensible and clever at the same time. You could write a PhD thesis on the options analysis implicit in her insight that if the lunar surface wouldn't support a straightforward lander, we had more than a design problem—the whole U.S. program of landing a man there would be in deep trouble. Writing the history of Surveyor, Oran W. Nicks said, "The engineering model of the lunar surface actually used for Surveyor design was developed after study of all the theories and information available. Fortunately, this model was prepared by engineers who were not emotionally involved in the generation of scientific theories, and the resulting landing system requirements were remarkably accurate."[4]

This lunar surface specification absorbed much of the ambiguity in the situation, passing on to the designers a simpler problem. Not a problem easily solved, or to which a solution already existed, but a problem that was solvable. It would take time and effort, but we knew that we could build a machine to land on Phyllis's moon.

Surveyors were built by Hughes Aircraft Company, and five made successful landings on the moon in 1966 and 1967. *Surveyor* 3 landed in the Ocean of Storms in 1967. Just a bit more than two years later, *Apollo 12* landed two hundred yards away, and Commander Pete Conrad walked over to the machine and took its picture.

Phyllis's insight that "the engineers can't work without a specification" applies to most organized human effort. Like the Surveyor design teams, every organization faces a situation where the full complexity and ambiguity of the situation is daunting. An important duty of any leader is to absorb a large part of that complexity and ambiguity, passing on to the organization a simpler problem—one that is solvable. Many leaders fail badly at this responsibility, announcing ambitious goals without resolving a good chunk of ambiguity about the specific obstacles to be overcome. To take responsibility is more than a willingness to accept the blame. It is setting proximate objectives and handing the organization a problem it can actually solve.

TAKING A STRONG POSITION AND CREATING OPTIONS

Many writers on strategy seem to suggest that the more dynamic the situation, the farther ahead a leader must look. This is illogical. The more dynamic the situation, the poorer your foresight will be. Therefore, the more uncertain and dynamic the situation, the more *proximate* a strategic objective must be. The proximate objective is guided by forecasts of the future, but the more uncertain the future, the more its essential logic is that of "taking a strong position and creating options," not of looking far ahead. Herbert Goldhamer's description of play between two chess masters vividly describes this dynamic of taking positions, creating options, and building advantage:

> Two masters trying to defeat each other in a chess game are, during a large part of the game, likely to be making moves that have no immediate end other than to "improve my position." One does not win a chess game by always selecting moves that are directly aimed at trying to mate the opponent or even at trying to win a particular piece. For the most part, the aim of a move is to find positions for one's pieces that (a) increase their mobility, that is, increase the options open to them and decrease the freedom of operation of the opponent's pieces; and (b) impose certain relatively stable patterns on the board that induce enduring strength

> for oneself and enduring weakness for the opponent. If and when sufficient positional advantages have been accumulated, they generally can be cashed in with greater or less ease by tactical maneuvers (combinations) against specific targets that are no longer defensible or only at terrible cost.[5]

■ ■ ■

In 2005, I was invited to help a smaller business school with its strategic plan. Business schools teach strategy but rarely apply the concept to themselves. At this school, the overall ambition of the dean and faculty was to break out from being a local school to one ranked with the best in the region. The draft strategic plan was typical for the industry: it was a list of areas in which the school would announce initiatives and try harder. It called for increased research visibility, more alumni giving, the creation of a global business studies program, the enhancement of its entrepreneurial studies program, and a sustainability initiative. Looking more closely at the situation, one could see that the largest segment of students took jobs in accounting firms and small-to-medium-sized local service businesses.

Strategic planning was the responsibility of the dean and the faculty executive council. I met with this group and explained the concepts of pivotal issues and the proximate objective. Then I asked the group to imagine that they were allowed to have only one objective. *And the objective had to be feasible*. What one single feasible objective, when accomplished, would make the biggest difference?

After a morning's deliberation they had two. They weren't quite as feasible as I would have liked, but they were a big step forward from their vague ambition to be a top school in the region. About one-half of the group had come up with an obvious, yet potentially pivotal, objective: "getting the students into better jobs." If students got better jobs, it was argued, they would be happier, faculty would be happier teaching happier students, alumni would give more money to the school, better students would be attracted to the school, and more resources would flow into the school to fund research and hiring. The other half of the group was in favor of a public-relations objective. They believed that focusing on getting more coverage of the school in business magazines and newspapers would raise its profile, yielding a number of favorable results.

Importantly, both objectives represented strong positions within a field of action and were each pregnant with options for future strategizing and action.

I praised both objectives and asked the group to make either or both even more proximate—more like tasks and less like goals. By the end of the day, the group had combined the two ideas. They decided that the primary objective of the school would be to get the students into better jobs. They would select ten target firms that should be hiring their graduates but presently were not. Faculty committees would be created to study these firms' recruiting practices and create programs to meet their needs and standards. Secondly, instead of global studies and sustainability, the school committed itself to a new course of studies on media management. The idea was that such a program would attract media people to visit the school, and if students got jobs in the media, it would naturally help raise the school's profile. Two of the ten target firms would be media companies.

HIERARCHIES OF OBJECTIVES

In organizations of any size, high-level proximate objectives create goals for lower-level units, which, in turn, create their own proximate objectives, and so on, in a cascade of problem solving at finer and finer levels of detail.[6] Proximate objectives not only cascade down hierarchies; they cascade in time. For instance, when Nestlé purchased British chocolate company Rowntree, top management made a judgment that Nestlé's transnational food-marketing skills would be able to take Rowntree's Britain-centered brands and move them into many other countries. The first steps in that direction were very successful, and the combined managements then developed more subtle and nuanced objectives. Anytime a company enters a new business or market, there is necessarily this cascade of adjusting and elaborating proximate objectives.

What is proximate for one nation, one organization, or even one person may be far out of reach to another. The obvious reason is differences in skills and accumulated resources. My understanding of this was sharpened during an afternoon discussion about helicopters.

A man I know only as PJ lives on the East Cape of Baja California, about thirty miles north of San Jose del Cabo, on the Sea of Cortez. He is now a surfer and fisherman, but PJ was once a helicopter pilot, first in Vietnam, and then in rescue work. The land in Baja California is unspoiled by shopping malls, industry, paved highways, or fences. Sitting on a hilltop in the warm winter we could see the gray whales jump and hear their tails slap on the water. Making conversation, I offered that "helicopters should be safer than airplanes. If the engine fails, you can autorotate to the ground. It's like having a parachute."

PJ snorted. "If your engine fails you have to pull the collective all the way down, get off the left pedal and hit the right pedal hard to get some torque. You have about one second to do this before you are dropping too fast." He paused and then added, "You can do it, but you better not have to think about it."

"So, everything has to be automatic?" I asked.

"Not all," he replied. "When an engine fails you have a lot to work out. You have to concentrate on where you are going to land and on maintaining a smooth sliding path down to the flare. That stuff takes a lot of concentration. But the basic act of controlling the helicopter, yes, that has to be automatic. *You can't concentrate on the crisis if flying isn't automatic*."

PJ opened another Corona and then expanded on his point. "To fly a helicopter you've got to constantly coordinate the controls: the collective, the cyclic, and the pedals, not to mention the throttle. It is not easy to learn, but you've got to get on top of it. You've got to make it automatic if you're going to do more than just take off and land. After you can fly, *then* you can learn to fly at night—but not before! After you can fly at night with ease, maybe *then* you're ready to learn to fly in formation, and then in combat."

As he spoke, PJ spread his fingers, overlapped his thumbs, then swooped this miniature formation around to illustrate his point.

"Master all that—make it automatic—and you can begin to think about landing on a mountain in high wind in the late evening, or landing on a rolling, pitching deck of a ship at sea."

As PJ spoke, I could visualize him landing on a ship at sea, timing the swells and pitches of the deck. Having long ago mastered the coordination of cyclic, pedals, and collective, he could concentrate on the coordination between his aircraft and the ship.

To concentrate on an objective—to make it a priority—necessarily assumes that many other important things will be taken care of. PJ was able to concentrate on the coordination between his helicopter and the rescue vessel because he already possessed layer upon layer of competences at flying that had become routine.

After this discussion, I came to see skills at coordination as if they were rungs on a ladder, with higher rungs in reach only when the lower rungs had been attained. Indeed, PJ's concept of a layering of skills explains why some organizations can concentrate on issues that others cannot. This understanding has helped shape the advice I offer clients. For example, when I work with a small start-up company, their problems often revolve around coordinating engineering, marketing, and distribution. Asking the CEO of such a firm to concentrate on opening offices in Europe may be pointless, because the company has not yet mastered the basics of "flying" the business. Once the firm stands firmly on that rung, it can move abroad and develop international operations. But, in turn, asking that newly international firm to move knowledge and skills around the world, as does a global veteran such as Procter & Gamble, may also be pointless. It must first master the complexity of operating in various languages and cultures before it can begin to skillfully arbitrage global information.

CHAPTER EIGHT

CHAIN-LINK SYSTEMS

A system has a *chain-link* logic when its performance is limited by its weakest subunit, or "link." When there is a weak link, a chain is not made stronger by strengthening the other links.

For the space shuttle *Challenger,* the weakest link was a solid rubber O-ring. On January 28, 1986, the O-ring in *Challenger*'s booster engine failed. Hot gas knifed through the structure; the rocket exploded. *Challenger* and its crew, the "pride of our nation" President Reagan called them, tumbled out of the clear blue sky and shattered on the ocean sixty-five thousand feet below.

If a chain must not fail, there is no point in strengthening only some of the links. Similarly, for *Challenger,* there could be no gain to making the booster engines stronger if the O-ring was weak. There was little point in improving guidance, or communications, or increasing the quality of crew training, if the O-ring was weak. The logic of the chain is at work in situations ranging from mountain climbing to the space shuttle to aesthetic judgment—situations in which the quality of components or subparts matters.

Quality matters when quantity is an inadequate substitute. If a building contractor finds that her two-ton truck is on another job, she may easily substitute two one-ton trucks to carry landfill. On the other hand, if a three-star chef is ill, no number of short-order cooks is an adequate replacement. One hundred mediocre singers are not the equal of one top-notch singer. Keeping children additional hours or weeks in broken schools—schools that can neither educate nor control behavior—does not help and probably increases resentment and distrust.

Talking with real estate experts and contractors about home remodeling, I learned that in assessing a property's potential, one should identify the *limiting factors*. If a house is near a noisy highway, that is a limiting factor. No matter how much marble is put in the bathrooms or how fine the cabinetry is in the kitchen, the noise will limit the house's value. Similarly, if a room has wonderful hardwood floors and classic architecture, a less-than-excellent paint job will limit its attractiveness. As an investor, one wants to find limiting factors that can be fixed, such as paint, rather than factors that cannot be fixed, such as highway noise. If you have a special skill or insight at removing limiting factors, then you can be very successful.

GETTING STUCK

There are portions of organizations, and even of economies, that are chain-linked. When each link is managed somewhat separately, the system can get stuck in a low-effectiveness state. The problem arises because of *quality matching*.[1] That is, if you are in charge of one link of the chain, there is no point in investing resources in making your link better if other link managers are not.

To make matters even more difficult, striving for higher quality in just one of the linked units may make matters worse! Higher quality in a unit requires investments in better resources and more expensive inputs, including people. Since these efforts to improve just one linked unit will not improve the overall performance of the chain-linked system, the system's overall profit actually declines. Thus, the incentive to improve each unit is dulled.

For instance, the various problems at General Motors from 1980 to 2008 had strong chain-link features. Increasing the quality of an automobile transmission does little good if the knobs fall off the dashboard and door panels continue to rattle. Improving fit and finish, along with the drivetrain, may offer little overall improvement as long as the designers continue to produce pedestrian designs. Improving the look of the automobiles may only increase costs unless the complex technology of design for manufacturability is mastered. And so on.

As another example, many of the thorny problems of economic development arise from chain-linked issues:

- It is of little use to supply advanced machinery to unskilled workers, but it is also useless to educate people for jobs that do not exist.

- Government bureaucracy can be a terrible burden, but improvement in its effectiveness can be won only if there is an efficient private sector.

- Without corruption, it would be impossible to get around the stifling bureaucracy, but bureaucracy is a necessary counter to nepotism and a culture of corruption.

- Improving the roads puts a strain on poor port facilities, and better ports without good roads are of little value. Improve both the roads and ports, and corrupt officials and unions will demand payments for letting shipments through.

Policy problems with chain-link logic are not restricted to the developing world. In the United States, dysfunctional inner cities, decayed schools, and prison systems that institutionalize race-based gangs, violence, and sexual assault can each be subjected to a chain-link analysis. The Department of Homeland Security has beefed up passport inspections at airports, a high-profile practice that can have little total payoff as long as more than four thousand miles of border and as much coastline remain virtually uncontrolled. Stopping two out of three radiological attacks won't be good enough.

GETTING UNSTUCK

Expertise is not evenly distributed in the world. If you seek the most efficient automobile makers, you must travel to the Kanto plain in Japan, where they cluster. Chemical expertise clusters in Europe where Germany, France, and Switzerland come together. Travel to the Santa Clara valley to find expertise in microprocessors and to the English Midlands for Formula 1 racing machines. And on the Italian Lombard plain, where Italy and Switzerland come together, you will find world-class expertise in mechanical systems—from fast cars to specialized industrial equipment.

Marco Tinelli is the general manager of a Lombardy machine company, operating on the outskirts of Milan. One day in 1997 I toured Marco's company and lunched with him at Savini, the classical restaurant in Galleria Vittorio Emanuele II, next to the duomo in Milan. Over a perfect risotto, Marco explained the turnaround at his family's company:

> When my uncle passed away, the responsibility for the company passed to me. Things were not good. The quality of the machines had declined, especially compared with our best competitors. Costs were too high and the sales personnel were not technically sophisticated. To sell a sophisticated machine with microprocessor controls takes a sophisticated salesperson. If we didn't change, we would slowly go out of business. But it seemed as if everything had to change. Where to start?

As he spoke, I realized that Marco Tinelli's diagnosis was that his machinery company had chain-link logic and that it was stuck. Any payoff from better-quality machines was diluted because the sales force could not accurately represent their qualities and performance. A better sales force, by itself, would have added little value without better machines. And improvements in quality and sales would not save the firm unless costs were reduced.

"Where did you start?" I asked, echoing his own question. Marco explained:

> I conducted three campaigns, one after another. In the first campaign we spent twelve months just on quality. I told the employees that everything we did for the next year would be to make our machines the best in the industry, the most reliable and the fastest.
>
> Once we had good quality machines, I focused entirely on the sales function. The salespeople had been involved in the quality campaign, and now the engineers and manufacturing people worked with sales to build skills, selling tools, and communications links back to the factory. Market results were slow in coming, but I knew we had to make these investments first to reap benefits later.

If one has not internalized the concept of quality matching and the problems of change in chain-link systems, then Marco's explanation of his actions may seem banal—he identified the three problems and worked on them in turn. But if one has these concepts, then Marco's statement is dense with meaning.

The first logical problem in chain-link situations is to identify the bottlenecks, and Marco did that—quality, sales' technical competence, and cost. The second, and greatest, problem is that incremental change may not pay off and may even make things worse. That is why systems get stuck. Marco's solution to this problem was to take personal responsibility for the final result and direct others' attention to the three bottlenecks, one after another. There were no immediate returns to the first campaign, but he did not stop nor did he operate a system that heaped blame on his department managers. Instead, he congratulated them for achieving the proximate goal of the first campaign and moved on to the second. There are little or no payoffs to incremental improvements in chain-link systems, but Marco avoided this problem by shutting down the normal system of local measurement and reward, refocusing on *change itself* as the objective.

One of the tasks of the interviewer is to listen for what is not said. Marco did not say, "We turned it around by increasing the pressure for profit." He did not say, "We developed new measures of quality and demanded improvements." He did not say, "I brought in new, more skilled, managers." Instead, Marco described a turnaround in which *he* provided the overall definition of what had to be done and in which he anticipated and absorbed the costs of change. In any organization there is always a managed tension between the need for decentralized autonomous action and the need for centralized direction and coordination. To produce a turnaround of a chain-link system, Marco Tinelli tipped the balance, at least for a while, strongly toward central direction and coordination.

Marco's explanation of his third campaign was also intriguing. In particular, Marco saw logical and temporal connections that dictated that the cost-reduction campaign come last:

> Finally, we spent nine months working just on cost. There was no other goal during this third campaign. I left cost cutting to the last because I wanted the cost-reduction campaign to work with, but not define, the type of machines we build. To reduce costs, we reviewed each component and each step in the manufacturing process. The big improvements came from cutting two products out of the line and bringing in-house some tools and dies we had been buying from other companies. By making our own dies we increased the speed of the machines, and thus increased their value to our customers. The price of the machine did not fall, but the cost to the user did. It took a sophisticated sales-engineering team to get this point across to our customers, which was another reason for making this type of cost reduction the last step.

Marco's efforts paid off, and the family company is a growing profitable firm with an excellent reputation in its industry. Chain-link systems can be changed and made excellent. It takes insight into the key bottlenecks. Plus, it takes leadership and the willingness to absorb short-term losses in the quest for future gains. At Marco Tinelli's company, he personally took the responsibility for the costs of change and plowed ahead, guided by the eventual end state to be achieved rather than monthly or quarterly profit.

EXCELLENCE

As we learn from Marco Tinelli, turning around a chain-link system requires direct leadership and design. Conversely, *the excellence achieved by a well-managed chain-link system is difficult to replicate*.

Consider IKEA. Formed in Sweden in 1943, the company designs ready-to-assemble furniture it sells through special IKEA-owned stores, advertised by its own catalogs. Giant retail stores located in the suburbs allow huge selections and ample parking for customers. In the stores, the catalogs essentially substitute for a sales force. Its flat-pack furniture designs not only reduce shipping and storage costs; they also help keep the stores in stock and let the customers pull their own stock out of inventory and take their purchases home, eliminating long waits for delivery. The company designs much of the furniture it sells, contracting out manufacturing, but managing its own worldwide logistics system.

IKEA's strategy is an effective way to coordinate policies, but it is hardly secret. Won't other companies see how it works and copy it, perhaps even improve it? The explanation for its continued excellence and the lack of any effective me-too competition is that its strategy builds on chain-link logic.

IKEA's adroit coordination of policies is a more integrated design than anyone else's in the furniture business. Traditional furniture retailers do not carry large inventory, traditional manufacturers do not have their own stores, normal retailers do not specify their own designs or use catalogs rather than salespeople, and so on. Because IKEA's many policies are different from the norm and because they fit together in a coherent design, IKEA's system has a chain-link logic. That means that adopting only one of these policies does no good—it adds expense to the competitor's business without providing any real competition to IKEA. Minor adjustments just won't do—to compete effectively with IKEA, an existing rival would have to virtually start fresh and, in effect, compete with its own existing business. No one did. Today, more than fifty years after IKEA pioneered its new strategy in the furniture industry, no one has really replicated it.

For IKEA's set of policies to be a source of sustained competitive excellence, three conditions must hold:

- IKEA must perform each of its core activities with outstanding efficiency and effectiveness.

- These core activities must be sufficiently chain-linked that a rival cannot grab business away from IKEA by adopting only one of them and performing it well. That is, a traditional furniture manufacturer that adds a ready-to-assemble line is no real threat to IKEA, nor is a traditional retailer that adds a catalog.

- The chain-linked activities should form an unusual grouping such that expertise in one does not easily carry over to expertise at the others. Thus, a traditional furniture retailer that did add a catalog would still have to master design and logistics and build vastly larger stores to begin to compete with IKEA. Plus, looking beyond traditional furniture companies, there are no potential competitors that possess this mix of resources and competencies.

IKEA teaches us that in building sustained strategic advantage, talented leaders seek to create constellations of activities that are chain-linked. This adds extra effectiveness to the strategy and makes competitive imitation difficult. What is especially fascinating is that both excellence and being stuck are reflections of chain-link logic.

In the case of excellence, like IKEA, a series of chain-linked activities are all maintained at a high level of quality, each benefiting from the quality of the other and the whole being resistant to easy imitation. On the other hand, when a series of chain-linked activities are of low quality, as in General Motors circa 2007, the system can be stuck, because there is little gain to improving only a fraction of the activities. Marco Tinelli's success demonstrates that to unstick a stuck chain-linked system, a strong leader must possess the insight and fortitude to make the necessary investments in each link of the chain.

CHAPTER NINE

USING DESIGN

The word "strategy" comes to us from military affairs. Unfortunately, humans have put more effort, over more time, into thinking about war than any other subject. Much of this knowledge has very little to tell us about strategy in nonmilitary situations. In particular, the primary way business firms compete is by placing their offers in front of buyers, each trying to offer a more attractive deal. This is a process more like a dance contest than a military battle. Businesses do not bomb one another's factories or kill one another's employees. While business employees can quit on a moment's notice, soldiers are indentured. Employees are not expected to stand and give up their lives to protect the company. And the impact of size is radically different. Other things being equal, the larger army has the advantage whereas the winning business tends to be the one whose offerings are most preferred by customers, its size being more the consequence than the cause of its success. Despite all these cautions, I believe that if you are careful about the level of abstraction, you can take certain fundamental lessons from military history and be the wiser for doing so.

THE FATHER OF STRATEGY

To begin at the beginning, armies, together with the authority structures supporting them, first arose in the Bronze Age in parallel with complex urban societies. Just as humans discovered that organized agriculture paid great dividends, they also found that organizing and coordinating the actions of fighters greatly magnified their effect. Properly organized and led, ordinary men could defeat skilled warriors who fought as individuals or as small bands.

The classic example of design in battle strategy, one that is still studied today, is Hannibal's victory over the Roman army at Cannae in 216 B.C. At that time, the Roman Republic controlled a series of territories and city-states in Italy. Carthage was a city-state of Phoenicians located in what is today Tunisia. Fifty years earlier, Carthage had lost a war with Rome over control of the southern Mediterranean. Seeking to restore Carthage's power and honor, Hannibal took an army to Spain, then through Gaul (France), and crossed the Alps into Italy. There, he raided towns up and down the Italian peninsula, seeking favorable terms from Rome.

After tiring of a policy of avoiding pitched battles, the Roman senate chose consuls Varro and Paullus, and gave them an unprecedented eight legions to defeat Hannibal.[1] The location of the battle was an open field, near the ruins of a fortress called Cannae, on the Adriatic Sea. To find the spot on a modern map, look for Monte di Canne, located at the back of the ankle of Italy's boot.

As the morning of August 2 dawned, eighty-five thousand or more Roman soldiers faced about fifty-five thousand of Hannibal's troops. Each army's front was about one mile long, and the two armies were about one-half mile apart. Hannibal had arranged his troops in a broad arc, bulging out in the center toward the Romans. In that central bulge, Hannibal placed troops from Spain and Gaul, soldiers who had been liberated from Roman rule or hired during his march from Spain to Italy and along the Po River. On the flanks, or sides, of this central bulge he placed his Carthaginian heavy infantry.

When the advancing Romans met Hannibal's army, the outward-arced center of Hannibal's front line was the first point of contact. There, the Gauls and Spaniards slowly fell back, not holding the line, just as Hannibal had ordered. Encouraged, the Roman army moved forward with shouts of victory, rushing to exploit this apparent weakness. Simultaneously, Hannibal's horse cavalry, placed on the sides of his mile-wide army, began its preplanned gallop in wide two-mile arcs around the sides of the Roman army, engaging and defeating the smaller Roman cavalry.

As the Roman legions pushed into the Carthaginian center, the original outward arc was reversed, and it began to bow inward under the pressure. As the center line bowed inward, Hannibal's heavy infantry units, positioned on either end of the central arc, maintained their positions but did not engage. Then, at Hannibal's signal, reinforcements moved to bolster the Carthaginian bowed-in center. The troops in the center stopped their retreat and held. Their aspect changed from that of panicky barbarians to that of hard, disciplined troops. Hannibal's heavy infantry flanks then moved to engage the sides of the Roman army, which was now surrounded on three sides. Then Hannibal's cavalry rode in from behind and closed the Roman's rear as well.

The ruthless genius of Hannibal's strategy was then revealed. Not only was the Roman army surrounded, but as their superior numbers pressed into the arc of Hannibal's bowed-in center, the Roman ranks were squeezed together. They became so tightly massed that many Roman soldiers could not move to raise their weapons. The Romans had lost coherence and mobility. Encircled and compressed together, their numerical superiority had been nullified.

The men at the very center of the compressed mass waited helplessly for death, unable to move. The Romans did not surrender or ask for mercy. At least fifty thousand Roman soldiers were killed that day, more soldiers than have died in any single day of battle before or since—more on that one day than at Gettysburg or the Somme. One-tenth that number of Hannibal's troops died. The Roman dead included consul Paullus, several former consuls, forty-eight tribunes, and eighty senators. In a few hours, one-fourth of the Republic's elected leadership was slaughtered at Cannae. Rome's defeat was so great that most southern city-states in Italy declared allegiance to Hannibal. The Greek cities in Sicily went over to Hannibal as did Macedon in the east.

To grasp the magnitude of the defeat, imagine that the 1944 German army, commanded by General Erwin Rommel, totally destroyed all Allied forces in Europe, that one-fourth of the U.S. Congress had been killed, and that Russia, northern Europe, and eastern Europe had turned to become German allies.

Rome and Hannibal fought in Italy for ten long years after Cannae, and Hannibal won further significant victories, never losing an engagement.[2] Biographer Theodore Dodge named Hannibal the "father of strategy," because, over this long conflict, Rome learned and, gradually, came to master strategy through Hannibal's painful teachings.[3] Roman society was hardened and militarized by this prolonged struggle, and Rome went on to conquer and dominate the known world for five hundred years. In turn, the rest of the Western world learned strategy from Rome.

■ ■ ■

The concept of strategy has many faces, and there are some we do not see in the story of Cannae. The history of this battle tells us little about longer-range considerations and little about how the strategy was created. The full design for the battle, at least in the available histories, seems to have been created by Hannibal, and its implementation was by his personal command. From Roman historians, we learn that Hannibal was considered noble and admired by all who met him, even Romans. Beyond that, we know almost nothing of his interpersonal abilities or methods. In particular, one wonders at how he persuaded the Gauls and Spaniards in his central arc to stage a mock retreat, an action that these men would have viewed as expensive in both blood and honor. We do not know.

However, what we *do* see in the story of Cannae are three aspects of strategy in bold relief, presented in their purest and most essential forms—premeditation, the anticipation of others' behavior, and the purposeful design of coordinated actions.

Premeditation

Cannae was not an improvisation; it was designed and planned in advance. Hannibal executed such choreographed strategies not just once, but many times in his years of war with Rome. There are furious debates over the best balance, in a strategy, between prior guidance and on-the-spot adaptation and improvisation, but there is always some form of prior guidance. By definition, winging it is not a strategy.

Anticipation

A fundamental ingredient in a strategy is a judgment or anticipation concerning the thoughts and/or behavior of others. The simplest way of looking at Cannae is that Hannibal surrounded, or enveloped, the Romans. But that is incomplete, for the Roman legions were the more mobile infantry on that field. Actually, the legions were enticed into becoming enveloped, enticed into a trap, their own mobility, courage, and even initiative turned against them. The very essence of Cannae was that the bars of the trap—the compression of the legions' ranks—were forged, in part, by the Romans' own vigorous responses to Hannibal's enticements.

In game theory one presumes that the opponent is as rational as oneself. It is clear that Hannibal did not make that presumption. However individually rational the Romans might have been, he saw the Roman army as an organization with a history, traditions, doctrine, and standardized training. Furthermore, that organization's leaders had identifiable motivations and biases. Consul Varro, for example, was known to be proud and a bit impetuous.

Hannibal knew these things because Carthage had fought Rome ten years earlier and came to understand its military system. The son of a military family, Hannibal was highly educated and had written several books in Greek and Punic. Also, part of the Roman behavior at Cannae was predictable because Hannibal had worked to shape it, raiding Varro's camp the night before, angering and embarrassing the consul in front of his troops, pushing him to seek immediate battle. Finally, elements of Roman behavior were predictable because the battle developed quickly, giving the Romans little time to study the situation and no time to learn new lessons and alter their methods.

Design of Coordinated Action

Hannibal's strategy at Cannae was an astoundingly adroit construction of coordinated actions orchestrated in time and in space. In 216 B.C., the fundamental formula for military success was fairly basic: keeping in formation, keeping discipline, and keeping troops from panicking and running. Therefore, when a Roman saw the enemy retreat, it looked like victory. The idea that a commander could convince warlike Gauls and Spaniards into a mock retreat was almost unthinkable. Furthermore, the normal pattern in ancient battle was that cavalry, after vanquishing the opposing cavalry, would chase fleeing disorganized horsemen and soldiers. It was not expected that they would re-form and attack the main body of infantry. The Carthaginian army's competence and discipline at carrying out a complex series of movements by different units—units that were physically separated but acting in preplanned cohesion around a central design—was a surprise. No army before Hannibal's had executed such choreographed multiple movements in time and space.[4]

It is often said that a strategy is a choice or a decision. The words "choice" and "decision" evoke an image of someone considering a list of alternatives and then selecting one of them. There is, in fact, a formal theory of decisions that specifies exactly how to make a choice by identifying alternative actions, valuing outcomes, and appraising probabilities of events. The problem with this view, and the reason it barely lightens a leader's burden, is that you are rarely handed a clear set of alternatives. In the case at hand, Hannibal was certainly not briefed by a staff presenting four options arranged on a PowerPoint slide. Rather, he faced a challenge and he *designed* a novel response. Today, as then, many effective strategies are more designs than decisions—are more constructed than chosen. In these cases, doing strategy is more like designing a high-performance aircraft than deciding which forklift truck to buy or how large to build a new factory. When someone says "Managers are decision makers," they are not talking about master strategists, for a master strategist is a designer.

THE PARTS OF A WHOLE

Business and corporate strategy deal with large-scale design-type problems. The greater the challenge, or the higher the performance sought, the more interactions have to be considered. Think, for instance, of what it takes to give a BMW 3 Series car that "driving machine" feel. The chassis, steering, suspension, engine, and hydraulic and electrical controls all have to be tuned to one another. You can make a car out of high-quality off-the-shelf parts, but it won't be a "driving machine." In a case like this there is a sharp gain to careful coordination of the parts into a whole.[5]

Form an image in your mind of the BMW's driver; see her taking the curves on the winding Angeles Crest Highway. Look at her face and imagine sensing her pleasure or displeasure with the automobile. Now, begin to vary the design. Make the car bigger, quieter, a bit less responsive but more powerful, heavier. Now, lighter, quicker, more responsive. To do so, you have to change the chassis, the engine weight and torque, the suspension, the steering assembly, and more. It will sway less and hug the road; the steering wheel will provide more tactile feedback. Now adjust the chassis: make it stiffer to dampen longitudinal twist and soften the front suspension just a bit to reduce road shock. Varying forty or fifty parameters, you will eventually find a sweet spot, where everything works together. She will smile and like her car.

But there is more. Her driving pleasure depends upon the price paid, so we begin to include cost in our design. We concentrate on her smile per dollar. Many more interactions must be considered to find the sweet spot that gives the largest smile per dollar. You cannot search the entire space of possibilities; it is too complex. But you can probably, with effort, produce a good configuration. To get more sophisticated, you should also include the pleasure the driver takes in buying a premium brand, backed up by image advertising and swank dealers. You should also consider her buying experience and the car's expected reliability and resale value. More design elements to adjust, more interactions to consider. And then, of course, you should consider other drivers with other tastes and incomes, a huge step upward in complexity and interaction.

That difficult exercise was design. But in seeking the best smile per dollar, we took a monopoly view. Yes, we went beyond product to include manufacturing and distribution in the design, but our strategy was tuned to please the customer, not to deal with competition. To deal with competition, expand your vision again to include other automobile companies. Now you are looking for a competitive sweet spot. You have to adjust the design—the strategy—to put more smile per dollar on a driver's face than she can get from competing products.[6] That driver might not be the young woman we first envisioned on the Angeles Crest Highway. Another firm may more easily meet her demands, so a critical issue becomes the identification of the particular set of buyers—our target market—where we have a differential advantage. Competitive strategy is still design, but there are now more parameters—more interactions—to worry about. The new interactions are the offerings and strategies of rivals. Very quickly, you are going to focus on what you, or your company, can do more effectively than others. It will normally turn out that competition makes you focus on a much smaller subset of car models, manufacturing setups, and customers.

I am describing a strategy as a design rather than as a plan or as a choice because I want to emphasize the issue of mutual adjustment. In design problems, where various elements must be arranged, adjusted, and coordinated, there can be sharply peaked gains to getting combinations right and sharp costs to getting them wrong. A good strategy coordinates policies across activities to focus the competitive punch.

■ ■ ■

I first discovered the discipline of design in my first job out of college, working as a systems engineer at the Jet Propulsion Laboratories. It was a dream job, doing conceptual designs of a mission to Jupiter, a project that would later be named Voyager.

JPL was organized around the subsystems of a spacecraft—

communications, power, structures, attitude control, computing and sequencing, and so on.* I was in the systems division, where the job of a systems engineer was the overall architecture of the spacecraft and working out the coordination among the specifications of all the different subsystems.

Our basic constraint was weight. We expected that the Titan IIIC rocket would launch about 1,200 pounds into a trajectory toward Jupiter. If we could use the larger Saturn 1B, then we could plan on a 3,000-pound spacecraft. Over a year, I sketched out two designs. Each was a different configuration based on a different weight budget.

With 3,000 pounds to work with, the design work was relatively easy. We could essentially bolt together fairly well-understood subsystems. Consequently, the divisions would not have to coordinate very much because the design challenge was relatively low. But if we had only 1,200 pounds to work with, things were more difficult. Interactions began to play a big role.

Most of the work in systems design is figuring out the interactions, or trade-offs, as they were called. The moment you tried to optimize any one part, that choice immediately posed problems for other parts. The weight constraint made the whole thing a web of competing needs, and it all had to be considered together. Cutting the weight of the radioactive thermal power unit meant less power for the radio, limiting it to about 35 watts. To compensate for the low-powered radio, we could try for a more focused dish antenna and seek greater accuracy in pointing the dish at Earth. That meant better sensors, more complex control logic, and more fuel for attitude control were required. Try to cut the shielding on the spacecraft by putting the radioactive power source on a longer boom and you would find that the boom sways, making guidance more difficult.

Each part of the system had to be reconsidered and shaped to the needs of the rest of the system. A great deal of work went into trying to create clever configurations that avoided wasteful duplication. For

* Attitude control referred to keeping the spacecraft oriented so that its solar panels (if any) pointed to the sun, its antenna to Earth, and its cameras and science to the target.

example, if a single device could perform multiple duties, acting as a shield from both sunlight and micrometeorites, and serve as a container for propellant, weight could be saved. Similarly, we sought ways to mitigate competition among subsystems for electrical power through the clever timing of operations.

Nothing I had learned in engineering school at UC Berkeley prepared me for thinking about this kind of design problem. There, I had learned how to mathematically model systems and then minimize something, such as cost or least-squared error. But this work at JPL was different. I had to learn enough about all the subsystems and their possible interactions, and *hold it all in my mind*, in order to imagine a configuration that might be effective. This was difficult, to say the least. I didn't know it at the time, but I was beginning to learn strategy.

Voyager 1 was launched fourteen years after those initial studies. It weighed 1,588 pounds—more than 1,200 because of improvements in the Titan IIIC launch vehicle. It took photographs and measurements of Jupiter and Saturn. The mission plan cleverly used one of the scientific television cameras to aid navigation by sending back pictures of the positions of Jupiter's moons against the background of stars. It is still operational and is presently 7.8 billion miles from the sun, beyond the edge of the solar system. *Voyager 2* took a slower path but visited Jupiter, Saturn, Uranus, and Neptune.

The Trade-Off

The lesson I took from systems engineering at JPL was that performance is the joint outcome of capability and clever design. In particular, given existing capabilities, such as rocket throw weight or power supply efficiency, to get more performance out of a system you have integrate its components and subsystems more cleverly and more tightly. On the other hand, if capabilities (technologies) could be improved, the demand for tight, clever integration was lessened. That is, more powerful booster rockets or lighter components would let us meet the weight constraint with less work on tight integration. This trade-off way of thinking about design has, for me, become central to my view of strategy:

> A design-type strategy is an adroit configuration of resources and actions that yields an advantage in a challenging situation. Given a set bundle of resources, the greater the competitive challenge, the greater the need for the clever, tight integration of resources and actions. Given a set level of challenge, higher-quality resources lessen the need for the tight integration of resources and actions.

These principles mean that resources and tight coordination are partial substitutes for each other. If the organization has few resources, the challenge can be met only by clever, tight integration. On the other hand, if more resources are available, then less tight integration may be needed.[7] Put differently, the greater the challenge, the greater the need for a good, coherent, design-type strategy.

Implicit in these principles is the notion that tight integration comes at some cost. That is, one does not always seek the very highest level of integration in a design for a machine or a business. A more tightly integrated design is harder to create, narrower in focus, more fragile in use, and less flexible in responding to change. A Formula 1 racing car, for example, is a tightly integrated design and is faster around the track than a Subaru Forester, but the less tightly integrated Forester is useful for a much wider range of purposes. Nevertheless, when the competitive challenge is very high, it may be necessary to accept these costs and design a tightly integrated response. With less challenge, it is normally better to have a bit less specialization and integration so that a broader market can be addressed.

THE ARC OF ENTERPRISE

Companies buy pickup trucks, office equipment, vertical milling machines, and chemical processing equipment, and they hire the services of warehouses, masses of high school and college graduates, lawyers, and accountants. None of these inputs are normally *strategic* resources. These kinds of assets and services cannot, in general, confer a competitive advantage, because competitors have access to virtually identical assets and services on the same terms. A strategic resource is a kind of property that is fairly long lasting that has been constructed, developed over time, designed, or discovered by a company and that competitors cannot duplicate without suffering a net economic loss.

A high-quality strategic resource yielding a powerful competitive advantage makes for great strategic simplicity. Consider Xerox's patents on plain paper copying. By the mid-1950s these patents were rock solid, and it became clear that buyers would be willing to pay three thousand dollars or more for a Xerox machine—a device that cost about seven hundred dollars to manufacture. Given this large and protected competitive advantage, Xerox did the obvious—it made and sold Xerox machines.

Xerox built factories, produced Xerox plain-paper photocopiers, and built sales and service networks. It experienced no meaningful competition from any of the old-line wet-process copier companies. It produced documents called "strategic plans," but they were merely financial projections. Its challenge was low. It did not need much in the way of a design-type strategy because its resource position—its patent—insulated it from competition and because the product's value to buyers was so much greater than the cost of making one.

Resources are to coordinated activity as capital is to labor. It takes a great deal of labor to build a dam, but the dam's services may then be available, for a time, without further labor. In the same way, Xerox's powerful resource position—its knowledge and patents regarding plain-paper copying—was the accumulated result of years of clever, focused, coordinated, inventive activity. And, like a dam, once that well-protected resource position was achieved, it persisted for many years. As one senior Xerox manager told me in 1977, "The factory sold its machines to the sales division at a transfer price that was double its full cost of production. Then, the sales division doubled or tripled that transfer price to set a price for the customer."

Thus, a strong resource position can obviate the need for sophisticated design-type strategy. If, instead, there is only a moderate resource position—perhaps a new product idea or a customer relationship—the challenge is to build a sensible and coherent strategy around that resource. Finally, the cleverest strategies, the ones we study down through the years, begin with very few strategic resources, obtaining their results through the adroit coordination of actions in time and across functions.

The peril of a potent resource position is that success then arrives without careful ongoing strategy work. Own the original patent on the plain-paper photocopier, or own the Hershey's brand name, or the Windows operating system franchise, or the patent on Lipitor, and there will be many years during which profits will roll in almost regardless of how you arrange your business logic. Yes, there was inventive genius in the creation of these strategic resources, but profits from those resources can be sustained, for a time, without genius.

Existing resources can be the lever for the creation of new resources, but they can also be an impediment to innovation. Well-led firms must, from time to time, cast aside old resources, just as they retire obsolete machinery. Yet strategic resources are embedded deeply within the human fabric of the enterprise, and most firms find this a difficult maneuver. Xerox, for example, built a world-class fast-response repair and maintenance service to take care of its installed base of copying machines. Thus, its initial resource—the patent on plain-paper copying—was used to create a new strategic resource. But the service system's value lay in keeping the base of failure-prone leased machines running. And its complement was a profitable business in "special" Xerox-brand plain paper, which jammed the copiers less frequently. The next step should have been to build a world-class paper-handling capability. That would have opened the door to an early position in personal copiers, printers, fax machines, and so on. But it would also have reduced the immediate value of the Xerox service-system resource. Resting on its laurels, Xerox let Canon, Kodak, and IBM develop superior paper handling technology, while it struck off in the futile search for a way to enter the computer business with a resource base specialized around maintaining failure-prone mechanical devices.

A very powerful resource position produces profit without great effort, and it is human nature that the easy life breeds laxity. It is also human nature to associate current profit with recent actions, even though it should be evident that current plenty is the harvest of planting seasons long past. When the profits roll in, leaders will point to their every action with pride. Books will be written recommending that others immediately adopt the successful firm's dress code, its vacation policy, its suggestion-box policies, and its method of allocating parking spaces. Of course, these connections are specious. Were there such simple, direct connections between current actions and current results, strategy would be a lot easier. It would also be a lot less interesting, for it is the *disconnect* between current results and current action that makes the analysis of the sources of success so hard and, ultimately, so rewarding.

Success leads to laxity and bloat, and these lead to decline. Few organizations avoid this tragic arc. Yet it is this fairly predictable trajectory that opens the door to strategic upstarts. To see effective design-type strategy, you must usually look away from the long-successful incumbent toward the company that effectively invades its market space. There you will find a tightly crafted and integrated set of actions and policies. Look at Canon, working around Xerox's patents and creating a radically new business model based on reliable desktop copying, rather than centralized high-speed high-volume copiers. Look at the young Microsoft besting IBM; the young Wal-Mart besting Kmart; the young Dell taking business away from HP, Compaq, and IBM; upstart FedEx pushing aside the traditional air-freight carriers; Enterprise Rent-A-Car competing effectively with Hertz and Avis with a new business model; Nvidia coming out of nowhere to steal domination of the graphics chip market away from Intel; and Google redefining the search business and taking it away from Microsoft and Yahoo! In each case you will find the upstart wielding a tightly coordinated competitive strategy.

In our longing for immortality, we ask that these strategic upstarts extend their success forever—the aging businessperson's quixotic search for *sustained* competitive advantage. But the incumbent laxity and inertia that gave these upstarts their openings applies to them as well. In time, most will loosen their tight integration and begin to rely more on accumulated resources and less on clever business design. Relying on the profits accruing to accumulated resources, they will lose the discipline of tight integration, allowing independent fiefdoms to flourish and adding so many products and projects that integration becomes impossible. Faced with the natural slowing of growth over time, they will try to create an appearance of youthful vigor with bolt-on acquisitions. Then, when their resource base eventually becomes obsolete, they, too, will become prey to another generation of upstarts. It is the cycle of life. Its important lesson is that we should learn design-type strategy from an upstart's early conquests rather than from the mature company's posturing. Study how Bill Gates outsmarted the giant IBM or how Nucor became a leader in the declining steel industry and you will learn design-type strategy. Study Microsoft today and you will see a mature giant, reaping the benefits of past victories but just as tied to its installed base and a rich mix of conflicting initiatives and standards as was IBM in 1985.

ORDER OUT OF CHAOS

One example of good strategy in which you can see the coordinated elements of design is the U.S. heavy-truck business. Daimler AG is the market-share leader (38 percent). It got that large by buying Ford's troubled heavy-truck business in 1977. The next largest producer is Paccar (25 percent), followed by Volvo (20 percent), and then Navistar (16 percent). Plumb in the middle of a low-growth, mature, very competitive industry, Paccar nevertheless turns in a solid performance. Its return on equity over the past twenty years has averaged 16 percent, compared with an average return of 12 percent earned by its competitors. Even more important, Paccar's profits have been remarkably stable in an industry plagued by strong upswings and downswings in demand. Paccar has not lost money since 1939, and its profit roll continues despite the recession of 2008–9.

The driving element in Paccar's strategy is quality, with its Kenworth and Peterbilt brands widely recognized as the highest-quality trucks made in North America. Paccar has received J. D. Power awards for its heavy trucks and for its service. The company prices accordingly, maintaining its strong market position despite premium prices.

How can you sell a truck at a premium price? In theory it is simple—your trucks have to run better and last longer so that the owner's cost to operate the truck is lower. Fleet operators look at differences of a fraction of a cent per mile in making purchase decisions, and the swing in costs is mostly fuel and wages. For example, if you buy a 2008 Kenworth T2000 sleeper for $110,000, and drive it 125,000 miles that year, you will probably pay *another* $115,000 each year in operating expenses for fuel, maintenance, repair, and insurance. And that is before wages and benefits. Because of this, Kenworth pioneered low-drag aerodynamic truck cabs thirty years ago as a way to cut fuel costs.

It is not easy to hold this kind of quality leadership for three big reasons. First, no one will believe you have the longest-lasting trucks until they have already lasted a long time on the road. It's a reputation that takes a while to earn and can be lost quickly. Second, designing a very high-quality piece of machinery is not a textbook problem. Designers learn from other designers over time, and the company accumulates these nuggets of wisdom by providing a good, stable place to work for talented engineers. Third, it is usually quite difficult to convince buyers to pay an up-front premium for future savings, even if the numbers are clear. People tend to be more myopic than economic theory would suggest.

Paccar's strategy—its design—is its way of dealing with these three obstacles to being a quality leader. The first element of its strategy is a subtle shift away from seeing quality purely in terms of operating cost. Instead, Paccar views quality through the eyes of the owner-driver. Owner-drivers increase their wages by pushing themselves harder, driving sixteen hours a day or more. Owner-drivers care about efficiency but also look beyond cost per mile, because the truck is their home, office, lounge, and TV room on the road. In addition, drivers prize the special sense of classic American style—a Harley-Davidson-type aura—that attaches to Paccar's brands, even as the interiors now have more of a Lexus look and feel. Owner-drivers buy Kenworth and Peterbilt trucks from experienced dealers who use 3-D computer displays to select from hundreds of customizing options. Paccar builds each truck to order, keeping inventories low and using a network of suppliers for its main components and parts. The trucks are designed with as many parts in common as practicable.

Truck fleet operators don't care about aura very much; they do care about turnover and idle time among their drivers. Fleet managers find that by using two drivers, idle time is cut in half or more. That means one of the drivers is sleeping or resting in the sleeper compartment a good part of the time, raising the same concerns about comfort the owner-driver has. Plus, when truck drivers meet at a stop, the owner-drivers have the highest status and their opinions have the most weight. The beauty of Paccar's positioning is that although fleet buyers pay more attention to cash cost per mile than owner-drivers do, many are pushed in some of the same directions by their drivers' preferences. Whatever the fleet owner's opinion, many of their drivers prefer Paccar trucks.

Paccar's strategy is based on doing something well and consistently over a long period of time. That has created difficult-to-replicate resources: its image, its network of experienced dealers, its loyal customers, and the knowledge embedded in its staff of designers and engineers. This position and these kinds of slow-build resources are simply not available to companies, mesmerized by the stock market, who want big results in twelve months.

A flexible approach to manufacturing makes Paccar's variable costs higher than competitors' but provides stability for its designers and engineers. In addition, its higher margins create a loyal, more dedicated network of dealers. All of this works, in part, because it is *not* in a high-growth industry that would attract large new investments from outside. To attack it directly, a rival would have to create new brands and new designs, and, quite possibly, sign up new dealers. The high-end market isn't big enough to warrant that kind of investment.

Paccar's design is expressed in actions that are consistent with its positioning and that are consistent over time. It does not make small trucks, only large ones. Within the large-truck segment, it does not make cheaper economy trucks. The product-buyer focus is maintained by its dealers, designers, and engineers. Because it is not diversified, the talk and knowledge in the design studio, in manufacturing, and in the executive suite are about truckers and heavy trucks. They don't need to hire a consulting firm to figure out their core competence or to find out who their buyers are.

The various elements of Paccar's strategy are not general purpose—they are designed to fit together to make a specialized whole. The design is clearest if you imagine a truck manufacturer assembled out of generic bits of various truck companies, a sort of Frankenstein's monster truck company. With medium-priced truck designs aimed at fleet buyers, dealers aimed at picky owner-drivers, and design engineers trained to cut costs to the bone, it would not last long. Good strategy is design, and design is about fitting various pieces together so they work as a coherent whole.

There is nothing magical about Paccar's strategy. It is classic "hold the high ground" positioning. This defensive structure can probably be maintained as long as there are no significant structural changes in the industry's economics or buyer behavior. Day-to-day competition in the industry is always important, and Paccar must introduce new features and models, strive to improve its quality and reduce its costs, and maintain its flexibility. But good strategy looks past these issues to what is fundamental. From that perspective, the threats to the company are not specific new products or competitive moves, but changes that undermine the logic of its design. If, for example, the NAFTA treaty encourages more and more shippers to use Mexican trucks rather than U.S. owner-drivers, Paccar's position is at risk. Similarly, the new sophisticated computer selling introduced into dealerships may be necessary, but there is a concern that it undermines the importance of the dealer's knowledge and expertise.

CHAPTER TEN

FOCUS

It is a bright April morning and my upcoming session is for executive MBAs. Some are already there, Web browsing, reading newspapers, or studying. Today's case is on Crown Cork & Seal, a maker of metal containers.[1] It is one of the oldest cases in the strategy collection. Updated many times, the case today takes the company through 1989.

My objectives are not to show my class how to manage a can company, or even how to create a good strategy. Instead, they are (1) to teach them how to *identify* a company's strategy, (2) to deepen their skills at analyzing qualitative information, and (3) to explore a particular mixture of policy and positioning called *focus*.

Crown's strategy had been crafted in the early 1960s by John F. Connelly, whose tight-fisted direction of Crown had become virtually a folktale in American business. It had been, for example, a favorite of legendary stock picker Peter Lynch, manager of Fidelity's Magellan Fund. Over thirty-five years, the company had achieved a phenomenal record, providing an average return to shareholders of 19 percent per year—an especially impressive performance given the intense competition in its industry.

What was Crown's secret? The case repeats the conventional wisdom that Crown specialized in containers for hard-to-hold products such as aerosols and carbonated soft drinks. While true, of course, this description is neither complete nor terribly useful in understanding how Crown competed. Nevertheless, most analysts stop there, gladly accepting this description of Crown's strategy. They will not have noticed that the details of Crown's policies point in other directions as well. In general, people will not push further because the analysis of unstructured information is hard, time-consuming work that requires both a rich knowledge of facts and well-developed skills in logic, deduction, and induction. Today my opening is the predictable gap between the analysis done by the participants and what can be done with a more disciplined effort.

I start by saying, "Our job today is strategy identification. To begin identifying a company's strategy, it is usually most helpful to examine the competitive environment. That is, to look at how the major competitors make their livings. Let's begin with the three major can companies: Continental Can, National Can, and American Can. The case says that 'most beverage companies had at least two sources of can supply. Further, can manufacturers often set up plants to supply a particular customer.'"[2]

To illustrate that a beverage company might have two dedicated suppliers, I sketch a diagram on the whiteboard. It has a box in the center labeled "Miller Brewing" and two can suppliers, represented by circles on either side of the box.

Pointing to the diagram, I say, "It doesn't take a PhD in industrial economics to see that this is a terrible industry structure. There is very direct competition between close-by can makers, whose products have to be essentially indistinguishable. Plus, there is the constant threat that the buyer may simply purchase a can line and do the job itself. Why in the world would a company invest in such a difficult setting?"

After some discussion, the class concludes that the big can makers have accepted being captive producers because of the benefits of long production runs—there is a large cost to changing a line from making one type of can to another. At the same time, they notice that the major can companies have very low profit rates—4 to 5 percent return on assets.

I say, "This is a difficult industry with low returns for the major players. But Crown Cork & Seal"—I make a show of looking in the case for its performance numbers—"beats the big three by a substantial margin. On average, it seems to be fifty to sixty percent more profitable. It's doing something right—something we call a *strategy*.

"What is Crown Cork & Seal's strategy?"

Todd, a real estate developer, asserts that "Crown is a low-cost producer." He goes on to argue, "You can't differentiate a can, so the reason it makes more money *must be* that its costs are lower. It keeps its costs down by running its plants 24/7 and keeping close to the customer."

He is dead wrong, for Crown's unit cost per can is almost certainly higher, not lower, than its competitors' cost per can. I say nothing, writing "low-cost producer" on the whiteboard.

Martin, an executive in the entertainment industry, says, "Crown specialized in hard-to-hold applications—aerosols and soft drinks. It had great customer service. There was lots of technical assistance for customers and great responsiveness, with an emphasis on speed. In the case, Connelly, the CEO, is willing to jump on a plane to help sort out one customer's problem."

"Excellent, Martin. That is indeed what the case says. There is actually a section, entitled 'Connelly's Strategy,' where it says that the company focused on containers for hard-to-hold applications—soft drinks and aerosols. It also says that it emphasized customer service and technical assistance.

"So, I guess we are done." I go to the podium and gather up my notes, then pause and look around. "Unless anyone has a problem with the official explanation."

Melissa, in the front row, is slowly shaking her head. I rarely hear from her, so I don't press for a hand, but simply ask, "Melissa?"

"Well," she starts, glancing at Martin, "I don't really see that putting soda in a can is all that much of a big technical feat. Crown isn't the only company that can do this. Why would that be a high-profit business?"

I nod in the affirmative and put my papers back on the podium. With a little prodding, Melissa has made a key step. She has questioned Martin's and the conventional view. She has noticed that a can for a hard-to-hold application isn't necessarily hard to make.

I say, "Suppose *Fortune* magazine, Harvard Business School case writers, and stock analysts all say Crown's strategy is a focus on hard-to-hold applications—carbonated beverages and aerosols. But also suppose that we are very stubborn. We want to do our own analysis. If you are serious about strategy work, you must always do your own analysis. A strategy is not necessarily what the CEO intended or what some executive says it is. Sometimes they are hiding the truth, sometimes they are misstating it, and sometimes they have taken a position as leader without really knowing the reasons for their company's success.

"If we are not going to automatically accept the opinions of others, how can we independently identify a company's strategy? We do this by looking at each policy of the company and noticing those that are different from the norm in the industry. We then try to figure out the common target of such distinctive policies—what they are coordinated on accomplishing." I go to the whiteboard and write "policy" over the two policies Martin called out—*technical assistance* and *rapid response*. Then I place a new column to the right labeled "Target."

Policy	Target
Technical assistance Rapid response	

Everyone will have noted that Crown emphasized technical assistance and rapid response, but, like Martin, will have thought of these policies only as some sort of "good things" that the company does. But they will not have noticed that not all customers need or benefit from such policies. Now comes the real work of figuring out its focus.

"Let's start with technical assistance," I say. "Melissa pointed out that putting soda in a can is not atomic science. What kind of customer needs technical help to get their product into a can?" My question only evokes blank looks. I have lectured on how to tackle seemingly formless questions like this. The first trick is to replace general nouns with specific examples. I wait a moment, and then I do it for them, a concrete example of replacing the abstract with the concrete. "What about Coors, does it need technical assistance from can companies?" The trick works—hands are up.

Reza is an aerospace engineer whose contributions are usually sound. He says, "The major beer companies can probably teach the can companies a thing or two. It was Coors that actually figured out how to make two-piece aluminum cans by a double-draw process. It's smaller companies that need technical assistance—companies without big technical staffs and without internal canning experience of their own."

"OK," I reply, and write "Smaller businesses" across from "Technical assistance," under the "Target" column. "And what about the rapid response policy, is that also focused on smaller companies?"

"Sure," says Reza. "Small companies may have less stable demand and may plan less well."

Reza's second response is quick but not careful. When faced with a question or problem to which there is no obvious answer, it is human nature to welcome the first seemingly reasonable answer that pops into mind, as if it were a life preserver in a choppy sea. The discipline of analysis is to not stop there, but to test that first insight against the evidence. Reza's explanation that rapid response favors small firms agrees with some of the facts on the table, but not all. I don't write anything down on the whiteboard.

There is an uncomfortable pause. Then, a student says, "Maybe the target is seasonal producers." I move slightly toward the board. Another says, "New products?" I am at the board with marker poised. I ask, "A hotter than normal summer, a new product—these mean . . . ?" Two or three students say "Rush orders" together. I write "Rush orders" across from "Rapid response" and under "Target."

"All right," I say. "We are making progress. The technical assistance policy seems to have small companies as a target and the rapid response policy seems to target rush orders. These two targets are not quite the same thing. Let's take a look at another policy." I add "Manufacturing" to the left-side column of policies.

The information about manufacturing policy is scattered throughout the case. It takes a while to surface the basics: Crown's plants are smaller than those of its rivals; none of Crown's plants are captive—each has at least two customers; Crown had excess lines set up and waiting for orders.

David, a private equity analyst, has been working a spreadsheet and helps clarify the implications. "Compared with the majors," he says, "Crown's plants are smaller but have more customers. So Crown's production of cans per customer must be a lot lower than the majors'. Also, since revenues per plant are higher, Crown's price per can must be considerably higher than the majors' average prices—maybe forty to fifty percent higher."

On the whiteboard I write "Speed" and "Less production per customer" as the targets of the cluster of manufacturing policies.

Now it is time to pull things together. I point to the list of policy targets on the whiteboard and ask, "Given *all* this, what is Crown Cork & Seal's focus?" The class has all the pieces, but I want them to tie these pieces to the fundamental economics of the industry. It is not easy to see this pattern, and I don't expect anyone to put it together on the spot. So I continue to speak, giving some leading hints. "What ties all of these observations together? *Smaller customers . . . rush orders . . . speed . . . less production per customer . . . higher prices*?"

I wait for perhaps twenty seconds, an eternity of silence in a classroom. Then I ask, "What is it that drove the majors to accept becoming captive producers?" This last clue is enough.

"Crown does short runs," exclaims Julia, an entrepreneur. "The majors accept long runs of standard items to avoid costly changeovers. Crown does the opposite and has a focus on shorter runs."

I say, "Great," as I draw a big circle around all of the elements on the target list—small customers, rush orders, and less shipments per customer—and label the circle "Shorter runs," and sign the label "Julia," recognizing her inductive insight.

The phrase "Shorter runs" ties the company's focus to the essential

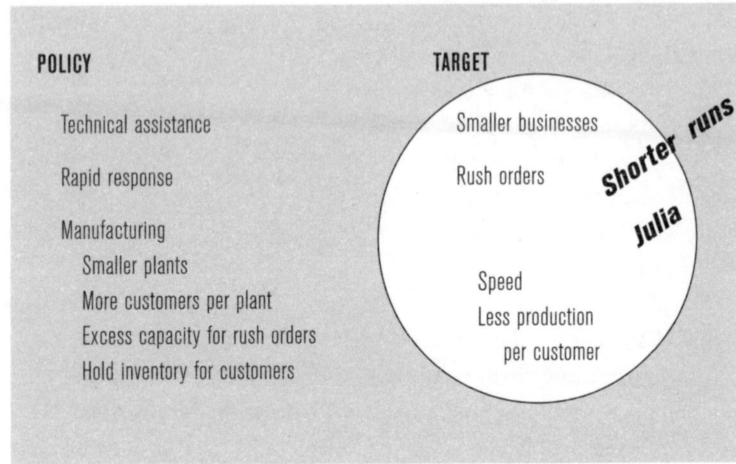

problem faced by producers in the industry—the very high costs of switching a can line from making one product to another, or even printing one label and then setting up to print another. "So we are finding that while Crown specialized in soft drink and aerosol cans, it also has a complex focus around *shorter runs*. The runs may be shorter because the customer is smaller, because the product is newer, because it is a low-volume high-value product, or because it is a rush order to cover seasonal or other unexpected demand, and so on."

After testing this idea against other company policies, I return to the issue of cost. Everyone can now see that shorter runs mean more changeovers. That, and Crown's policies of excess capacity, lots of technical assistance, and rapid response all drive costs up, not down. So we have a company focused on shorter runs with higher costs per can balanced by higher prices.

I say, "It would be nice if focus always meant more profit. But it just isn't so. It's time to figure out how all of this allows Crown to earn higher margins."

I go to the whiteboard and draw a circle, representing Crown Cork & Seal, with a ring of squares around it, each representing a customer. The contrast with the nearby picture of "Miller Brewing" with its two suppliers is sharp.

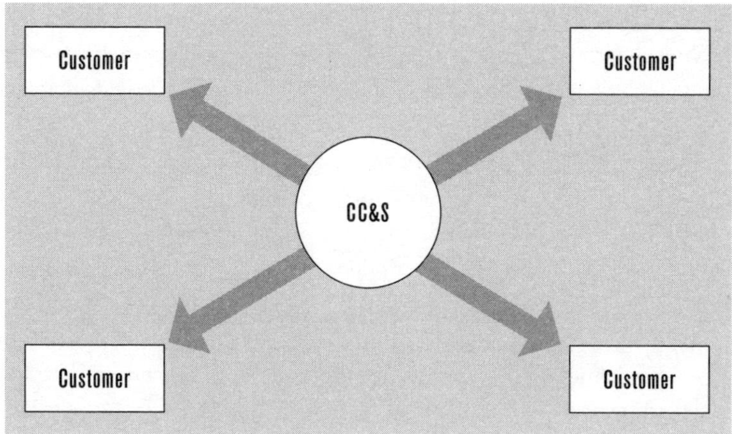

"We know that none of Crown's plants are captive. Who is in the better position? American Can selling to Miller Brewing or Crown selling a special order to a local soft drink bottler?"

Cheryl, a financial analyst for Sony, gets it right away: "Crown. By focusing on short runs, Crown avoids the captive squeeze. Instead of one customer with several competing suppliers, Crown is a supplier with several customers per plant. Going for long runs made the majors captive. Short runs turn the situation around. *Crown hasn't given up its bargaining power like the captives have.*"

Using the diagrams for emphasis, I summarize what we have discovered. Crown and the majors are in the same industry but are playing by different rules. By concentrating on a carefully selected part of the market, Crown has not only specialized, it has increased its bargaining power with respect to its buyers. Thus, it captures a larger fraction of the value it creates. The majors, by contrast, have larger volumes of business but capture much lower fractions of the value they create. Thus, Crown crafted a competitive advantage in its target market. It isn't the biggest can maker, but it makes the most money.

This particular pattern—attacking a segment of the market with a business system supplying more value to that segment than the other players can—is called focus. Here, the word "focus" has two meanings. First, it denotes the coordination of policies that produces extra power through their interacting and overlapping effects. Second, it denotes the application of that power to the right target.*

As the students discover Crown Cork & Seal's focus strategy, there is a sense of surprise. The inner logic is visible after our analysis, although it was not beforehand. The logic of this strategy was not visible in the company's own self-description, nor in the pronouncements of Wall Street analysts. It wasn't a secret; it was just that it is hard work to fit the pieces together. Virtually drowning in a twenty-four-hour barrage of superficial news and commentary, the students are surprised that the real world can sometimes have an inner logic that is not secret but that nevertheless remains unremarked.

"Is it always this way?" a student asks me. "If you do the work, can you find the real strategic logic of every business?"

"No," I reply, "not of every business. If the business is really successful, then there is usually a good strategic logic behind that success, be it hidden or not. But the truth is that many companies, especially large complex companies, don't really have strategies. At the core, strategy is about focus, and most complex organizations don't focus their resources. Instead, they pursue multiple goals at once, not concentrating enough resources to achieve a breakthrough in any of them."

* This meaning of "focus" was introduced by Michael Porter in his book *Competitive Strategy*.

CHAPTER ELEVEN

GROWTH

In 1989, John Connelly, in poor health, stepped down from active management at Crown Cork & Seal, appointing his longtime protégé, William Avery, as CEO. One year later, Connelly died at age eighty-five.

Upon taking over the leadership of Crown, Avery immediately began a program of growth through acquisition. Interviewed four years later, he recalled, "When I became president in 1989, I had to light a fire and get the company going again. The company's growth had slowed down in the 1980s."[1] The fire Avery lit was fueled by people with expertise in deals and acquisitions. The new team he assembled was led by acquisition specialist Alan Rutherford, who moved from the Brussels office to become Crown's chief financial officer. In addition, Craig Calle moved from investment bank Salomon Brothers to become Crown's treasurer, and Torsten Kreider left investment bank Lehman Brothers to run planning and analysis.

During 1990 and 1991, Avery doubled Crown's size with the acquisition of Continental Can's domestic and foreign businesses. In 1992 and 1993, Crown spent $615 million to buy Constar, a leading maker of plastic containers for the soft drink and bottled water industries, and another $180 million on Van Dorn, a maker of plastic, metal, and composite containers. It paid $62 million for Tri-Valley Growers, a traditional maker of metal food cans.

In 1995, Crown began an eighteen-month effort to acquire Carnaud-

MetalBox S.A., the largest maker of plastic and metal containers in Europe. CarnaudMetalBox was the outcome of a difficult merger between two-hundred-year-old Metal Box of the United Kingdom and Carnaud of France. It was a leading can maker in both countries, with much of its production being traditional metal food cans.

Commenting on the purpose of the combination, Avery said, "We want to grow bigger and get a better use of our resources. As the global leader in the metal and plastic segments of the packaging industry . . . we will have a worldwide foundation for continued international growth."[2] Few executives have been so clear in stating that they want to grow in order to have a platform for further growth.

By 1997, Avery's team had completed twenty acquisitions and Crown had become the largest container manufacturer in the world. Avery had predicted that its size would allow it to get better prices from suppliers and that Crown's traditional skill at cost control would let it trim excess overhead and capacity from French-run CarnaudMetalBox. No one mentioned the awkward fact that Crown's traditional competence had been flexibility and short runs, not cost control.

In 1998, troubles appeared. Crown's foray into plastic containers had paralleled the rapid growth in this business. The new blow-molded polyethylene terephthalate (PET) containers were taking significant business away from traditional glass and metal containers in soft drinks and certain foods categories (for example, ketchup and salad dressing). But this growth was not powered by a basic increase in the demand for containers. Rather, it came from replacing metal and glass with plastic. Growth based upon substitution has a clear ceiling and, once the conversion to the substitute has taken place, the growth grinds to a sudden halt. This happened to Crown's PET business just as Crown became the world's largest producer. And not only were conversions from metal to plastic pretty much complete, but unit sales of PET containers actually started to shrink as large two-quart plastic soda bottles replaced several single-drink containers.

To add insult to injury, whereas management and analysts had hoped for firmer prices from the more consolidated industry of metal cans, prices began to fall instead of rise, cutting profits dramatically. Several factors were to blame. No competitor seemed willing to close European plants, each facing labor problems if a plant closed and each wanting to increase its market share. In addition, competition from cheaper PET containers was spilling over to virtually eliminate the already razor-thin margins in traditional metal cans. All of this—the slowdown of growth, the industry overcapacity, and the spillover of price competition from plastic back to metal cans—is basic industry analysis and could have been easily predicted by the use of the popular Five Forces framework developed by Michael Porter.[3]

Between 1998 and 2001, Crown's stock price dropped catastrophically, falling from $55 to $5 (see the chart below). In mid-2001, Avery retired, replaced by John Conway, a longtime Crown employee with training in economics and law. The era of rapid expansion by acquisition was over, and it was up to Conway to find some way to make the now gigantic Crown profitable again. Whereas Avery's mantra had been grow, Conway stressed cost, quality, and technology. From 2001 through the end of 2006, sales and profits were essentially flat, about $1 billion in

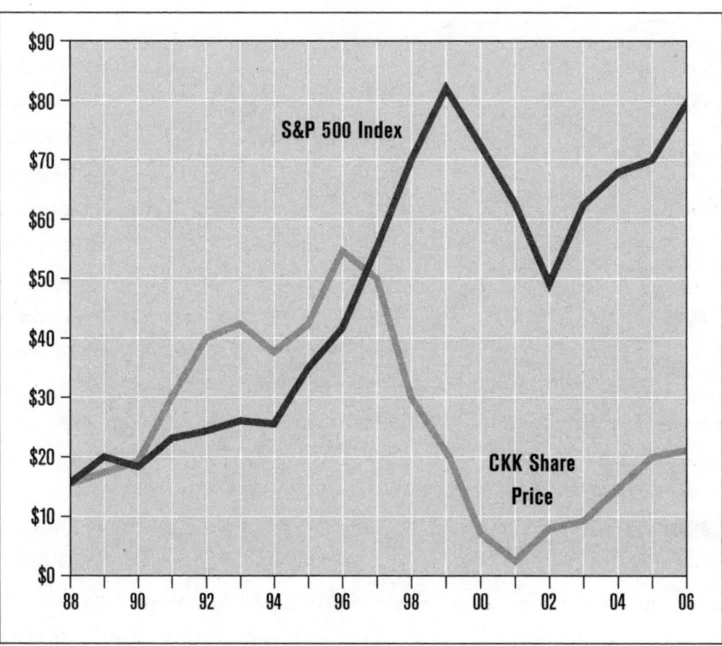

debt was repaid, and the value of a share of common stock climbed gradually from $5 to $20, about $5 higher than it had been seventeen years earlier when the program of expansion began.

As quoted earlier, when Avery took over at Crown he complained that "the company's growth had slowed down." It had. During the ten years (1980–89) before Avery become CEO at Crown, revenues grew at only 3.1 percent per year. However, it had nevertheless generated an annual average return to shareholders of 18.5 percent, enormously more than the 8.6 percent achieved by the S&P 500 during the same period. During the seventeen years after Connelly stepped down, from 1990 to 2006, the company grew rapidly, becoming the "leading" container maker in the world. But an owner of Crown's common stock received a return of only 2.4 percent per year, much lower than the 9 percent provided by the S&P 500 Index. The chart below shows how Crown's rapid run-up in sales revenue was accompanied by a dramatic fall in return on capital—the ratio of profit to investments.[4] That ratio was a respect-

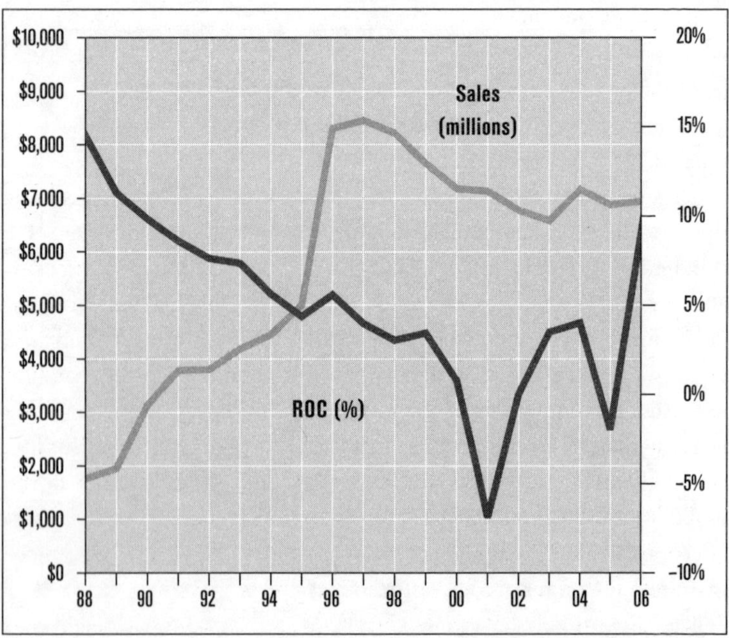

able 15.3 percent when Avery took over, but it fell almost immediately to below 10 percent, then to below 5 percent after the acquisition of CarnaudMetalBox.

Crown's long record of superior performance under Connelly's leadership had rested upon its carefully designed strategy that, through a coordinated set of policies, focused the company on products and buyers where the customer's bargaining power was lessened. When Avery took over leadership of Crown, he found that the new PET bottles were making big inroads into the market for soft drink containers. Product changeover costs in plastics were much lower than in metal containers, so the basis of Crown's traditional advantage was eroding. What to do?

Avery chose to grow the corporation by acquisition with an emphasis on the PET business, attracted by the growth in that industry. The problem was that he left the company's traditional competitive advantage behind without replacing it. Asked about a loss of focus, CFO Calle showed no concern, interpreting focus as merely a restriction on the product line: "It's currently fashionable to focus, but we've always been there. We operate in a $300 billion industry and serve only the metal and plastic portion, which amounts to $150–200 billion."[5] He did not choose to understand the deeper meaning of focus—a concentration and coordination of action and resources that creates an advantage. Instead, he and CEO Avery were mesmerized by the prospects of expansion.

The problem with diving into the growing PET industry was that growth in a commodity—such as cement or aluminum or PET containers—is an industry phenomenon, driven by an increase in overall demand. The growing demand pulls up profit, which, in turn, induces firms to invest in new capacity. But most of the profits of the growing competitors are an illusion because they are plowed back into new plant and equipment as the business grows. If high profits on these investments can be earned after growth slows, then all is well. But in a commodity industry, as soon as the growth in demand slows down, the profits vanish for firms without competitive advantages. Like some sort of economic black hole, the growing commodity industry absorbs more cash from the ordinary competitor than it ever disgorges.

The proposition that growth itself creates value is so deeply entrenched in the rhetoric of business that it has become an article of almost unquestioned faith that growth is a good thing. CEO Avery's description of his problem ("The company's growth had slowed down in the 1980s") and his goals ("We want to grow bigger . . . a worldwide foundation for continued international growth") are little more than the repetition of the word "growth"—magical invocations of the name of the object of desire.

■ ■ ■

The problem with engineering growth by acquisition is that when you buy a company, especially a public company, you usually pay too much. You pay a premium over its ordinary market value—usually about 25 percent—plus fees. If you have friendly investment bankers and lenders, you can grow as fast as you like by acquisition. But unless you can buy companies for less than they are worth, or unless you are specially positioned to add more value to the target than anyone else can, no value is created by such expansion.

Corporate leaders seek growth for many reasons. They may (erroneously) believe that administrative costs will fall with size. A poor, but common, reason for acquisitions is to move key executives to the periphery rather than let them go. The leaders of larger firms tend to be paid more. And, in a decentralized company, making acquisitions is a lot more fun than reading reports on divisional performance. In addition to all these reasons, key corporate advisers—investment bankers, consultants, mergers and acquisitions law firms, and anyone who can claim a "finder's fee"—can earn a king's ransom by being "helpful" in a major deal.

In 1998, I was retained by Telecom Italia as a special consultant on strategy. Telecom Italia was then the fifth largest fixed-line telecommunications operator and Europe's largest and most innovative mobile operator. It had been privatized in a series of steps beginning in 1994 and ending in the sale of public shares in 1997.

At that moment the strategic problems facing traditional fixed-line European operators were considerable. Many still earned the juicy gross margins typical of monopoly national carriers, but the future held the possibility of dramatically increased competition and technological change. Deregulation was allowing foreign entry into national markets, and the Internet was blossoming. Companies such as Telecom Italia had large cash flows based on past investments, and a critical issue was where to invest those cash flows. More fixed lines seemed unwise. Optical fiber rings around cities looked promising, but three foreign firms already had plans for regional centers like Milan. Competing against them would simply cannibalize existing business revenue. The Internet was growing rapidly, but income was small—its growth was based on very low prices, much lower than those charged for voice or traditional data traffic.

The chairman and CEO, Gianmario Rossignolo, had been talking about an alliance with Cable & Wireless, a company begun in the nineteenth century as a provider of undersea telegraph links across the British Empire. Nationalized in 1947, it had been reprivatized in 1981 by Margaret Thatcher. Cable & Wireless CEO Richard Brown was an American, brought in to break an internal political logjam that had kept the company operating like a set of independent fiefdoms. Brown had been seeking a major alliance, first flirting with British Telecom, then AT&T, then Sprint. The (fluffy) argument was that telecommunications was globalizing and that there would be value in a global brand.

Brown and Rossignolo had begun their alliance discussions with talk of a series of cross holdings in France, the Caribbean, and other locations. By late summer, their informal proposal had escalated into what would effectively be a merger of the two companies, with Richard Brown emerging as chairman.

Rossignolo had been slotted into his position as Telecom Italia's chief by the influential Agnelli family, which led the small group of "core" shareholders. By early October 1998, however, some board members, including Agnelli agents, had become disenchanted with him. They were particularly concerned about the proposed merger with Cable & Wireless. In this context, I was asked to meet with Joseph Silver (not his real name), a managing director of Morgan Stanley Dean Witter, which was the lead investment banker involved in the deal. A board member told me, "Wall Street has the global view of the industry." My assignment was to find out Morgan Stanley's rationale for the merger.

Joseph Silver and I met in a plain conference room in Milan. I started the discussion with a straightforward question. In his view, what was the rationale for the proposed deal?

"Economies of scale," he replied.

"But these companies operate in totally different regions," I responded. "Where are the economies of scale in combining a Caribbean operator with one in Italy, or Brazil?"

"Telecom Italia," he replied, "needs to move traffic from South America to Europe. Cable & Wireless has cables that can handle that traffic."

This response surprised me. It was a flunking response to a standard question in an MBA course midterm exam. You don't need to own a cattle ranch to get fertilizer for your rose garden and you don't need a $50 billion merger to move communications traffic. A contract will suffice.

"It seems to me," I said, "that we could simply write a contract, right now as we sit here, to move some Telecom Italia traffic on certain Cable & Wireless cables. We don't need a major merger to do it."

"Well, professor," he said, "the issue is larger than traffic. The fundamental rationale for the merger is really . . . economies of mass."

"I am not familiar with that term."

"What I mean by 'economies of mass' is that the two companies will, together, be larger. The combined company will have much greater cash flow."

Again, I was surprised at his argument. Combining any two companies sums their cash flows—that's arithmetic. It is not an argument for why a specific deal is worth the price.

"Telecom Italia," I said, "already has substantial cash flow. In fact, the major reason its stock price is not higher is because analysts and investors doubt that the company has good uses for all that cash. For example, Telecom Italia just overbid for an important license in South America. There was over $1 billion between its offer and the next highest bid. Cable & Wireless is in about the same position, generating more cash than it can wisely invest. I just don't see any 'economies of mass' in combining these cash flows."

Joseph Silver closed his slim briefcase. He was clearly uninterested in further discussion. He looked at me as if I were a child, someone who just didn't understand the big leagues. He said, "With more cash flow you can do a bigger deal." Then he left the room.

Pressed to explain why the deal made sense, Silver could only suggest that it was a gateway to an even bigger deal. Morgan Stanley, of course, stood ready to collect a healthy fee, skimmed from the billions that would flow in this deal and any larger deals to follow. Two days after our meeting, the board rejected the proposed merger and, in a stormy session, accepted Gianmario Rossignolo's resignation.

■ ■ ■

Healthy growth is not engineered. It is the outcome of growing demand for special capabilities or of expanded or extended capabilities. It is the outcome of a firm having superior products and skills. It is the reward for successful innovation, cleverness, efficiency, and creativity. This kind of growth is not just an industry phenomenon. It normally shows up as a gain in market share that is simultaneous with a superior rate of profit.

CHAPTER TWELVE

USING ADVANTAGE

Two equally skillful chess players sit waiting for the game to begin—which one has the advantage? Two identical armies meet on a featureless plain—which one has the advantage? The answers to these questions is "neither," because advantage is rooted in differences—in the asymmetries among rivals. In real rivalry, there are an uncountable number of asymmetries. It is the leader's job to identify which asymmetries are critical—which can be turned into important advantages.

WRESTLING THE GORILLA

In 2000 I was working with a start-up company that had developed a new microporous material where the size of the pores adjusted with temperature. The hope was that clothing incorporating this material would shed rain, like Gore-Tex, but would also be warmer in really cold conditions and cooler when it became hot. As a start-up, this had been the company's only activity and the team was justly proud of their accomplishment. They were excited about the possibility of taking their patented idea and developing a line of textiles and outdoor wear. They had already picked a brand name and were negotiating with designers.

At the venture-capital firm that had backed the start-up, Susan had been their strongest supporter and she knew the most about both the team and its technology. However, when the start-up team met with Susan to work out third-round financing, or even an initial public offering of stock, she was not enthusiastic. "I think it would be smarter," she said, "to take our samples and work out license arrangements. Or even to sell the company outright to a major textile manufacturer."

The start-up team fought back. The CEO led the charge, arguing, "We have shown what we can do. This is a real opportunity to build a great company."

"You have done a fantastic job," Susan replied. "You have created a wonderful new technology. No one can deny your skills at development—they are world class. But building a textile company, or a clothing company, is a completely different game."

The air in the room was taut with frustration. Susan might be right, but they wanted to move forward. Hadn't they proved themselves?

"Look," Susan said, "it's like this. You have won an Olympic gold medal in the 1,500-meter run. You have a good chance at winning the 10,000-meter run and I might back you at that. But you want to switch from running to wrestling gorillas. That's not a good idea and I can't back you at it."

Susan's powerful image helped sway the team. They wanted to move ahead, but they certainly didn't want to wrestle the gorilla.

■ ■ ■

No one has an advantage at everything. Teams, organizations, and even nations have advantages in certain kinds of rivalry under particular conditions. The secret to using advantage is understanding this particularity. You must press where you have advantages and side-step situations in which you do not. You must exploit your rivals' weaknesses and avoid leading with your own.

After 9/11 the United States formulated an objective of destroying the Afghanistan-based al Qaeda leadership and the Taliban government that had protected them. In military conflict, the United States has enormous resources and skills that enable it to quickly deliver stupendous amounts of force. The United States had a clear strength and used it to kill al Qaeda operatives and drive the Taliban from power. Top-level leaders failed, however, to press this advantage and allowed Osama bin Laden to escape from his mountain hideout in Tora Bora into northwest Pakistan.[1]

Nine years after 9/11, Osama bin Laden remains uncaught and the United States is involved in a continuing low-intensity war in Afghanistan against the Taliban. The present strategy of the United States in Afghanistan is based on turning the populace against the Taliban and toward the central government. This approach had traction in Iraq where the populace was accustomed to a strong central government. By contrast, Afghanistan is a medieval warlord-based society where loyalty and power is local. After years of U.S. support, the Afghan central government remains corrupt and ineffective outside of Kabul. Thus, the Taliban's terror tactics against the population are brutally effective because any protection against the Taliban can only be temporary and geographically limited. Even more seriously, the Taliban is not an army, it has no uniform, and everyone in Afghanistan is both armed and probably related to someone in the Taliban.

All of these obstacles can be overcome with time and resources. But both ordinary citizens and the Taliban know that the United States will withdraw. It will withdraw for political reasons and because staying in Afghanistan is stupendously expensive. The U.S. military, carefully designed to inflict crushing high-intensity force, spends $1 million per year to put each soldier in Afghanistan. You don't want to have been a tool of the United States when these forces are drawn down and the Taliban return to power.

In Afghanistan, the United States is "wrestling the gorilla" because it has allowed itself to be drawn into a conflict in support of an almost nonexistent ally and where advantage lies with the side with the most patience and with the least sensitivity to casualties and collateral damage. In this situation, the Taliban has the advantage and is using it.

COMPETITIVE ADVANTAGE IN BUSINESS

The term "competitive advantage" became a term of art in business strategy with Michael Porter's 1984 insightful book of that title. Indeed, Warren Buffett has said that he evaluates a company by looking for "sustainable competitive advantage."

The basic definition of competitive advantage is straightforward. If your business can produce at a lower cost than can competitors, or if it can deliver more perceived value than can competitors, or a mix of the two, then you have a competitive advantage. Subtlety arrives when you realize that costs vary with product and application and that buyers differ in their locations, knowledge, tastes, and other characteristics. Thus, most advantages will extend only so far. For instance, Whole Foods has an advantage over Albertsons supermarkets only for certain products and only among grocery shoppers with good incomes who place a high value on organic and natural foods.

Defining "sustainability" is trickier. For an advantage to be sustained, your competitors must not be able to duplicate it. Or, more precisely, they must not be able to duplicate the resources underlying it. For that you must possess what I term an "isolating mechanism," such as a patent giving its holder the legally enforceable right to monopolize the use of a technology for a time.[2] More complex forms of isolating mechanisms include reputations, commercial and social relationships, network effects,* dramatic economies of scale, and tacit knowledge and skill gained through experience.

As an example, Apple's iPhone business is protected by the Apple and iPhone brand names, by the company's reputation, by the complementary iTunes service, and by the network effects of its customer group, especially with respect to iPhone applications. Each of these resources has been crafted by Apple executives and put in place as part

* A "network effect" increases the value of a product as the number of buyers or users gets larger. It is like an economy of scale, but instead of reducing the producer's cost, it increases the buyer's willingness to pay. We see very strong network effects in businesses like Amazon and Facebook.

of a program for building a sustained competitive advantage. These resources are scarce in that competitors find it difficult, if not impossible, to create comparable resources at a reasonable cost.

Claims in advertising or sales pitches that a particular IT system or product or training program will provide a competitive advantage are misusing the term since an "advantage" on sale to all comers is a contradiction in terms.

"INTERESTING" ADVANTAGES

Stewart Resnick, the chairman of privately held Roll International Corporation, and his wife, Lynda, are serial entrepreneurs. Not only have they established several very successful companies, they have also used their wealth to support medical research, education, and the arts. Being able to create successful strategies, not just once but over and over again, is a rare skill. And it is clear that their skills are not rooted in any one industry—they have been able to succeed in alarm services, flower delivery, collectibles, agribusiness, and bottled water.

As I drive to Roll's headquarters in West Los Angeles, I review what I know about the Resnicks. Stewart's father had owned a bar in New Jersey, and Stewart's first business was a janitorial service based on a friend's floor scrubber. The business grew, paying his way through law school at UCLA. He sold it in 1969 for about $2.5 million and invested in an alarm services firm. Lynda's first business was an advertising agency, and when Stewart sold the alarm services firm, they worked together to acquire Teleflora in 1979.

For Teleflora, Stewart and Lynda created the concept of flowers arranged in keepsake containers, an approach that dramatically increased profits for them and their florists. In 1985, they bought the Franklin Mint, a producer of collectors' coins. Lynda spearheaded the expansion into pop-culture keepsakes, precision model cars, and a host of other items. (The Resnicks sold the Franklin Mint in 2006.)

During the 1980s, the Resnicks began to invest in agribusiness: citrus orchards, pistachio and almond orchards, and pomegranates. Over time, these businesses have become their biggest profit makers. Today, Roll is the largest citrus grower in California and the largest nut grower in the world. During the 2000s, Roll began marketing pure pomegranate juice and juice products under the POM Wonderful brand. It acquired Fiji Water, a company that bottles water from native aquifers in Suva, Fiji. And it acquired Suterra, an Oregon maker of pheromones that disrupt insect mating behavior, protecting crops without the need for insecticides. Today, Roll International is one of the two hundred largest private companies in America.

Roll's headquarters is an oasis of art and sculpture in an ordinary West Los Angeles office district. Stewart is casual, soft-spoken, and self-confident. His grasp of the details of each of Roll's businesses is unusual for the chairman of a firm of Roll's size and complexity.

Stewart tells me that Teleflora had been competing on price when he acquired the business. "We changed to a service model," he says, explaining that Teleflora provides florists with the largest member network, an Internet-based IT system, keepsake products to hold and include with flowers, Web hosting services, credit card processing services, and point-of-sale technologies. "There is more competition now than ever," he says, "but Teleflora is a much more successful business than it was when we bought it. Then it was one-tenth the size of FTD; now it is twice as large."

I ask him if there is a common lesson that can be taken from businesses as disparate as Teleflora and Fiji Water. Stewart opens his hands palms up and tilts his head to the side, a gesture meaning "How can I explain?" After a pause, he says, "By providing more value you avoid being a commodity. The bottled water field is crowded, but Lynda saw something unique in this product—water from a deep aquifer in Fiji that has been naturally filtered for several hundred years. Water that fell to earth before the industrial age, before pollution and chemicals. It is a unique proposition that the original owners had not exploited."

I understand about avoiding being a commodity. Yet, Roll has become the largest citrus grower in California and the largest almond and pistachio grower in the world. I ask, "Aren't these agricultural products, by definition, commodities?"

Stewart says that he began to buy agricultural land in 1978 as a passive hedge against inflation. The breakthrough came when he realized that these businesses were actually quite "interesting."

"Interesting?" I ask. If human ears could perk up, mine would.

After thinking for a moment, Stewart says, "To me, a business is 'interesting' when I can see ways to increase its value. The typical nut farmer can't control his own destiny. He simply accepts what the trees yield and the market's prices.

"A small nut farmer can't afford the investments needed to develop the market or do research on yields or do efficient processing. But we had a large holding. We were large enough to earn back the costs of research on yields and quality. And I realized that if we could stimulate the demand for almonds and pistachios, then there would be a real benefit. Of course, all California nut farmers would benefit from the increased demand, but we were the only grower with the size to make the investment worthwhile. And it has worked. Consumption keeps growing and exports are up. Our 'Wonderful' brand commands a price premium. Almonds and pistachios are healthy snacks, and there is still a huge potential for expansion."

I suggest that stimulating the demand for nuts would provide only a temporary benefit to Roll. Wouldn't the advantage dissipate once other growers increased their production to match the higher demand?

"Things don't happen with lightning speed in agriculture," Stewart explains. "It takes seven to ten years for newly planted trees to mature. That gave us time to invest in planting, branding, processing, and merchandising. Then, as demand grew, we aggressively built nut-processing capacity. The scale economies in processing make it hard for smaller farmers to build their own processing facilities. And unless you can do processing, packaging, marketing, branding, and distribution, it may not pay to buy more land and plant new trees."

I could see that Stewart's approach to the nut business was a complex coordinated maneuver over a decade of time. His original large-scale holdings enabled him to capture the lion's share of benefits from investments in research, market development, advertising, and promotion. The seven-to-ten-year lag in competitive response provided both the financing and a window of opportunity to build large-scale nut-processing facilities. The economies of scale in processing have so far prevented smaller competitors from achieving equivalent costs.

It must have taken iron nerve to wait years for the strategy to work. "You are still looking five to ten years ahead?" I query.

"It is one of the big benefits of being a private company. When I first bought these lands from major oil companies, they were looking ahead one quarter or one year. They wanted to get the assets 'off their books' to make their financial ratios look better. We can do more with these businesses because we don't suffer the crazy pressures that are put on a public company."

Some Advantages Are More "Interesting" Than Others

When another person speaks you hear both less and more than they mean. Less because none of us can express the full extent of our understanding, and more because what another says is constantly mixing and interacting with your own knowledge and puzzlements. When Stewart Resnick explained what made a business "interesting" to him, I made an unexpected connection to aspects of the concept of competitive advantage that I had been puzzling over for some time. I felt something click into place in my mind. To explain, I have to go back to 2002 when my UCLA colleague Steven Lippman and I created a thought experiment about competitive advantage.

Our thought experiment* concerned an imaginary "silver machine" left behind by a passing UFO. It could produce $10 million per year in raw silver at no cost—it used no inputs of energy, materials, or labor. There were no taxes and the constant interest rate was 10 percent. The original finder of the silver machine sold it to a new owner for $100 million. Did this new owner, we asked, have a competitive advantage in the silver business?

The silver machine problem became an underground puzzle in the strategy field. The silver machine was obviously a low-cost producer—zero cost is about as low as it goes. The conundrum was that this advantage did not make the new owner any wealthier. Yes, the machine paid

* A thought experiment tests ideas for logical consistency and logical implications.

out $10 million per year, but that was just an ordinary 10 percent return on what had been paid to buy it. Its competitive advantage seemed to have evaporated because of the change in ownership. Yet the machine continued to produce silver at zero cost.[3]

It took some time, but I can unravel the puzzle. The silver machine does have a competitive advantage in the silver business.[4] The conundrum disappears when you carefully distinguish between competitive advantage and financial gain—many have assumed that they are the same thing, but they are not. But it was Stewart Resnick who helped me see another even more important fact about the silver machine—that its advantage, though real, wasn't *interesting*.

The silver machine's advantage gives it value, but the advantage isn't interesting because there is no way for an owner to engineer an *increase* in its value. The machine cannot be made more efficient. Pure silver cannot be differentiated. One small producer cannot pump up the global demand for silver. You can no more increase the value of the silver machine than you can, by yourself, engineer an increase in the value of a Treasury bond. Therefore, owning this advantage is no more interesting than owning a bond.

For Stewart Resnick, and now for me, a competitive advantage is interesting when one has insights into ways to increase its value. That means there must be things you can do, on your own, to increase its value.

To see an example of a major competitive advantage that is, presently, not increasing in value, look at eBay. It should be obvious that eBay has a considerable competitive advantage in the global person-to-person auction business. eBay invented this business and remains by far the worldwide dominant firm in it. More specifically, eBay's competitive advantage lies in its unrivaled ability to offer the least expensive, most effective solution to just about anyone who wishes to buy or sell a personal item online. Its broad user base, easy-to-use software, the PayPal payment system, and its methods of rating sellers all give it a considerable advantage over any competing platform. Over the years, eBay has been very profitable. During the year ending in December 2009, the company had an operating cash flow of $2.9 billion, an after-tax sales margin of 26 percent, and a healthy after-tax return on assets of 13 percent. Yet, despite its competitive advantage, the company's market value had been stagnant or declining for more than seven years. By operating, eBay definitely provides a service whose cost of provision is well below the value placed on it by customers, and does this so efficiently that others can not horn in on its core business. Nonetheless, it has not been creating new wealth for its owners.

Like the silver machine, eBay's value has been static, indicating that its competitive advantage has been static. However, eBay is a lot more "interesting" than the silver machine. Although there are no ways (by definition) to alter the silver machine's advantage, there are a myriad of ways to change eBay's services, its efficiency, and the uses to which its resources and skills are put. So, eBay's advantage is potentially interesting. It will become truly interesting when someone gains special insights into unexploited ways to expand the value of eBay's already considerable competitive advantages.

VALUE-CREATING CHANGES

Many strategy experts have equated competitive advantage with high profitability. The example of eBay (and of the imaginary silver machine) shows that this is not necessarily so. Despite all the emphasis on "competitive advantage" in the world of business strategy, you cannot expect to make money—to get wealthier—by simply having, owning, buying, or selling a competitive advantage. The truth is that the connection between competitive advantage and wealth is dynamic. That is, wealth *increases* when competitive advantage *increases* or when the demand for the resources underlying it *increases*. In particular, increasing value requires a strategy for progress on at least one of four different fronts:

- deepening advantages,
- broadening the extent of advantages,
- creating higher demand for advantaged products or services, or
- strengthening the isolating mechanisms that block easy replication and imitation by competitors.

Deepening Advantage

Start by defining advantage in terms of surplus—the gap between buyer value and cost. *Deepening* an advantage means widening this gap by either increasing value to buyers, reducing costs, or both.*

It would be foolish to attempt to summarize the vast variety of methods and approaches that can be used to make improvements in cost and/or value. It is more useful to highlight the two main reasons this process stalls.

First, management may mistakenly believe that improvement is a "natural" process or that it can be accomplished by pressure or incentives alone. As Frank Gilbreth pointed out in 1909, bricklayers had been laying bricks for thousands of years with essentially no improvement in tools and technique.[5] By carefully studying the process, Gilbreth was able to more than double productivity without increasing anyone's workload. By moving the supply pallets of bricks and mortar to chest height, hundreds or thousands of separate lifting movements per day by each bricklayer were avoided. By using a movable scaffold, skilled masons did not have to waste time carrying bricks up ladders. By making sure that mortar was the right consistency, masons could set and level a brick with a simple press of the hand instead of the time-honored multiple taps with a trowel. Gilbreth's lesson, still fresh today, is that incentives alone are not enough. One must reexamine each aspect of product and process, casting aside the comfortable assumption that everyone knows what they are doing. Today, this approach to information flows and business processes is sometimes called "reengineering" or "business-process transformation." Whatever it is called, the underlying principle is that improvements come from reexamining the details of how work is done, not just from cost controls or incentives.

The same issues that arise in improving work processes also arise in the improvement of products, except that observing buyers is more difficult than examining one's own systems. Companies that excel at product development and improvement carefully study the attitudes,

* When looking at costs, include the buyer's costs of searching for the product, evaluating it, traveling to buy it or waiting for it to arrive, switching to it, installing it, and learning how to consume it.

decisions, and feelings of buyers. They develop a special empathy for customers and anticipate problems before they occur.

The second reason firms may fail to engage in a process of improvement occurs when isolating mechanisms surrounding important methods are weak. Companies in such situations sensibly hope to catch a free ride on the improvements of others. To benefit from investments in improvement, the improvements must either be protected or embedded in a business that is sufficiently special that its methods are of little use to rivals.

Broadening the Extent of Advantage

Extending an existing competitive advantage brings it into new fields and new competitions. For example, cell phone banking is a growing phenomenon outside of the United States, especially in the less developed countries. eBay holds substantial skills in payment systems embedded in its PayPal business. If eBay could build on these to create a competitive advantage in cell phone payment systems, it would be *extending* a competitive advantage.

Extending a competitive advantage requires looking away from products, buyers, and competitors and looking instead at the special skills and resources that underlie a competitive advantage. In other words, "Build on your strengths."

The idea that some corporate resources can be put to good use in other products or markets is possibly the most basic in corporate strategy.[6] Its truth is undeniable yet it is also the source of great mischief. Bemused by the idea that their company's competitive strength lies in vaporous generalities such as "transportation," "branded consumer products," or "management," companies may diversify into products and processes they know nothing about.

The basis for productive extensions often resides within complex pools of knowledge and know-how. For example, DuPont started as a specialist in explosives. After World War I, its skills at chemistry and chemical production led DuPont to manufacture cellulose, synthetic rubber, and paints. The work in synthetics led to new skills in polymer chemistry, which, in turn, led to Lucite and Teflon in 1935. Further developments in polymers led to nylon, Mylar, Dacron, Lycra, and more. Similar patterns of accumulating and extending technological resources can be found in General Electric, IBM, 3M, and many pharmaceutical and electronics companies.

Extensions based on proprietary know-how benefit from the fact that knowledge is not "used up" when it is applied; it may even be enhanced. By contrast, extensions based on customer beliefs, such as brand names, relationships, and reputation, may be diluted or damaged by careless extension. Although great value can sometimes be created by extending these resources, a failure in the new arena can rebound to damage the core.

A good example of the care management must take in extending its brands and reputation is that of the Walt Disney Company. It has long enjoyed a substantial competitive advantage in the entertainment industry because of its ability and reputation in family-friendly fare. To appreciate the magnitude of this advantage, note that no other film company is able to pull viewers to its movies by its brand name alone. Many kids go to (or are taken to) the newest Disney film without much regard to its content. By contrast, no one goes to a movie because it is a Sony Pictures Studios product or because it was made by Paramount. Those brands have some power in financial circles and in distribution channels, but none with the consumer.

A brand's value comes from guaranteeing certain characteristics of the product. But those characteristics are not easy to define. What, exactly, is a "Disney" film? How far can the brand be stretched without losing value? Mark Zoradi is president of the Walt Disney Motion Pictures Group (formerly Buena Vista Motion Pictures Group), which markets and distributes motion pictures under the Walt Disney, Touchstone, and Miramax imprints. It also oversees the operations of the Disney and Pixar animation studios. In late 2008, Mark and I were discussing the Disney brand and strategies for extending it. He told me this:

> The most valuable thing we have is the Disney brand. Several years back, Dick Cook [then chairman of Walt Disney Studios] got us thinking hard about how to build on that strength without diluting it. Some people think a Disney movie has to be suitable

for very young children. But they forget that Walt made *20,000 Leagues Under the Sea,* a film that was probably much too scary for very young kids. We looked at the whole list of the most successful films in history and discovered that we would have been proud to release a surprising number under the Disney name—films like *E.T., Superman,* and the *Indiana Jones* movies.

To keep the faith and still expand the brand we came up with three basic guidelines. *No bad language.* It's OK for people to get angry and red in the face, but no cursing. *No uncomfortable sexual situations.* We want romance but we will leave making dirty movies to others. *No gratuitous violence.* We are all in favor of swashbuckling adventure but there will be no beheadings or spurting blood. It is this broader view that let us release *Pirates of the Caribbean, National Treasure,* and *Prince Narnia* under the Disney brand.

Mark Zoradi's three guidelines are intended to help the company extend the Disney brand into the increasingly successful action-adventure genre without damaging the brand's value in its more traditional sector.

Creating Higher Demand

A competitive advantage becomes more valuable when the number of buyers grows and/or when the quantity demanded by each buyer increases. Technically, it is the scarce resources underlying the advantage that increase in value. Thus, more buyers for small airplanes will increase the value of Embraer's (Brazil) brand name and its specialized skills in design and production. Note that higher demand will increase long-term profits only if a business already possesses scarce resources that create a stable competitive advantage.

Because so many strategy theorists have mistakenly equated value-creating strategy with "having" a sustainable competitive advantage, they have largely ignored the process of engineering increases in demand. Engineering higher demand for the services of scarce resources is actually the most basic of business stratagems.

Stewart and Lynda Resnick's POM Wonderful pomegranate business is an example of acting creatively to generate more demand. In 1987, they bought 18,000 acres of nut orchards from Prudential Life Insurance. Among the almond and pistachio trees were 120 acres of pomegranate bushes. "I first wanted to replant this acreage with nut trees, but we decided to keep the bushes," Stewart recalled. "Our company reports split results by crop and, after a few years, I noticed that we were consistently making more money per acre from the pomegranates than from the nuts."

In the 1990s, pomegranates were a very minor crop in the United States, and Americans were largely unfamiliar with them. The fruit had its ancient origins in the Middle East, and many associated it with life-giving properties. In 1998, the Resnicks began to fund research on the properties of pomegranates. The researchers reported that the juice contained even more antioxidants than red wine. Further study suggested that the juice might lower blood pressure and that its concentration of flavonoids might help prevent prostate cancer. Since 1998, the Resnicks have donated more than $30 million to research into the fruit's health benefits.

The Resnicks developed a strategy of dramatically increasing the national demand for pomegranates. Like their previous success in nuts, this would create value if they owned a substantial fraction of pomegranate production and if new competitive production did not swiftly appear. To implement this strategy, the Resnicks began to buy more acreage. By 1998, they had six thousand acres committed to the future production of pomegranates—a sixfold increase in U.S. productive capacity.

The company also began to study ways of packaging and marketing pomegranate juice. The standard industry approach was to dilute an expensive strong-flavored juice with much larger quantities of blander white grape, apple, and pear juices. That was how Ocean Spray sold its cranberry juice. Lynda Resnick suggested a different concept. Their main pomegranate offering would be 100 percent pure with no fillers. It would deliver 100 percent of the health benefits. It would not be marketed as a soft drink or kids' sugar kick. Rather, it would be a new category—a fresh, refrigerated antioxidant juice, distributed beside fresh produce. The brand name would be POM with the "O" shaped like a heart. The Resnicks decided to bet on Lynda's concept.

POM's president Matt Tupper recently recalled that the massive plantings, cresting in 2000–2001, created the threat of a "red tide" of unsold pomegranate juice if the strategy of dramatically increasing demand didn't work. "It was daunting," he said. "We had to go all out. Lynda worked tirelessly to shape the concept, the package, and the marketing approach. She wrote, gave interviews, and introduced POM to every mover and shaker in her huge network of contacts. *It worked*. Demand surged. By 2004 we were the dominant producer in a new hot category of product. And, even better, it's good for you."

Strengthening Isolating Mechanisms

An isolating mechanism inhibits competitors from duplicating your product or the resources underlying your competitive advantage. If you can create new isolating mechanisms, or strengthen existing ones, you can increase the value of the business. This increased value will flow from lessened imitative competition and a consequent slower erosion of your resource values.

The most obvious approach to strengthening isolating mechanisms is working on stronger patents, brand-name protections, and copyrights. When a new product is developed, its protection may be strengthened by stretching an already powerful brand name to cover it. When an isolating mechanism is based on the collective know-how of groups, it may be strengthened by reducing turnover. When protections are unclear, legislation or courtroom verdicts may clarify and strengthen certain positions.

An example of *collective* action to strengthen property rights is the history of the U.S. petroleum industry. As soon as oil was first pumped in Pennsylvania in 1859, the issue of ownership came to the fore. In the case of a mineral like coal the rule was clear—a person owned the coal beneath their land. But oil, the courts decided, moved and flowed like a wild beast—no one could really tell where a particular drop of oil had come from. Applying the age-old Anglo-Saxon "rule of capture," oil legally belonged to whoever pumped it out of the ground.

Because oil reservoirs extend beyond property boundaries, most wells are drilled into what amounts to being a large common reservoir. Since the rule-of-capture said that the oil belonged to whoever pumped it, each successful driller had to pump as fast as possible. If a well was not pumped, others would empty the reservoir anyway. This created the forests of oil rigs and fantastic rates of development in early U.S. oil fields where overpumping was the rule of the day. For example, soon after the great East Texas field was discovered in 1930, there were forty-four separate wells pumping on one square city block in the town of Kilgore. Within eighteen months, the price of oil had fallen from one dollar to 13 cents per barrel, the field's pressure had collapsed, and water was seeping into the reservoir. Many members of the industry wanted some way of stopping the "arms race," but courts threw out plans to control production as illegal price fixing. In late 1931, the governor of Texas declared martial law in the East Texas field and used the National Guard to halt production.

Eventually, over decades, oil producers, state governments, and the federal government struggled to work out the present rules for controlling oil field production and the sharing of revenue among property owners. The task was complicated because not all oil producers had the same interests or information. In particular, larger holdings had better information about the ultimate reserves in the field.[7] Nevertheless, the obstacles were overcome. In this case, it took cooperative action to alter the legal isolating mechanisms protecting each driller's discoveries.

Another broad approach to strengthening isolating mechanisms is to have a moving target for imitators. In a static setting, rivals will sooner or later figure out how to duplicate much of your proprietary know-how and other specialized resources. However, if you can continually improve, or simply alter, your methods and products, rivals will have a much harder time with imitation. Consider, for example, Microsoft's Windows operating system. Were this to remain stable for a long period of time, there is little doubt that clever programmers around the world could, over time, create a functionally equivalent substitute. However, by continually changing the program—even if the changes are not improvements—Microsoft makes it very costly to engineer a continuing series of functional equivalents. Windows is a moving target.

Along the same lines, continuing streams of innovations in methods and products are more difficult to imitate when they are, themselves, based on streams of proprietary knowledge. For example, a company that innovates by using scientific knowledge will have, in general, weaker isolating mechanisms than one that combines science with information fed back from lead customers or proprietary information gleaned from its own internal operations.

CHAPTER THIRTEEN

USING DYNAMICS

In classical military strategy the defender prefers the high ground. It is harder to attack and easier to defend. The high ground constitutes a natural asymmetry that can form the basis of an advantage.

Much of academic strategy theory concerns more and more intricate explanations for why certain types of economic high ground are valuable. But such discussions sidestep an even more important question: how do you attain such an advantaged position in the first place? The problem is that, as valuable as such positions are, the costs of capturing them are even higher. And an easy-to-capture position will fall just as easily to the next attacker.

One way to find fresh undefended high ground is by creating it yourself through pure innovation. Dramatic technical inventions, such as Gore-Tex, or business model innovations, such as FedEx's overnight delivery system, create new high ground that may last for years before competitors appear at the ramparts.

The other way to grab the high ground—the way that is my focus here—is to exploit a wave of change. Such waves of change are largely *exogenous*—they are mostly beyond the control of any one organization. No one person or organization creates these changes. They are the net result of a myriad of shifts and advances in technology, cost, competition, politics, and buyer perceptions. Important waves of change are like an earthquake, creating new high ground and leveling what had been high ground. Such changes can upset the existing structures of competitive positions, erasing old advantages and enabling new ones. They can unleash forces that may strengthen or radically weaken existing leaders. They can enable wholly new strategies.

An exogenous wave of change is like the wind in a racing boat's sails. It provides raw, sometimes turbulent, power. A leader's job is to provide the insight, skill, and inventiveness that can harness that power to a purpose. You exploit a wave of change by understanding the likely evolution of the landscape and then channeling resources and innovation toward positions that will become high ground—become valuable and defensible—as the dynamics play out.

To begin to see a wave of change it helps to have some perspective. Business buzz speak constantly reminds us that the rate of change is increasing and that we live in an age of continual revolution. Stability, one is told, is an outmoded concept, the relic of a bygone era. None of this is true. Most industries, most of the time, are fairly stable. Of course, there is always change, but believing that today's changes are huge, dwarfing those in the past, reflects an ignorance of history.

For example, compare the changes during your life to those that occurred during the fifty years between 1875 and 1925. During those fifty years, electricity first lit the night and revolutionized factories and homes. In 1880, the trip from Boston to Cambridge and back was a full day's journey on horseback. Only five years later, the same trip was a twenty-minute ride on an electric streetcar; with the streetcar came commuting and commuter suburbs. Instead of relying on a single giant steam engine or water wheel to power a factory, producers switched to electric motors to bring power into every nook and cranny. The sewing machine put decent clothing within everyone's reach. And electricity powered the telegraph, the telephone, and then the radio, triggering the first significant acceleration in communications since the Roman roads. During that fifty-year period, railroads knit the country together. The automobile came into common use and revolutionized American life. The airplane was invented and commercialized. Modern paved highways were built and agriculture was mechanized. IBM's first automatic tabulating machine was developed in 1906. A huge wave of immigration changed the face of cities. Modern patterns of advertising, retailing, and consumer branding were developed—hundreds of famous brands, such as Kellogg's, Hershey's, Kodak, Coca-Cola, General Electric, Ford, and Hunt's, date from this era. Most of the foundations of what we now see as the "modern world" were put in place, and great still-standing industrial empires were established. All of this took place in the fifty years between 1875 and 1925.

Now, look at another, more modern, period of fifty years. Since I was born in 1942, television has reshaped American culture, jet air travel has opened the world to ordinary people, the falling costs of long-distance transport have generated a rising tide of global trade, retail stores the size of football fields now dot the landscape, computers and cell phones are ubiquitous, and the Internet has made it possible to work, seek out entertainment, and shop without leaving home. Millions can instantly tweet about their evanescent likes and dislikes. Yet, all in all, the last fifty years' changes have had a smaller impact on everyday life and the conduct of business than did the momentous changes that occurred from 1875 to 1925. Historical perspective helps you make judgments about importance and significance.

After a wave of change has passed, it is easy to mark its effects, but by then it is too late to take advantage of its surge or to escape its scour. Therefore, seek to perceive and deal with a wave of change in its early stages of development. The challenge is not forecasting but understanding the past and present. Out of the myriad shifts and adjustments that occur each year, some are clues to the presence of a substantial wave of change and, once assembled into a pattern, point to the fundamental forces at work. The evidence lies in plain sight, waiting for you to read its deeper meanings.

When change occurs, most people focus on the main effects—the spurts in growth of new types of products and the falling demand for others. You must dig beneath this surface reality to understand the forces underlying the main effect and develop a point of view about the second-order and derivative changes that have been set into motion. For example, when television appeared in the 1950s it was clear that everyone would eventually have one and that "free" TV entertainment would provide strong competition to motion pictures. A more subtle effect arose because the movie industry could no longer lure audiences out of their homes with "just another Western." Traditional Hollywood studios had been specialized around producing a steady stream of B-grade movies and did not easily adapt. By the early 1960s, movie attendance was shrinking rapidly. What revived Hollywood film was a shift to independent production, with studios acting as financiers and distributors. Independent producers, freed from the nepotism and routines of the traditional studio, could focus on assembling a handpicked team to make a film that might be good enough to pull an audience off of their family-room sofas. Thus, a second-order effect of television was the rise of independent film production.

SENSING THE WAVE'S SWELL

It is a wet winter day in 1996 and I have driven from my office in Fontainebleau to Paris in order to meet with executives of Matra Communications. Several years earlier, the French government had sold off its controlling interest in the Matra Group, a large high-tech military, aerospace, electronics, and telecommunications equipment firm. Canada-based Northern Telecom had bought a 39 percent stake in Matra Communications, the company's telecommunications equipment subsidiary.

Jean-Bernard Lévy, the chairman and CEO of Matra Communications, welcomes me into his office. At forty he is young for his position by American standards. But the French system is different. Anyone who is very smart and very good in math gets a free world-class education at one of the Grand Écoles and is virtually guaranteed a fast track in government or industry. Lévy has served in government and France Telecom, and was general manager of Matra's satellite business for several years. By 2002, he had become CEO of Vivendi, the media conglomerate controlling Universal Music Group, Canal+, Activision Blizzard, and other businesses, and by 2005 he became chairman of Vivendi's management board.

Lévy, his chief financial officer, and I discuss the challenges facing

Matra Communications in the rapidly changing world of telecommunications. He explains that "the telecommunications business has been, along with mainframe computing, an industry in which economies of scale—at a global level—have been determinative. If a company doesn't have a significant market presence in at least two legs of the triad [Japan, Europe, and North America], then it struggles along as a niche player, offering very specialized equipment." Then, with a wry smile, he adds, "Or it depends upon the government forcing the local telephone monopoly to buy from the local supplier."

"That seems," I say, "to put Matra in a difficult position. Matra is not one of the top ten telecommunications equipment makers in the world."

"No, it is not," he says. "But there are big changes afoot. Cellular telephony will shake up the industry. European deregulation will change the rules of the game. And the Internet will blur the lines between communications, data, and entertainment."

"So, network and cellular equipment are the key opportunities?"

"Those are the immediate changes. More are coming."

Change can mean opportunity. Yet recent changes have not been especially good for Matra. I ask a pointed question. "I am trying to understand the forces that are changing the structure of the industry. For instance, look at the amazing success of Cisco Systems. It sits right on the interface between telecommunications and computing—a position that everyone thought would be the big battleground between AT&T and IBM. And yet, instead of a battle of titans we have this upstart grabbing the business.

"As you said, the critical barrier to becoming a major player in telecommunications equipment and computing has been scale," I continue. "Yet, Cisco Systems, started by two university staff members, has broken right through the scale 'barrier.' It has grabbed the internetworking equipment market right out from under the nose of giants like IBM, AT&T, Alcatel, NEC, and Siemens. *And* Matra. How has that happened?"

The CFO argues that Cisco offered stock option incentives that were out of reach of larger, more established firms. That enabled Cisco to attract the top technical talent in the world.

Jean-Bernard Lévy shakes his head. He has a different slant on the issue. "We have had Matra engineers working on inter-networking equipment. The basic principles are well understood. Yet we cannot seem to replicate the performance of Cisco's multi-protocol network routers."

"Are there key patents?" I ask.

"There are patents, but they aren't the crucial thing," he replies. "The heart of the Cisco router is firmware—software burned into read-only memory or implemented in programmable arrays. Cisco's product embodies, perhaps, one hundred thousand lines of code that is very skillfully written. It was created by a very small team—maybe two to five people. That chunk of very clever code gives the product its edge."

Later that evening, back in my office, I transcribed my interview notes and reflected on what I had been told. A router, I knew, was really just a small computer—it used microprocessors, memory, and input-output ports to manage the flow of data over a digital network. Its performance had little to do with the specific microprocessors, memory, and logic chips inside it. After all, everyone in the industry had access to similar chips. The part of the Cisco router that is so hard to duplicate was the software. Well . . . no, it was the *skill* embodied in the software that was so hard to duplicate.

Then I saw it. I had been talking about Cisco as if it were a single example of skill countering scale. But the forces Cisco had harnessed to its advantage were much deeper than the skills of any one company, much broader than any one industry.

In the computing and telecommunications equipment sectors, economic success had traditionally been based on capabilities at coordinating hordes of engineers in vast billion-dollar development projects and in managing large workforces in the manufacture of complex electronic equipment. That had been the basis of the power of IBM and AT&T and had been central to the engineering-intensive success of Japan. But now, in 1996, the basis of success in many areas was shifting to software—to the cleverness of chunks of code written by small teams. It was a shift from economies of size to the know-how and skill of single individuals. It was as if military competition suddenly shifted from large armies to single combat. A chill moved up and down my spine. There was the unnerving sense of hidden subterranean forces at work, twisting the landscape.

Three years earlier, I had lived and worked in Tokyo for several months. Then, the conviction that Japan would be the economic superpower of the twenty-first century had been alive and well. But now the locus of innovation had shifted to the small-team entrepreneurial culture of Silicon Valley. My mind's eye saw this wave of change spreading to affect machine tools, bread makers, furnaces, toasters, and even automobiles. The forces at work were not only altering the fortunes of companies, they were shifting the very wealth of nations.

DISCERNING THE FUNDAMENTALS

The work of discerning whether there are important changes afoot involves getting into the gritty details. To make good bets on how a wave of change will play out you must acquire enough expertise to question the experts. As changes begin to occur, the air will be full of comments about what is happening, but you must be able to dig beneath that surface and discover the fundamental forces at work. Leaders who stay "above the details" may do well in stable times, but riding a wave of change requires an intimate feel for its origins and dynamics.

For many years, telecommunications had been one of the most stable industries. But in 1996, when Jean-Bernard Lévy and I were discussing Cisco Systems, the structure of the computing and communications industry had suddenly become fluid and turbulent. Of the visible trends, the rise of personal computing and data networking were on everyone's radar. The deregulation of telecommunications and its shift to digital technology had been long anticipated. The two more mysterious shifts were the rise of software as a source of competitive advantage and the deconstruction of the traditional computer industry.

It seems obvious in hindsight. Both the rise of software's importance and the computer industry's deconstruction had a common cause: the microprocessor. Yet these connections were far from obvious in the beginning. Everyone in high tech could see the microprocessor, but understanding its implications was a much more difficult proposition. Let me share with you a personal view of some of the steps along that path.

Software's Advantage

How had software become such a sharp source of advantage? The answer is that millions of microprocessors, in everything from PCs to thermostats, bread machines to cruise missiles, meant that their programming determined the performance of these devices.

When I was an undergraduate studying at UC Berkeley in 1963, two of the main areas of excitement within electrical engineering were integrated circuits and computing. The first integrated circuits had been demonstrated in 1958, and devices created for the Minuteman missile project had integrated hundreds of transistors onto a single chip. With regard to computing, there was nothing mysterious about making a computer's central processor—the circuit patterns had been common knowledge since the 1950s.

All of my Berkeley classmates understood that if one could push integration from hundreds of transistors to *thousands* of transistors on a single chip, it would be possible to have a one-chip computer processor. Silicon Valley historians and patent attorneys love to argue over who "invented" the first microprocessor, but the idea of putting all the components of a processing unit onto one chip was in the air as soon as integrated circuits appeared. In any event, the first microprocessor offered for sale was Intel's 4-bit 4004 in 1971, containing 2,300 transistors.

At that time, the chip market had two segments. Standardized chips such as logic gates and memory were produced in high volume but were commodities. Specialized proprietary chips or chipsets provided much higher margins but were only produced to order in low volumes. And the rights to a complex proprietary chip belonged to the customer who had ordered it and sometimes designed it.

Significantly, and often sadly, many crucial decisions do not appear to be decisions at the time. Instead, managers simply apply standard operating procedures to the situation. Within Intel, the 4004 microprocessor was classified as a specialized proprietary design, so the rights to it belonged to customer Busicom, which intended to build it into its line of calculators. As luck would have it, Busicom came under profit pressure and asked Intel for a price reduction. Intel lowered the price in return for the right to sell the chip to others. Then, amazingly, this pattern was repeated with Intel's next microprocessor, the 8-bit 8008. This microprocessor had been created as a proprietary chip for CTC, the maker of Datapoint computer terminals. Running out of money, CTC traded the rights to the 8008's design for the chips it needed. In this case, CTC had actually designed the chip's instruction set—you can still see echoes of that instruction set in Intel's most advanced x86 processors.

It took years for Intel's management, and the rest of the industry, to fully appreciate the implications of a general-purpose chip that could be specialized with software. Instead of each customer paying to develop a specialized proprietary chip, many could use the same general-purpose microprocessor, creating proprietary behavior with software. Thus, the microprocessor could be produced in high volume. Instead of being a job shop for other companies' designs, Intel could be a product-based technology company. Speaking about the 4004, and microprocessors in general, then chairman Andy Grove said, "I think it gave Intel its future, and for the first fifteen years we didn't realize it. It has become Intel's defining business area. But for . . . maybe the first ten years, we looked at it as a sideshow."[1]

Intel cofounder Gordon Moore became famous for his "law" predicting the rate of progress in speed and manufacturing costs in integrated circuits. He was less well known for his observation that design costs for custom chips were becoming larger than fabrication costs and were escalating at an unsupportable rate. He wrote, "Two things broke the crisis for semiconductor component manufacturers . . . the development of the calculator [microprocessor] and the advent of semiconductor memory devices." To Moore, the beauty of these devices was that, although complex, they could be sold in high volumes.

In a discussion with a group of managers at Qualcomm, a San Diego maker of mobile phone chips, I reviewed Moore's point about the escalating costs of designing more and more complex special-purpose chips. One manager was puzzled and asked if it wasn't also expensive to create software. He went on to rhetorically ask "Are software engineers less expensive than hardware engineers?"

It was a good question. None of us had an instant answer. I sharpened the question with an example from my own experience. Rolls-Royce had wanted to create a sophisticated fuel monitoring and control unit to enhance the efficiency of its jet engines. It could have accomplished this through proprietary hardware embodying the necessary logic, or it could have used a general-purpose microprocessor, expressing its proprietary ideas by writing software to program it. Whether it chose to use a microprocessor plus software or proprietary hardware chips, it would have had to do a lot of engineering work for only a few thousand installations. Why prefer software?

As is often the case, restating a general question in specific terms helped. We quickly developed an answer that has since stood up to scrutiny by a number of other technical groups: Good hardware and software engineers are both expensive. The big difference lies in the cost of prototyping, upgrading, and, especially, the cost of fixing a mistake. Design always involves a certain amount of trial and error, and hardware trials and errors are much more costly. If a hardware design doesn't work correctly, it can mean months of expensive redesign. If software doesn't work, a software engineer fixes the problem by typing new instructions into a file, recompiling, and trying again in a few minutes or a few days. And software can be quickly fixed and upgraded even after the product has shipped.

Thus, software's advantage comes from the rapidity of the software development cycle—the process of moving from concept to prototype and the process of finding and correcting errors. If engineers never made mistakes, the costs of achieving a complex design in hardware and software might be comparable. But given that they do make mistakes, software became the much-preferred medium (unless the cutting-edge speed of pure hardware was required).

WHY COMPUTING DECONSTRUCTED

In 1996, soon after my conversation with Jean-Bernard Lévy in Paris, Intel chairman Andy Grove published his insightful book *Only the Paranoid Survive*. Grove drew on his expertise in both business and technology to forcefully describe how "inflection points" can disrupt whole industries. In particular, he described the "inflection" that had transformed the computer industry from a "vertical" to a "horizontal" structure.

In the old vertical structure, each computer maker made its own processors, memory, hard drives, keyboards, and monitors, and each wrote its own systems and applications software. The buyer signed up with a maker and bought everything from that manufacturer. You couldn't plug an HP disk drive into a DEC computer. By contrast, in the new horizontal structure, each of those activities had become an industry in its own right. Intel made processors, other firms made memory, others made hard drives, Microsoft made systems software, and so on. Computers were assembled by mixing and matching parts from competing manufacturers.

Grove was dead-on in understanding that "not only had the basis of computing changed, the basis of competition had changed too."[2] Still, as a strategist, I wanted to know more. Why had the computer industry deconstructed itself and become horizontal? Andy Grove wrote, "Even in retrospect, I can't put my finger on exactly where the inflection point took place in the computer industry. Was it in the early eighties, when PCs started to emerge? Was it in the second half of the decade, when networks based on PC technology started to grow in number? It's hard to say."[3]

I was puzzled over the cause of the computer industry's deconstruction. Then, about a year later, the reason snapped into focus. I was interviewing technical managers at a client firm and one said that he had formerly been a systems engineer at IBM. He then explained that he had lost that job because modern computers didn't need much systems engineering. "Why not?" I asked without thinking.

"Because now the individual components are all smart," he answered. Then I saw it.

The origin of Andy Grove's inflection point was Intel's own product—the microprocessor. The modularization of the computer industry came about as each major component was able to contain its own microprocessor—each part became "smart."

In many traditional computers, and early personal computers, the CPU—the active heart of the machine—did almost everything itself. It scanned the keyboard, looking for a keystroke. When it sensed one, it analyzed the row and column of the keystroke on the keyboard to determine the letter or number that had been pressed. To read a tape drive, the CPU constantly controlled the speed of the tape reels and the tension of the tape, stopping and starting the drive as it interpreted the data coming in and storing it in memory. To typewrite with a "daisy-wheel" printer, the CPU controlled the spin of the wheel and the timing of each separate hammer strike. In some cases, designers created custom mini-CPUs to manage these peripherals, but the integration among these devices remained complex and unstandardized and consumed a great deal of systems engineering effort.

After the arrival of cheap microprocessors, all that changed. The modern keyboard has a small microprocessor built into it. It knows when a key has been hit and sends a simple standardized message to the computer saying, in effect, "The letter X was pressed." The hard-disk drive is also smart so that the CPU doesn't need to know how it works. It simply sends a message to the hard disk saying "Get sector 2032," and the hard-disk subsystem returns the data in that sector, all in one slug. In addition, separate microprocessors control the video screens, memory, graphics processors, tape drives, USB ports, modems, Ethernet ports, game controllers, tape drives, backup power supplies, printers, scanners, and mouse controllers that make up modern computers.

Smart components operating within a de facto standard operating system meant that the job of systems integration became almost trivially simple. The skills at systems integration that IBM and DEC had built up over decades were no longer needed. That was why my engineer-informant had lost his job.

With the glue of proprietary systems engineering no longer so important, the industry deconstructed itself. Modules did not have to be custom designed to work with every other part. To get a working system, customers did not have to buy everything from a single supplier. Specialist firms began to appear that made and sold only memory. Others made and sold only hard drives or keyboards or displays. Still others made and sold video cards or game controllers or other devices.

Today, there are many academic researchers who look at the computer industry and see a network of relationships, each one a channel whereby one firm coordinates with another. The idea of a network especially enchants modern reductionist sociologists who count connections among people, skipping over the old-fashioned hard-to-quantify questions about content and meaning. However, dwelling on this network of weak relationships confuses the background with the absent foreground. What is actually surprising about the modern computer industry is not the network of relationships but the absence of the massively integrated firm doing all the systems engineering—all of the coordination—internally. The current web of "relationships" is the ghostly remnant of the old IBM's nerve, muscle, and bone.

CISCO SYSTEMS RIDES THE WAVE

As I mentioned to Jean-Bernard Lévy that day in 1996, Cisco Systems was a recent start-up that had "grabbed the inter-networking equipment market right out from under the nose" of industry giants. The story of how Cisco Systems came into being and how it came to beat the giants vividly demonstrates the power of using waves of change to advantage. The particular waves Cisco used were the rise of software as a critical skill, the growth in corporate data networking, the shift to IP networks, and the explosion of the public Internet.

In the early 1980s, Ralph Gorin, the director of Stanford University's computer facilities, wanted a way of hooking together separate networks of Apple, Alto, and DEC computers as well as various printers. Each type of computer network used different kinds of wires, plugs, timing, and, most important, different proprietary protocols for encoding information. Gorin's request was for a way to interconnect these proprietary networks. The solution, called the *blue box*, was engineered by Stanford staff members Andy Bechtolsheim and William Yeager.[4]

Two other Stanford staff members, Len Bosack and Sandy Lerner, began to refine the blue box, moving the improved designs into their newly formed company, Cisco Systems. After an acrimonious split with Stanford in 1987, Cisco Systems received full legal rights to the software in return for a payment to Stanford of $167,000 and the promise of discounts on Cisco products. It was thought that Cisco would sell some of its boxes, now called routers, to other research universities, but there was no expectation that Cisco would make much money. There was certainly no expectation that Cisco would become, for a brief moment in 2000, the most valuable corporation in the world.

Soon after receiving its first injection of venture capital in 1988, Cisco's management was turned over to professionals. John Morgridge was CEO from 1988 to 1995, followed by John Chambers. Both CEOs skillfully guided Cisco to take advantage of the powerful forces at work in its industry. During the 1988–93 period, Cisco rode three simultaneous waves. The first wave was the microprocessor and its key implication—the centrality of software. Cisco outsourced the manufacture of its hardware, concentrating on software, sales, and service. Ralph Gorin remarked that "Cisco cleverly sold software that plugged into the wall, had a fan, and got warm."

The second wave lifting Cisco in its early years was the rise of corporate networking. Just as at Stanford, corporations were discovering the need to connect mainframes, personal computers, and printers that used different network protocols. The Cisco router's ability to handle multiple protocols was in growing demand.

The third wave was IP (Internet Protocol) networking. In 1990, most network protocols had corporate owners and sponsors. IBM had SNA (Systems Network Architecture), Digital Equipment Corporation had DECnet, Microsoft had NetBIOS, Apple had AppleTalk, Xerox had developed the Ethernet, and so on. By contrast, IP was created in the late 1970s to handle traffic on ARPANET, the precursor to the Internet. IP was pure logic—it had no wires or connectors, no timing specifications or hardware. Plus, it was free and was no company's proprietary product. As corporations began to hook disparate computers into networks, corporate IT departments began to see the value in a protocol that was vendor neutral. Increasingly, corporations made IP their backbone network protocol and, at the same time, Cisco began to make IP the central hub protocol on its routers.

Critically, none of the industry incumbents jumped to forcefully occupy this space. Each had its own proprietary network protocol and each was loath to totally abandon it. And each was even more loath to produce equipment that would help a competitor's equipment onto the network.

If three waves were not enough, Cisco literally exploded under the force of a fourth wave that hit in 1993: the rise of Internet use by the general public. Inside corporations, computer users suddenly wanted Internet access. Not just dial-up access over a modem, but a direct always-on connection to the IP backbone. As universities and corporations scrambled to make this happen, IP won the battle for internal network standards, and Cisco routers captured two-thirds of the corporate networking market. At the same time, traffic on the Internet backbone was skyrocketing and Cisco was there, providing the high-speed routers to handle the flow of Internet data on a continental scale. Where there were competitive barriers, Cisco maneuvered around them. In 1992–94, Cisco worked with IBM to add support for IBM's proprietary SNA protocol to its routers and worked with AT&T and others to make sure that its equipment supported telecommunications industry protocols (for example, Asynchronous Transfer Mode and Frame Relay).

When faced with a corporate success story, many people ask, "How much of the success was skill and how much was luck?" The saga of Cisco Systems vividly illustrates that the mix of forces is richer than just skill and luck. Absent the powerful waves of change sweeping through computing and telecommunications, Cisco would have remained a small niche player. Cisco's managers and technologists were very skillful at identifying and exploiting these waves of change, and were lucky enough to make no fateful blunders. Key competitor IBM was pulling its punches after thirteen years of antitrust litigation. The Internet came along at just the right time to accelerate Cisco's upward climb. And various incumbents were held in check by their own inertia, their strategies of supporting a single or a proprietary protocol, and by the very rapidity of change.

SOME GUIDEPOSTS

It is hard to show your skill as a sailor when there is no wind. Similarly, it is in moments of industry transition that skills at strategy are most valuable. During the relatively stable periods between episodic transitions, it is difficult for followers to catch the leader, just as it is difficult for one of the two or three leaders to pull far ahead of the others. But in moments of transition, the old pecking order of competitors may be upset and a new order becomes possible.

There is no simple theory or framework for analyzing waves of change. In the words of my UC Berkeley junior-year physics professor, Nobel laureate Luis Alvarez, "This course is labeled 'advanced' because we don't understand it very well." He explained, "If there were a clear and consistent theory about what is going on here, we would call this course 'elementary' physics."

Working with industry-wide or economy-wide change is even more advanced than particle physics—understanding and predicting patterns of these dynamics is difficult and chancy. Fortunately, a leader does not need to get it totally right—the organization's strategy merely has to be *more right* than those of its rivals. If you can peer into the fog of change and see 10 percent more clearly than others see, then you may gain an edge.

Driving or skiing in the fog is unnerving without any source of orientation. When a single recognizable object is visible in the mist, it provides a sudden and comforting point of reference—a guidepost. To aid my own vision into the fog of change I use a number of mental guideposts. Each guidepost is an observation or way of thinking that seems to warrant attention.

The first guidepost demarks an industry transition induced by *escalating fixed costs*. The second calls out a transition created by *deregulation*. The third highlights *predictable biases in forecasting*. A fourth marks the need to properly assess *incumbent response* to change. And the fifth guidepost is the concept of an *attractor state*.

Guidepost 1—Rising Fixed Costs

The simplest form of transition is triggered by substantial *increases in fixed costs,* especially product development costs. This increase may force the industry to consolidate because only the largest competitors can cover these fixed charges. For example, in the photographic film industry, the movement from black-and-white to color film in the 1960s strengthened the industry leaders. One insightful analysis of this wave of change points is that in the previously mature black-and-white photo film industry, there was little incentive for competitors to invest heavily in R & D because film quality already exceeded the needs of most buyers.[5] But there were large returns to improvements in quality and the ease of processing color film. As the costs of color-film R & D escalated, many firms were forced out of the market, including Ilford in the United Kingdom and Ansco in the United States. That wave of change left behind a consolidated industry of fewer but larger firms, dominated by Kodak and Fuji.

A similar dynamic was IBM's rise to dominance in computing in the late 1960s, driven by the surging costs of developing computers and operating systems. Still another was the transition from piston to more sophisticated jet aircraft engines, cutting the field of players down to three: GE, Pratt & Whitney, and Rolls-Royce.

Guidepost 2—Deregulation

Many major transitions are triggered by major changes in government policy, especially *deregulation.* In the past thirty years, the federal government has dramatically changed the rules it imposes on the aviation, finance, banking, cable television, trucking, and telecommunications industries. In each case, the competitive terrain shifted dramatically.

Some general observations can be made about this kind of transition. First, regulated prices are almost always arranged to subsidize some buyers at the expense of others. Regulated airline prices helped rural travelers at the expense of transcontinental travelers. Telephone pricing similarly subsidized rural and suburban customers at the expense of urban and business customers. Savings and loan depositors and mortgage customers were subsidized at the expense of ordinary bank depositors. When price competition took hold, these subsidies diminished fairly quickly, but the newly deregulated players chased what used to be the more profitable segments long after the differential vanished. This happened because of the inertia in corporate routines and mental maps of the terrain, and because of poor cost data. In fact, highly regulated companies do not know their own costs—they will have developed complex systems to justify their costs and prices, systems that hide their real costs even from themselves. It takes years for a formerly regulated company, or a former monopolist, to wring excess staff expense and other costs out of its system and to stop its accountants from making arbitrary allocations of overhead expenses to activities and products. In the meantime, these mental and accounting biases mean that such companies can be expected to wind down some product lines that are actually profitable and continue to invest in some products and activities that offer no real returns.

Guidepost 3—Predictable Biases

In seeing what is happening during a change it is helpful to understand that you will be surrounded by *predictable biases in forecasting*. For instance, people rarely predict that a business or economic trend will peak and then decline. If sales of a product are growing rapidly, the forecast will be for continued growth, with the rate of growth gradually declining to "normal" levels. Such a prediction may be valid for a frequently purchased product, but it can be far off for a durable good. For durable products—such as flat-screen televisions, fax machines, and power mowers—there is an initial rapid expansion of sales when the product is first offered, but after a period of time everyone who is interested has acquired one, and sales can suffer a sharp drop. After that, sales track population growth and replacement demand.

Predicting the existence of such peaks is not difficult, although the timing cannot be pinned down until the growth rate begins to slow.

The logic of the situation is counterintuitive to many people—the faster the uptake of a durable product, the sooner the market will be saturated. Many managers find these kinds of forecasts uncomfortable, even disturbing. As a client once told me, "Professor, if you can't get that bump out of the forecast, I can find a consultant who will."

Another bias is that, faced with a wave of change, the standard forecast will be for a "battle of the titans." This prediction, that the market leaders will duke it out for supremacy, undercutting the middle-sized and smaller firms, is sometimes correct but tends to be applied to almost all situations.

For example, the "convergence" of computing and telecommunications had been predicted for many years. One of the most influential forecasts in this regard was NEC chairman Koji Kobayashi's 1977 vision of "C&C" (computers and communications). He felt that IBM's acquisition of a communications switch maker and AT&T's acquisition of a computer maker illustrated the path forward. He imagined telephone systems with computing backup—telephones that would translate spoken sentences from one language to another. He predicted that convergence would parallel advances in integrated circuit technology (large-scale integration, very large-scale integration, and beyond). With this vision of convergence firmly in mind, Kobayashi pushed NEC in the direction of greater and greater computing power. NEC sought to build ever faster and more compact supercomputers. The U.S. government deregulated AT&T, in part to prepare for its anticipated battle with IBM.

The problem NEC, AT&T, IBM, and other major incumbents all encountered was that convergence didn't happen the way it was "supposed" to happen. Like two sumo wrestlers, AT&T and IBM advanced to the center of the ring, preparing to grapple. Then it was as if the floor beneath them crumbled, dropping both into a pit beneath. The very foundations they had stood upon were eaten away by waves of change—the microprocessor, software, the deconstruction of computing, and the Internet. Having a common fate was not the kind of convergence that had been envisioned.

Along the same lines, in 1998 many pundits were predicting the emergence of global megacarriers that would dominate world communications. Such companies, foreshadowed by the Concert Communications Services joint venture between AT&T and British Telecom, would offer global seamless carriage of data over complex managed intelligent networks. Of course, it turned out that there is no more reason for one company to own networks all over the world than there is for UPS to own all the roads on which its trucks travel.

A third common bias is that, in a time of transition, the standard advice offered by consultants and other analysts will be to adopt the strategies of those competitors that are currently the largest, the most profitable, or showing the largest rates of stock price appreciation. Or, more simply, they predict that the future winners will be, or will look like, the current apparent winners.

- As aviation was deregulated, consultants advised airlines to copy Delta's Atlanta-based hub-and-spokes strategy. But, unfortunately for the copycats, Delta's profits had come from subsidized prices on the short-haul routes to rural towns it served from Atlanta—subsidies that were disappearing with deregulation.

- While WorldCom's stock price was flying high, consultants urged clients to emulate the company and get into the game of putting fiber-optic rings around cities (twenty-one around Denver!). "At 10 percent of the volume, WorldCom is already beating AT&T on per unit network costs" one report claimed.[6] That advice had to be withdrawn when sleepy telephone companies awoke and began to cut prices. WorldCom then crashed and burned.

- In 1999, the Web start-up advice was to create a "portal" such as Yahoo! or AOL—a website that acted as a guide to the Internet and provided a protected "playground" of specialized Web pages that users were herded toward. But although these companies were the stars of the moment, their initial strategies of capturing and channeling Web traffic were soon made obsolete by the sheer scale of the expanding Internet.

Guidepost 4—Incumbent Response

This guidepost points to the importance of understanding the structure of *incumbent responses* to a wave of change. In general, we expect incumbent firms to resist a transition that threatens to undermine the complex skills and valuable positions they have accumulated over time. The patterns of incumbent inertia are discussed in detail in chapter 14, "Inertia and Entropy."

Guidepost 5—Attractor States

In thinking about change I have found it very helpful to use the concept of an *attractor state*. An industry attractor state describes how the industry "should" work in the light of technological forces and the structure of demand. By saying "should," I mean to emphasize an evolution in the direction of efficiency—meeting the needs and demands of buyers as efficiently as possible. Having a clear point of view about an industry's attractor state helps one ride the wave of change with more grace.

During the 1995–2000 period, when the telecommunications industry was in turmoil, Cisco System's strategic vision of "IP everywhere" was actually a description of an attractor state. In this possible future, all data would move as IP packets, whether it moved over home Ethernets, wireless networks, telephone company ATM networks, or submarine cables. In addition, all information would be coded into IP packets, whether it was voice, text messaging, pictures, files, or a video conference. Other firms were envisioning a future in which carriers provided "intelligent" networks and "value-added services," terms that actually meant that carriers would provide special protocols, hardware, and software to support services such as video conferencing. By contrast, in the "IP everywhere" attractor state, the "intelligence" in the network would be supplied by the devices plugged into its endpoints—the network itself would be a standardized data pipeline.

An attractor state provides a sense of direction for the future evolution of an industry. There is no guarantee that this state will come to be, but it does represent a gravitylike pull. The critical distinction between an attractor state and many corporate "visions" is that the attractor state is based on overall efficiency rather than a single company's desire to capture most of the pie. The "IP everywhere" vision was an attractor state because it was more efficient and eliminated the margins and inefficiencies attached to a mishmash of proprietary standards.

Two complements to attractor-state analysis are the identification of accelerants and impediments to movements toward an attractor state. One type of accelerant is what I call a *demonstration effect*—the impact of in-your-face evidence on buyer perceptions and behavior. For example, the idea that songs and videos were simply data was, for most people, an intellectual fine point until Napster. Then, suddenly, millions became quickly aware that a three-minute song was a 2.5 megabyte file that could be copied, moved, and even e-mailed at will.

As an example of an impediment, consider the problems of the electric power industry. Given the limited carrying capacity of the atmosphere for burned carbon compounds, the obvious attractor state for the power industry is nuclear power. The simplest path would be to replace coal- and oil-fired boilers with modern third- or fourth-generation nuclear boilers. The major impediment to the U.S. power industry moving in this direction is the convoluted and highly uncertain licensing process—at each stage, local, state, and federal authorities are involved as well as the courts. Whereas it takes France five years to license and build an *entire* nuclear plant, it would probably take ten years or more for a U.S. utility to just carry out a boiler changeover.

An interesting attractor-state analysis can be performed on the future of the newspaper industry. The special complexity of newspapers, television, websites, and many other media arises from their indirect revenue structure—they receive much of their income from advertising.

The challenge is especially acute for the bellwether *New York Times*, with a weekday circulation of about one million copies. The company's outsized subscription and newsstand fees garnered $668 million in 2008, more than enough to cover its newsroom and administrative expenses. The problem is the cost of physically printing and distributing the newspaper. These costs are roughly double or triple the subscription revenue and have been covered by advertisers. But in 2009, advertising revenues went into steep decline.

The forces at work are twofold. First, readership is slowing because today's readers have free access to 24/7 broadcast news, free online access to basic headline stories, and free online access to thousands of specialized blogs and articles that offer commentary and analysis. Just as the big-city midcentury department store was squeezed between the suburban mall and big-box discounters, readers can now skip the general-purpose newspaper in favor of both lower cost and more fascinating fare. Second, newspaper advertising has been declining since the mid-1980s. Today's advertisers are increasingly interested in more targeted media, ones that go beyond demographics and identify a consumer's specific interests. That is the power of Google—the ability to use the content of search requests to identify the interests of its users. General-purpose newspapers will suffer under this wave of change.

News media can be differentiated in three basic dimensions: territory (world, national, regional, local), frequency (hourly, daily, and so on), and depth (headline, feature story, in-depth expert analysis). I believe that the attractor state for news contains specialists along each of these dimensions rather than generalists trying to be all things to all people. With electronic access to information, there is simply no good reason to continue to bundle local, national, and world news together and add weather, sports, comics, puzzles, opinion, and personal advice to the mix. I believe that as we move toward this attractor state, general-purpose daily wide-circulation newspapers will fade away. Local news and more specialized news media will continue to exist and even flourish. The strategic challenge for the *New York Times* and the *Chicago Tribune* is not "moving online" or "more advertising," but unbundling their activities.

In this unbundled attractor state, it is very likely that there would be a continuing market for local news, weather, and sports reported by a daily newspaper, although it would have to operate with less overhead and less pretension than the current *New York Times*. It is likely that the appropriate vehicle for in-depth news analysis and investigative journalism would be a weekly magazine, ultimately delivered to a digital reader (and available free online after one month). By contrast, top national and world news will be most appropriately delivered online, especially to mobile platforms. An interesting complement would be a cable news channel. To reduce costs, partnerships with capital-city newspapers and independent journalists around the world will help (a strategy that would use the *New York Times'* brand as a bargaining tool). Similar online opportunities will exist for coverage of business, politics, the arts, and science.

In moving to an online model, a large traditional newspaper will need to place much more emphasis on aggregating content from a variety of sources and writers versus depending on staff journalists. Successful online media present the user with a carefully selected nest of links to articles, stories, blogs, and commentary. To date, there is no successful online source of revenue other than advertising. The more that advertising can be targeted based on user demographics and revealed interests, the more a media site can charge for its placement.

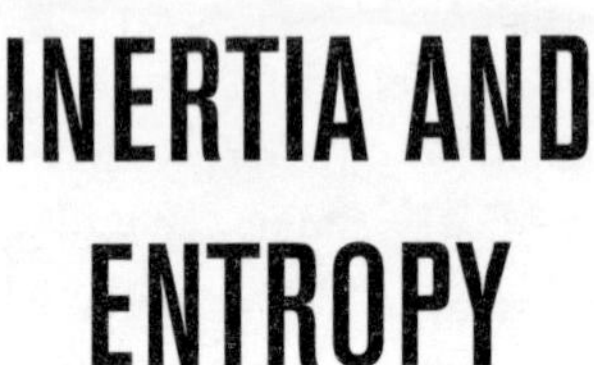

CHAPTER FOURTEEN

INERTIA AND ENTROPY

Even with its engines on hard reverse, a supertanker can take one mile to come to a stop. This property of mass—resistance to a change in motion—is *inertia*. In business, inertia is an organization's unwillingness or inability to adapt to changing circumstances. Even with change programs running at full throttle, it can take many years to alter a large company's basic functioning.

Were organizational inertia the whole story, a well-adapted corporation would remain healthy and efficient as long as the outside world remained unchanged. But, another force, *entropy*, is also at work. In science, entropy measures a physical system's degree of disorder, and the second law of thermodynamics states that entropy always *increases* in an isolated physical system. Similarly, weakly managed organizations tend to become less organized and focused. Entropy makes it necessary for leaders to constantly work on maintaining an organization's purpose, form, and methods even if there are no changes in strategy or competition.

Inertia and entropy have several important implications for strategy:

- Successful strategies often owe a great deal to the inertia and inefficiency of rivals. For example, Netflix pushed past the now-bankrupt Blockbuster because the latter could not, or would not, abandon its focus on retail stores. Despite having a large early lead in mobile phone operating systems, Microsoft's slowness in improving this software provided a huge opening for competitors, an opening through which Apple and Google quickly moved. Understanding the inertia of rivals may be just as vital as understanding your own strengths.

- An organization's greatest challenge may not be external threats or opportunities, but instead the effects of entropy and inertia. In such a situation, organizational renewal becomes a priority. Transforming a complex organization is an intensely strategic challenge. Leaders must diagnose the causes and effects of entropy and inertia, create a sensible guiding policy for effecting change, and design a set of coherent actions designed to alter routines, culture, and the structure of power and influence.

INERTIA

Organizational inertia generally falls into one of three categories: the inertia of routine, cultural inertia, and inertia by proxy. Each has different implications for those who wish to reduce inertia or those who seek to gain by attacking a less-responsive rival.

The Inertia of Routine

The heartbeat of any sizable business is the rhythmic pulse of standard procedures for buying, processing, and marketing goods. Its more conscious actions are guided by less rhythmic but still well-marked paths. Even the breathless chase after an important new client, the sizing of a new facility, and the formulation of plans are familiar moves in a game that has been played before. An organization of some size and age rests on layer upon layer of impacted knowledge and experience, encapsulated in routines—the "way things are done." These routines not only limit action to the familiar, they also filter and shape managers' perceptions of issues. An organization's standard routines and methods act to preserve old ways of categorizing and processing information.

The inertia created by standard routines can be revealed by sudden outside shocks: a tripling of the price of oil, the invention of the microprocessor, telecommunications deregulation, and so on. The shock changes the basis of competition in the industry, creating a significant gap between the old routines and the needs of the new regime.

U.S. airline deregulation, inaugurated in 1978, was such a shock. The routines for running airlines and concepts of competition had become set over decades of strong regulation. Deregulation acted to suddenly release many constraints on action, but many of the moves made in the first few years were guided by old rules of thumb rather than the realities of the new situation.

Two years after airline deregulation, I was asked to help Continental Airlines with some strategy issues, including the purchase of new aircraft. The company had a large fleet of DC-10s, but sought help in thinking through its options in spending an estimated $400 million on new equipment. The CEO, Al Feldman, had just jumped into Continental from the CEO position at Frontier Airlines, where he had been a strong supporter of deregulation.

In the decades of regulation, the government set fares and assigned routes to airlines; competition was more or less limited to image, food, and personal service. The standard unit of production in the airline industry is the available-seat-mile (ASM). Take a seat, lift it to thirty-two thousand feet, and move it one mile and you have produced one ASM. Airline operating costs per ASM fall with the length of a trip because many trip costs are fixed. The costs of servicing the aircraft, wear and tear, cleaning, food, and even some crew costs did not depend much on trip length. A 367-mile trip between Los Angeles and Phoenix might cost $0.22 per ASM while a much longer 2,000-mile trip to Detroit might cost only $0.09 per ASM. Congress wanted to promote air travel to small towns, so in the days of regulation the Civil Aeronautics Board (CAB) set fares that were below cost on short routes and forced each airline to fly them. The losses on short routes were covered by the profits on long-haul routes, where the CAB set prices above cost. Of course, the CAB forced each airline to fly a mix of routes.

Working with a small team, I developed a view of the near future of the industry. My analysis was that deregulated fares would shift to more closely parallel costs. Prices and margins on short-haul routes would rise, and they would fall on long-haul routes. The implication was that, with deregulation, profits would be made only in two ways: a low-cost operating structure or cleverness in grabbing short-haul routes that did not have enough volume to support vigorous competition. At that time, the dominant feeling in the industry was that low-cost strategies would pull in lots of consumers, but that the business traveler would remain relatively insensitive to price. My thinking was different. Of course business travelers wanted frequent, convenient, comfortable travel, but most business flyers didn't pay for their travel—their employers did. And employers might be more interested in travel cost than comfort. Business travelers liked comfort, but would their companies pay a premium for it? We thought that falling long-haul prices would make them less willing to do so. I forecast that even as load factors rose, prices and margins would fall.

This point of view directly contradicted the dominant wisdom in the newly deregulated industry. Long haul had always been profitable. Just a few months before, Dick Ferris, United Airlines' feisty CEO, had given a talk to Wall Street analysts, saying his strategy was to eliminate short feeder routes and "concentrate on the long-haul routes where the bucks are." He committed United to spending $3 billion to build a new long-haul fleet, centered in Chicago. Braniff International had also reacted to the new era by adding new long-haul routes. I hoped that our analysis would show how Continental could be smarter.

My ideas were not well received by the executive committee. The bottom line, announced from the top, was "You've got it all wrong. We have already run a planning model and we know coast-to-coast fares have to rise, not fall. The question is which new equipment we should be buying: Boeing, Airbus, or McDonnell Douglas."

At moments like this, one is never sure what to think. Perhaps I was missing something. What was this "planning model" that was forecasting higher prices on the long hauls? It took a week for me to chase down the model and its forecast. Sure enough, there it was in black and white: current long-haul fares were out of equilibrium and were forecast to rise.

Continental's "planning model" was a computer program called the Boeing Fleet Planner. The program was provided by Boeing to help airlines make equipment acquisition decisions. Given a route structure and equipment profile, it worked out operating costs and spat out predicted financial statements. Continental used McDonnell Douglas equipment, but the Fleet Planner program knew the operating characteristics of all major aircraft.

I sat down next to the finance-office specialist who explained how it worked. To run the program one had to tell it which routes would be flown, project a market share on each, and specify the equipment. The program combined this information with operating cost data and computed the cost per ASM on each route. Estimating that 55 percent of seats would be filled (the load factor), it then added in a 12 percent return on capital and projected a fare. That was the fare that "had to rise, not fall."

Incredulous, I said, "This is the predicted fare? But it's just cost plus a markup!"

"We have used this tool for a long time," the specialist coolly replied. "It has been pretty reliable."

I was astonished. "What happens to these numbers—where do they go from here?" I asked.

"They go to the CAB, along with a bunch of other stuff, as part of fare planning," he said.

Continental's system for projecting airfares for the new era of competition was the same one it had used all during the regulation era to suggest and justify fares in negotiations with the CAB. This projection had nothing to do with competition, supply, demand, capacity, or market forces. It took costs and added a markup. *It "predicted" what the CAB would do in setting fares*. The Boeing Planner was a fine tool, but it wasn't a fare predictor unless you had a regulator guaranteeing that you would make a 12 percent return flying half-full airplanes.

Despite deregulation, the CEO's animated speeches on how the company had a new, competitive spirit, and an aggressive posture assumed by the senior management group, the company's planning, pricing, and marketing routines were unchanged from the era of regulation. The new competitive spirit was pure aggressiveness, unalloyed by craft.

It took another month to uncover the dead, yet controlling, hand of another regulation-era rule of thumb. By setting fares to allow the airlines a "fair" 12 percent return on capital, where capital was equity *plus* debt, the CAB had, in effect, guaranteed that an airline's debt interest would always be paid. All a firm had to do was not deviate too much from the overall norm. Banks had a similar rule about airline debt being a good credit risk. This had a big influence on the attitude toward new equipment. When the airlines moved from props to jets, and when they again moved from narrow to wide-body aircraft, billions of dollars were spent on new aircraft, adding tremendous chunks of new capacity. In a normal industry, a surge of new equipment placed in service by all competitors would have forced a crash in prices and major losses. And, in a normal industry, competitors cannot all add capacity at the same time unless there is a remarkable surge in demand. But in the airline business, the CAB lent a hand, propping up prices—and even increasing them—in these periods of overcapacity. Reequipment by the regulated airlines had not been a strategic problem. A simple rule sufficed: *reequip when everyone else does*.

Deregulation meant that the old rules of thumb were obsolete. *Go for the long-haul routes*, *fares will cover total costs*, and *reequip when everyone else does* were not going to work in the future. From 1979 to 1983, the majors kept enacting the old rules. In 1981, United, American, and Eastern together lost $240 million, while all of the shorter-haul carriers (Delta, Frontier, USAir, and so on) made a profit. Over the next two decades, only Southwest would be consistently profitable. In 1984 and '85, fares on long-haul routes fell 27 percent. On short-haul low-volume routes, fares rose 40 percent, more than covering costs. Our team's analysis was essentially right. Not rocket science, but counter to the long-standing rules of thumb.

Being right doesn't always help the decision maker. In Continental's case, a nasty strike dragged management's attention away from market dynamics. The plan to buy new aircraft was scuttled when fares did not rise and losses mounted. Then, sensing the firm's plight, entrepreneur Frank Lorenzo of Texas Air initiated a hostile takeover of the company. Top management couldn't believe that tiny Texas Air could take over a major airline—it wouldn't be until the late 1980s that U.S. corporate managements got used to this idea. Frustrated, angry, and suffering a secret deep depression, Continental CEO Al Feldman shot himself at his desk in August 1981.

In 1982, Frank Lorenzo merged Continental and Texas Air in a reverse takeover. A year later the new company was bankrupt, in part a tactic to separate the equipment from the old union contracts. A new Continental Airlines emerged from bankruptcy in 1986 and soon consolidated with Frontier, People Express, and New York Air. Frank Lorenzo sold his interest in 1990.

■ ■ ■

Inertia due to obsolete or inappropriate routines can be fixed. The barriers are the perceptions of top management. If senior leaders become convinced that new routines are essential, change can be quick. The standard instruments are hiring managers from firms using better methods, acquiring a firm with superior methods, using consultants, or simply redesigning the firm's routines. In any of these cases, it will probably be necessary to replace people who have invested many years developing and using the obsolete methods as well as to reorganize business units around new patterns of information flow.

The Inertia of Culture

In 1984, I had a close-up look at one of the epicenters of corporate cultural inertia in that era—AT&T.* As the corporate inventor of Unix, which today underlies the open-source Linux and Apple's Mac OS X operating systems, AT&T should have been a major player, especially with regard to computer communications. Retained as a strategy con-

* At that moment, AT&T had been split off from its historic telephone system businesses. It consisted of Bell Labs research units, Western Electric manufacturing divisions, the consumer products businesses, computing products, network systems and services, and long-distance telephone services. Today, the AT&T label applies to a very different company—a combination of long-distance services, national wireless services, and many of the original local telephone companies. Bell Labs and Western Electric are today owned by Alcatel-Lucent. Business communications and network services have been spun off, becoming Avaya Inc.

sultant, I worked with the company on new products and strategies in computing and communications.

The strategic plans I helped formulate at AT&T included developing and bonding key software packages with the AT&T brand name. [1] In addition, we planned on making these packages and add-on modules available for sale electronically, over telephone lines, with AT&T "communicating computers."* Finally, we were interested in developing a simpler version of AT&T's Unix for the PC platform, one that would begin to support a graphical user interface.

As I developed working relationships at AT&T, some high-level managers let me in on what they saw as an embarrassing secret. AT&T wasn't competent at product development. Yes, the company was the proud owner of Bell Labs; the inventor of the transistor, the C programming language, and Unix; and was a marvelous place that probed deeply into the fundamentals of nature. But there was no competence within AT&T at making working consumer products. One story that was told concerned cellular phones. Starting in 1947, Bell Labs developed the basic ideas underlying mobile telephony. However, the first market test, in 1977, had to be undertaken using Motorola's equipment.

Another story concerned videotex. In 1983, AT&T had a joint venture with the Knight Ridder newspaper chain to test a videotex system (Viewtron). The system would provide news, weather, airline schedules, sports scores, and community information as text on a home TV screen. But Bell Labs had not been able to deliver software capable of handling even the light demands of the test market. The software to run the system was instead developed by a small company (Infomart) working under subcontract to Knight Ridder.

My personal lesson in this regard came with respect to the "communicating computer," a PC tied by a modem to network services. (This was a decade before the Internet came into widespread public use.) I wanted to demonstrate to senior management the potential for selling software via computer. The metaphor was an elevator: first floor games,

* In 1983–84, the Internet was an academic curiosity. The development of a national Internet backbone did not take place until the National Science Foundation began to fund it in 1986.

second floor utilities, third floor calculations, and so on. We talked with AT&T Bell Labs about a simple PC-based program to demonstrate this interface. They quoted three million dollars and two years. I suggested a simpler approach and was told by a Bell Labs representative "not to interfere with our design prerogatives." Frustrated, I wrote the straightforward code for the demonstration myself in three weeks.

The problem at AT&T was not the competence of individuals but the culture—the work norms and mindsets. Bell Labs did fundamental research, not product development. The reaction to a request for demonstration code was as if Boeing engineers had been asked to design toy airplanes. Just as in a large university, the breakthroughs of a tiny number of very talented individuals had been used to justify a contemplative life for thousands of others. Through the many decades during which AT&T had been a regulated monopoly, this culture grew and flourished. Now, with deregulation, competition, and the soaring opportunities in mass-market computing and data communications, this way of doing things was a huge impediment to action. To make matters even worse, the massive inertia of the system was not being countered. With no real understanding of technology, most senior managers at AT&T did not comprehend or appreciate the problem. And those few who did had almost no chance of changing the character of Bell Laboratories, a crown jewel of American R & D, a development center that produced Nobel laureates.

The strategy work I did at AT&T in 1984–85 was a waste. The hard-won lesson was that a good product-market strategy is useless if important competencies, assumed present, are absent and their development is blocked by long-established culture. The seemingly clever objectives I helped craft were infeasible. It would be at least a decade before AT&T slimmed down and gained enough engineering agility to support work on competitive strategy.

Western Electric and most of AT&T Bell Laboratories were spun off as Lucent Technologies in 1996. Wall Street loved the new company and drove its price from eight dollars to eighty dollars per share before a lack of profits became evident and its price collapsed to below one dollar in 2002. French telecommunications equipment maker Alcatel merged with Lucent in 2006. Since the merger, Alcatel-Lucent's value has declined by 70 percent, largely due to losses in Lucent's operations.

■ ■ ■

We use the word "culture" to mark the elements of social behavior and meaning that are stable and strongly resist change. As a blunt and vivid example, Khmer Rouge leader Pol Pot killed one-fifth of the Cambodian population, executed almost every intellectual, burned almost all books, and outlawed religion, banks, currency, and private property, but still did not much alter Cambodian culture. The cultures of organizations are more lightly held than those of nationality, religion, or ethnicity. Still, it is dangerous to think that organizational culture can be changed quickly or easily.

The first step in breaking organizational culture inertia is simplification. This helps to eliminate the complex routines, processes, and hidden bargains among units that mask waste and inefficiency. Strip out excess layers of administration and halt nonessential operations—sell them off, close them down, spin them off, or outsource the services. Coordinating committees and a myriad of complex initiatives need to be disbanded. The simpler structure will begin to illuminate obsolete units, inefficiency, and simple bad behavior that was hidden from sight by complex overlays of administration and self-interest.

After the first round of simplification, it may be necessary to fragment the operating units. This will be the case when units do not need to work in close coordination—when they are basically separable. Such fragmentation breaks political coalitions, cuts the comfort of cross-subsidies, and exposes a larger number of smaller units to leadership's scrutiny of their operations and performance. After this round of fragmentation, and more simplification, it is necessary to perform a triage. Some units will be closed, some will be repaired, and some will form the nuclei of a new structure. The triage must be based on both performance and culture—you cannot afford to have a high-performing unit with a terrible culture infect the others. The "repair" third of the triaged units must then be put through individual transformation and renewal maneuvers.

Changing a unit's culture means changing its members' work norms and work-related values. These norms are established, held, and enforced daily by small social groups that take their cue from the group's high-status member—the alpha. In general, to change the group's norms, the alpha member must be replaced by someone who expresses different norms and values. All this is speeded along if a challenging goal is set. The purpose of the challenge is not performance per se, but building new work habits and routines within the unit.

Once the bulk of operating units are working well, it may then be time to install a new overlay of coordinating mechanisms, reversing some of the fragmentation that was used to break inertia.

Inertia by Proxy

A lack of response is not always an indication of sticky routines or a frozen culture. A business may *choose* to not respond to change or attack because responding would undermine still-valuable streams of profit. Those streams of profit persist because of their customers' inertia—a form of inertia by proxy.

As an example, in 1980 the prime interest rate hit 20 percent. With the then-new freedom to create money market customer accounts, how did banks respond? Smaller and newer banks seeking retail growth were happy to offer this new type of high-interest deposit account. But many older banks with long-established customers did not. If their customers had been perfectly agile, quickly searching for and switching to the highest-interest accounts, they would have had to offer higher-interest accounts or disappear. But their customers were not this agile.

I was a consultant to the Philadelphia Savings Fund Society (PSFS) at the time and asked about its rate structure on deposits. A vice president tried to find the brochure describing the higher-interest money market accounts and then gave up. He said, "Our average depositor is a retired person and not that sophisticated. Those depositor funds make up the last giant pool of 5 percent money left on the planet!" What he meant was that he could loan out his depositors' money and earn 12 percent or more, while paying only 5 percent to the depositors. Sure, some depositors would depart, but most would not and the profits on their inertia were enormous. The important implication for competitors was that, at that moment, a rival could poach customers away from PSFS without triggering a competitive response.

In an example from telecommunications, the regional Bell operating companies varied in the number of business customers they served. With the advent of the Internet, which were the first to offer digital subscriber line services? The telephone companies' primary data offering to business had been T1 lines, priced at about four thousand dollars per month and offering 1.5 mbps. In 1998, DSL speeds were about one-third of T1 speeds, but DSL prices were one-thirtieth. That is, a customer could replicate a T1 line with three DSLs for one-tenth the cost. Rather than cannibalize their very profitable T1 business, telephone companies serving New York, Chicago, and San Francisco just punted—they didn't offer DSL. These telephone companies lost about 10 percent of their corporate data business each year to the new-wave carriers (WorldCom, Intermedia Communications, and dozens of digital competitive local exchange carriers, or CLECs), but the very high profits in the T1 business more than made up for the decline.*

Again, the apparent inertia of the telephone companies was actually inertia by proxy, induced because their customers were so slow to switch suppliers, even in the face of dramatic price differences. This inertia by proxy fooled hundreds of companies and investors. The fantastic rate of expansion of the "new network" carriers was taken as evidence of competitive superiority, unleashing a frenzy of investment and stock appreciation. When the telephone companies finally began to respond in 2000, the bubble popped. Once real competition began, it was a rout. Not a single CLEC survived.

■ ■ ■

Inertia by proxy disappears when the organization decides that adapting to changed circumstances is more important than hanging on to old profit streams. This can happen quite suddenly, as it did in telecommunications after 1999. Attackers who have taken business away from an

* Understanding this balance should allow you to predict that the first telephone company to offer DSL services to businesses would be U.S. West, the former Mountain Bell, headquartered in Denver. U.S. West had the fewest number of T1 lines on lease and served fast-growing corporate and residential markets. It was an innovator in creating and offering DSL services to businesses.

apparently sleepy firm may find themselves suddenly without any profits. This effect may be magnified because the customers who switched away from the inert incumbent are, by self-selection, the most sensitive to a better offer.

On the other hand, if the attacker has been successful in building bonds of cost and loyalty with newly acquired customers, then the incumbent's return to a competitive posture may fail to gain back its lost buyers.

ENTROPY

It is not hard to see entropy at work. With the passage of time, great works of art blur and crumble, the original intent fading unless skillful restorers do their work. Drive down a suburban street and it is easy to spot the untended home. Weeds grow in the garden, paint peels from a door. Similarly, one can sense a business firm that has not been carefully managed. Its product line grows less focused; prices are set low to please the sales department, and shipping schedules are too long, pleasing only the factory. Profits are taken home as bonuses to executives whose only accomplishment is outdoing the executive next door in internal competition over the bounty of luck and history.

Entropy is a great boon to management and strategy consultants. Despite all the high-level concepts consultants advertise, the bread and butter of every consultant's business is undoing entropy—cleaning up the debris and weeds that grow in every organizational garden.

Denton's

In 1997, I was retained by Carl and Mariah Denton to look at the overall performance and value of their family company. The company, Denton's Inc., operated a chain of garden and landscape supply outlets in four states. Denton's dated back to the 1930s, when a number of separate retailers combined as a way of surviving the Great Depression. Originally serving fairly rural communities, it had, over the years, expanded into exurban areas as well. The twenty-eight retail outlets operated under three separate brand names but were all actually quite similar. Each outlet had a retail store building that sold garden supplies and tools and a large outdoor space that sold plants, trees, soils, and landscaping materials. Denton's owned twenty of its locations outright and leased the remaining eight.

Carl and Mariah Denton were avid gardeners, and their home could have been an advertisement for the company's products and services. The air was heavy with the scent of flowers, and an artificial stream burbled down ledges of stone and rock. Under a large shady oak tree we talked about the company and their desire to "get it in shape" to hand over to their children. They gave me a CD-ROM containing five years of financial results for each store and the company as a whole.

Digging into the financial statements I began to untangle layers of complexity. The main source of confusion was the treatment of capital. The company's return-on-capital measure for each retail outlet mixed apples and oranges. One location purchased in 1950 had cost $5,000 per acre and one bought in 1989 had cost $95,000 an acre. The computed return-on-investment figures for these locations made the older one look like a huge winner compared with the newer one.[2] This way of measuring business performance confounded retailing with real estate investment gains.

To put each location on a comparable basis, I devised a new measure of operating profit I called *gain to operating* (GTO) that adjusted for these differences and for various allocations.[3] Denton's best store had a GTO of $1.05 million and its worst had a GTO of negative $0.97 million. That is, closing that store would yield $0.97 million more per year than continuing to operate it. Denton's whole chain showed a GTO of $0.32 million, a very different picture from the $8 million in net income the accounts showed.

The chart I prepared for Carl and Mariah Denton is reproduced on the following page. To build this chart I ranked outlets in order of their gains to operating, with outlet 1 having the highest and 28 having the lowest. The bars show, for each rank, the *cumulative* gain to operating all of the outlets at that rank or better. Thus, the first bar on the left represents the best outlet in the chain—its GTO was $1.05 million per year. The next bar represents the GTO of outlet 1 *plus* that of outlet 2, a total cumulative GTO of $1.05 + 0.63 = $1.68 million. The third best outlet earned $0.5 million, so the third bar shows the cumulative GTO of outlets 1, 2, and 3 (1.05 + 0.68 + 0.5 = $2.18 million). Outlets 4 through 14 added another $2.5 million to the cumulative total, bringing it up to $4.68 million. But, beginning with outlet 15, negative GTOs begin to drag down the cumulative total. In fact, the negative GTOs of outlets 15 through 28 summed to negative $4.4 million, almost totally canceling out the contributions of the positive GTO stores. As you can see, *the number one outlet's GTO was higher than that of the whole chain of twenty-eight!*

DENTON'S ADJUSTED CUMULATIVE GAIN TO OPERATING (MILLIONS OF $)

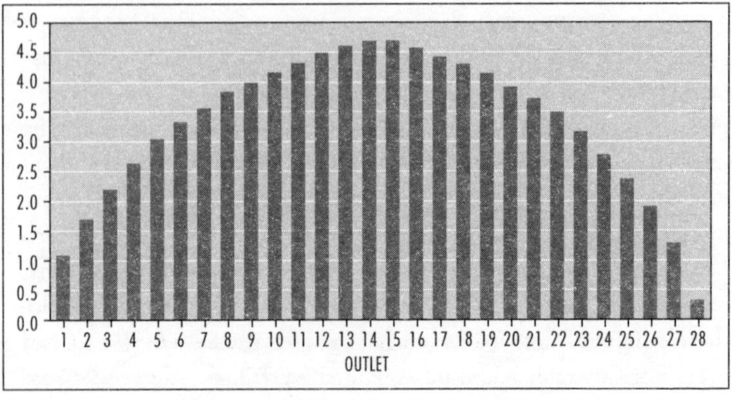

I call this a *hump chart*. Whenever you can assign profit or gain to individual products, outlets, areas, segments, or any other portion of the total, you can build a hump chart. I built my first hump chart in an analysis of Western Electric's pre-deregulation product mix. Since then, I have seen and helped build hump charts for planning military base closings, Sony products, telephone company customers, and a variety of other situations. If there are no cross-subsidies, the bars will rise smoothly to a maximum. But if some operations, some products, or some locations are subsidized by others, there will be a true "hump" on the chart—the bars will rise to a maximum and then begin to sag downward as the loss operations pull down the profits of the whole.

If the operations are separable, then a distinct hump, sustained over time, indicates a lack of management. It is a way to see entropy at work. At Denton's, the cross-subsidies were obscured by the measurement system and institutionalized over time. For example, in addition to the distortions caused by poor measures of space and land costs, Denton's measured the monthly and annual performance of each location by its "business operations profit," a figure that omitted employee incentive and bonus payments. Because incentive payments were set each year by corporate management, the logic was that they should not be charged directly to each location. But over many years incentive and bonus payments had become close to entitlements and were paid on the basis of total corporate profit, creating a subsidy from the more profitable locations to the less profitable.

Carl and Mariah were shocked by the hump chart. "You can't be suggesting that we drop half of the locations," Mariah said.

"No," I replied. "But it might make a great deal of sense to close the very worst performing locations. If you do that, and fix the other eight weak locations, you will double total earnings."

Improving the performance of the weaker locations took two years. The methods were straightforward data-driven management and transfer of best practices. The key at Denton's was to figure out why some locations performed better than others. Sales per square foot was a major driver of performance and it turned out to be strongly affected by location, the closeness of a competing Home Depot, the nursery layout, and the landscaping presentation. Better performing outlets, we discovered, had moved beyond the old-style grid layout and looked more like gardens. Plants were not simply labeled but described in detail along with planting suggestions and ideas about pairings with other plants. Plants were presented in attractive collections, promoting impulse buying. Landscaping supplies were not simply piled up but shown off in set-piece presentations, again helping customers to visualize how to use these materials at their own homes. Selling activities in the store, garden, and landscaping areas were separated because the knowledge bases of the sales personnel differed greatly across these activities.

At the end of two years, Denton's gain to operating had risen from $100,000 to more than $5 million and its accounting profit had doubled. About one-half of the increase came from dropping five weak outlets and the other half from a best-practices program. None of this improvement came from a deep entrepreneurial insight or from innovation. It was all just management—just undoing the accumulated clutter and waste from years of entropy at work.

Planning and planting a garden is always more interesting and stimulating than weeding it, but without constant weeding and maintenance the pattern that defines a garden—the imposition of a special order on nature—fades away and disappears.

General Motors

One of the clearest examples of entropy in business was the gradual decay of the order imposed on the early General Motors by Alfred Sloan. In this decay, one can see the value of competent management by its absence. Indeed, you cannot fully understand the value of the daily work of managers unless one accepts the general tendency of unmanaged human structures to become less ordered, less focused, and more blurred around the edges.[4]

In 1921, Henry Ford held 62 percent of the U.S. automobile market, having built a giant enterprise around the Model T. Ford's success came mainly from the Model T's low price, achieved by world-class industrial engineering of each aspect of automobile manufacturing.

General Motors was smaller than Ford and had been assembled through a number of acquisitions. In April 1921, the company's president, Pierre du Pont, asked Alfred Sloan (then vice president of operations) to undertake a study of "product policy" for the company. At that moment, the company produced ten lines of vehicles that together held about 12 percent of the automobile market. As can be seen in the following diagram, GM's Chevrolet, Oakland, Oldsmobile, Sheridan, Scripps-Booth, and Buick divisions all offered automobiles in the $1,800–$2,200 range. None produced a car that competed with Ford's $495 Model T. Plus, the Chevrolet, Oakland, and Oldsmobile divisions were badly in the red.

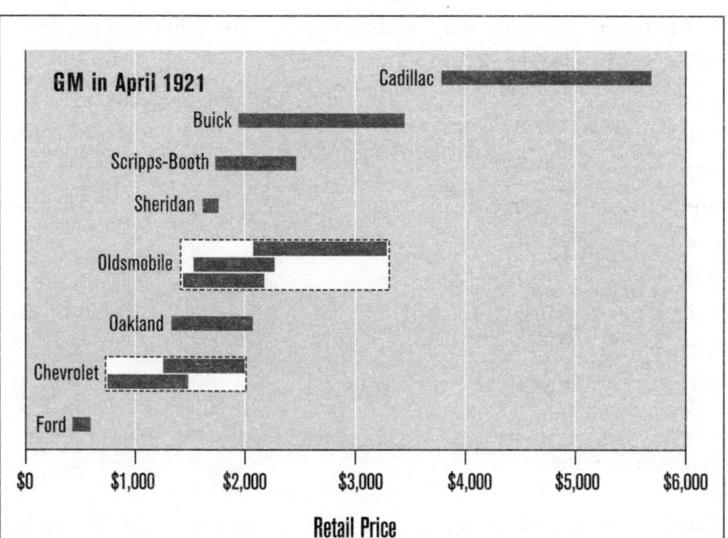

Two months later, Sloan presented his product policy to the executive committee. Sloan insisted that "General Motors' car line should be integral, that each car in the line should properly be conceived in its relationship to the line as a whole." More specifically, he wanted "quality competition against cars below a given price tag, and price competition against cars above that price tag."[5] Sloan's plan not only cut the prices of the cars in the line, it gave each brand a unique range of prices to work within. This new policy dramatically reduced the amount of intracompany competition and product clutter. Under Sloan's concept, there was no fuzziness or confusion about the difference between a Chevrolet, a Buick, and a Cadillac. Look at the diagram on the next page to see the logic and order Sloan's design imposed.

The executive committee adopted Sloan's plan, sold Sheridan Motors, and dissolved Scripps-Booth. Sloan became president in 1923. Oakland became Pontiac five years later. By 1931, General Motors had become the largest automaker and one of the leading corporations in the world. Throughout the 1940s and '50s, Sloan's concept became a part of American culture. Walking through a suburban neighborhood, you could tell who lived in each house by the car parked out in front:

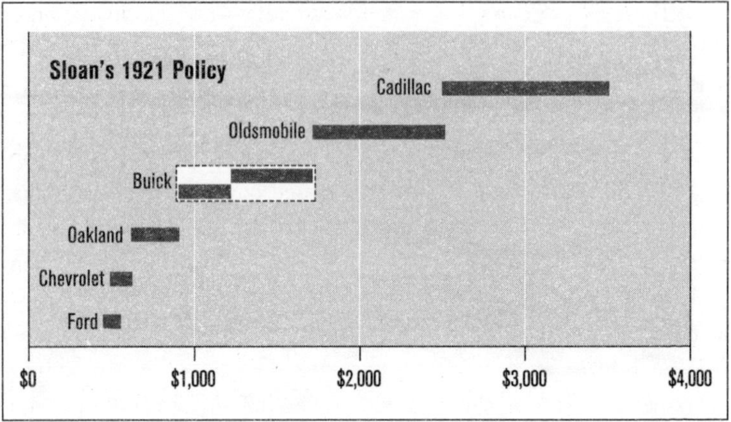

ordinary people drove Chevrolets, the foreman a Pontiac, the manager a Buick, and the CEO a Cadillac.

Sloan's product policy is an example of design, of order imposed on chaos. Making such a policy work takes more than a plan on a piece of paper. Each quarter, each year, each decade, corporate leadership must work to maintain the coherence of the design. Without constant attention, the design decays. Without active maintenance, the lines demarking products become blurred, and coherence is lost.

If the company is fully decentralized, this blurring of boundaries is bound to happen and the original design, based on brands defined around price ranges, becomes buried under a clutter of new products. For example, executives running the Chevrolet division knew that they could increase the Chevrolet division's sales and profit by offering some higher-priced models. This move might take some business away from Chrysler; it would also take business away from Pontiac and Oldsmobile. Conversely, executives running the Pontiac division saw that they could increase their division's revenues if they offered some lower-priced models, so they pushed in that direction. Like a parent who must resist fourteen-year-olds' pushing for beer at the party, corporate management's job is to resist these imprecations and preserve the design. If the design becomes obsolete, management's job is to create a new way of coordinating efforts so that the competitive energy is directed outward instead of inward.

By the 1980s, Sloan's design had faded away—a vivid illustration of the power of entropy. General Motors not only had blurred its brands and divisions, it engaged in badge engineering, offering essentially the same vehicle under several model and brand names.

More recent administrations worked to reduce the amount of overlap. In 2001, the Oldsmobile division was closed down, a stark recognition that its models had lost any distinction in either style or price. Lawsuits from displaced Oldsmobile dealers made this a very expensive proposition.

The 2008 product lineup at General Motors is shown on the next page, along with competitor Toyota's product lineup. Because GM's product mix was much more complex in 2008 than it had been in 1921, the display is restricted to sedans and coupes, omitting SUVs, vans, hybrid engine vehicles, and all trucks. Although Oldsmobile no longer existed in 2008, I have projected the price ranges of its models by adjusting its model year 2000 cars for GM's overall price inflation over the intervening eight years.

As can be seen, models were clustered around the mass-market \$20,000–\$30,000 range. In fact, at a price point of \$25,500, General Motors offered nine vehicles (two Chevrolets, one Saturn, four Pontiacs, and two Buicks). Toyota, by contrast, offered two cars at that price.

The loss of coherence in General Motors' product line dramatically increased the amount of internal competition among its brands. Business leaders tend to see competition as a cleansing wind, blowing away waste and abuse. But the world is not that simple. If you invest in advertising or product development to take business away from a competitor, that may increase the corporate pie. But if you invest to take business away from a sister brand or division, that may make the whole corporate pie smaller. Not only are the investments in advertising and development partially wasted, but you have probably pushed down the prices of both brands.

In June 2009, General Motors declared bankruptcy and was bailed out by the Obama administration, making the U.S. Treasury the majority owner of the company. Under the protection of bankruptcy, the company dropped the Saturn, Pontiac, and Hummer brands.

Reversing the effects of entropy at Denton's took work, but the problem was not compounded by substantial inertia. Once the issues became evident, both leaders and most managers were willing to remedy the situation. By contrast, the problems affecting General Motors in

TOYOTA AND GENERAL MOTORS MODELS IN 2008

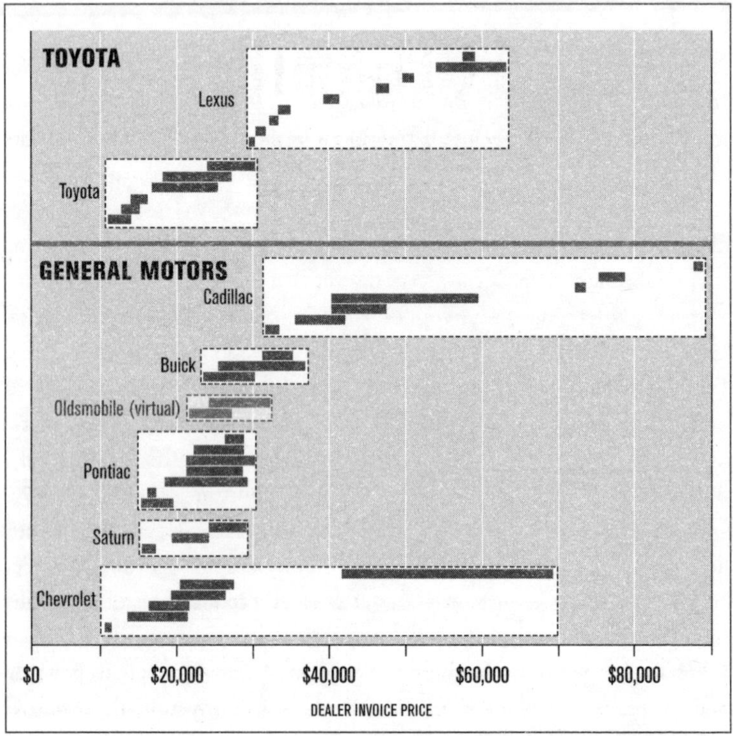

Each black bar is a model, and brands are collected within dotted rectangles. This chart leaves out SUVs, hybrid vehicles, vans, and all trucks. General Motors' Oldsmobile division was closed in 2001. The "virtual" products shown for Oldsmobile are the model year 2000 products price-inflated to 2008. The high-priced component of the Chevrolet division is the Corvette.

2008 were created by decades of entropy combined with inertia due to embedded obsolete routines, frozen culture, and chain-link systems. Bankruptcy may not be enough to fix this difficult situation. I expect to see the company fragment further and sell off valuable brand names over the next decade.

CHAPTER FIFTEEN

PUTTING IT TOGETHER

Nvidia, a designer of 3-D graphics chips, had a very rapid rise, shooting in a few short years past apparently stronger firms, including Intel, to dominate the high-performance 3-D graphics chip market. In 2007, *Forbes* named Nvidia the "Company of the Year," explaining that "Since Huang [CEO and founder] took the company public in 1999, Nvidia's shares have risen 21-fold, edging out even the mighty Apple over the same time period."[1]

Nvidia jumped from nowhere to dominance almost purely with good strategy. Follow the story of Nvidia and you will clearly see the kernel of a good strategy at work: diagnosis, guiding policy, and coherent action. You will also glimpse almost every building block of good strategy: intelligent anticipation, a guiding policy that reduced complexity, the power of design, focus, using advantage, riding a dynamic wave of change, and the important role played by the inertia and disarray of rivals.

There are chunks of commentary and analysis sprinkled through this story. They are set in smaller type and look just like this chunk of text. These commentaries shine a light on some of the strategic considerations revealed by the story, issues that may not be apparent on a first reading.

3-D GRAPHICS, UTAH, AND SGI

Nvidia's domain of 3-D graphics has nothing to do with wearing special glasses or with images that jump off the page or out of the movie screen. The "3-D" in 3-D graphics describes the process used to create an image appearing on a computer monitor. If you are looking at a still image, it may not be obvious that is was created with 3-D graphics technology—it is just a still image generated by dots of color. However, once you gain real-time control over the position of the imaginary camera, the difference is dramatic. Using a mouse or joystick to control the imaginary camera, you can explore a 3-D scene, viewing it from different positions, moving your viewpoint around objects to view them from behind or above, and moving into rooms and spaces at will. This is possible because the computer "knows" the three-dimensional structure of the whole scene.

Many of the fundamental components of modern 3-D graphics technology were developed at the University of Utah as part of a stream of research initiated by Professors Ivan Sutherland and David Evans in the late 1960s. While other computer science programs were teaching high theory, the Utah program was focused on the practical challenge of rendering 3-D images and building flight simulators. The program produced an astounding number of computer graphics superstars, including John Warnock, founder of Adobe Systems; Nolan Bushnell, founder of Atari; Edwin Catmull, cofounder of Pixar; and Jim Clark, founder of both Silicon Graphics and Netscape.

Jim Clark was at Stanford when he formed Silicon Graphics Inc. (SGI) in 1982. From its inception, SGI aimed to make the fastest high-resolution graphics workstations on the planet. SGI's influence on the graphics industry was immense. It not only provided the highest performing graphics hardware, it also developed a special graphics language (GL) that became the standard for many in the industry. Together, SGI's hardware and GL framed the problem of 3-D graphics in a way that became the dominant logic in 3-D graphics. Called the *graphics pipeline*, this approach rested on breaking the images in the scene into triangles, processing each triangle separately, and putting them back together again to form the final image. One famous use of this technology was rendering the velociraptors in *Jurassic Park*. In 1992, SGI finally realized the whole graphics pipeline in hardware—a system of banks of processors tied to a "triangle bus." Called the *Reality Engine*, the machine stood four feet high and was priced at over $100,000.

GAMERS

By the early 1990s it was evident that chips would eventually get fast enough to do good 3-D graphics on a PC. But would people use this capability? And, if they did, what would they use it for? Experts opined that, perhaps, people would take virtual trips to far-off cities via 3-D graphics, or that real estate agents would use 3-D graphics to give prospective buyers virtual walk-throughs of homes. But, as it turned out, the market was driven by a different application. The sudden rise of violent 3-D action games for the PC pulled 3-D chips onto the market.

Once, visiting a friend's home, I noticed his teenage son, Paul, playing a game called Myst on a personal computer. Paul's monitor showed a still picture of a scene. Paul clicked on the image of a bridge and the CD-ROM drive ground for a few seconds before the image changed to a view from the bridge. Music played, but nothing moved and each new scene took several seconds to render. It was the summer of 1994 and Myst was then a very popular game on personal computers.

Two weeks later, I visited again, and this time Paul was playing a game called Doom. The image on the screen showed a monster dropping into a room on a descending platform. The monster was firing red blobs at Paul, which streaked across the room. Paul was using the mouse and keyboard to bob and weave away from the red blobs. There was no delay. With each flick of his wrist, the image shifted as he scrambled around this three-dimensional space. He ran through a door and down a corridor. The monster followed. Paul ducked into an alcove, popping out into the corridor to let off a pistol shot and then back into the alcove to avoid return fire. He repeated this move three times and killed the monster. The visual effects were fast and the overall effect was a white-knuckle adrenaline rush.

Paul's father was a computer scientist at the prestigious École des Mines de Paris in Fontainebleau. Commenting on Doom, he said, "It is really remarkable. I would not have guessed one could render 3-D graphics that fast on a personal computer. There are programs that do 3-D rendering on PCs, but they take minutes or even hours to create a scene, not milliseconds."

Doom was the brainchild of John Carmack and John Romero, who had formed id Software in 1991. Their hit creations, especially Doom and Quake, redefined action games, introduced clever new technologies for displaying 3-D scenes on PCs, and moved the center of gravity of computer gaming innovation from the console industry to the PC platform. In addition, id Software was one of the first companies to adeptly exploit the then-new Internet. It distributed Doom, together with nine levels of play, without cost, online. Once addicted to the game, a player could purchase the registered version and play additional levels. With free distribution over the burgeoning Internet, Doom was an overnight sensation.

In 1996, id Software added online competitive play to its newly released game Quake. A player's PC, running Quake locally, could be connected via the Internet to other players so the group could share a game. Each player was able to move and to see the movements of the others' characters in real time—and to attack them. After Quake, most PC action games included online play as a feature.

Internet competitive gaming made the quality of 3-D graphics a high-stakes affair for the players. If you were a corporate executive reading research reports on the graphics industry, or studying statistics on chip sales, you would not appreciate this growing need. On the other hand, if you played Quake online, you quickly discovered that having a poor graphics system meant that your view of the situation was unclear and out of date—"lagged" in the jargon of the players—and you died over and over again. There is nothing like life-or-death stakes to generate a demand for an edge, and this online struggle among teenage boys created a sharply focused demand for high-performance 3-D graphics chips.

The first company to tap into this demand, and thereby cash in on PC-based 3-D graphics, was 1994 start-up 3dfx Interactive. Formed by three engineers, all alumni of Silicon Graphics, the company's first add-on graphics board, branded Voodoo, was tied to its own Glide proprietary graphics language. Glide was a cut-down version of Silicon Graphics' GL language, simplified so it could run on 3dfx's dedicated chips without help from the central processor. The first game written to use Glide was Tomb Raider, and the Voodoo board's real-time 3-D images of Lara Croft were the hit of the 1996 Electronic Entertainment Expo.

When a product gives a buyer an advantage in competition with others, there will be an especially rapid uptake of the product. When, for example, the first spreadsheet, VisiCalc, appeared in 1979, it provided an edge to MBA students, financial analysts, and other professionals who used it. VisiCalc was rapidly adopted and helped push personal computers from their hobby niche into the mainstream. Similarly, interactive online 3-D gaming created a demand for the edge provided by better and faster 3-D graphics.

3dfx's idea of setting a de facto standard came right off the pages of Geoffrey Moore's influential 1991 book, Crossing the Chasm: Marketing and Selling Technology Products to Mainstream Customers. *This book popularized academics' concepts of "network externalities" and "standards lock-in" and was the bible for people who wanted to be, or to spot, the next Microsoft. If enough game authors began to use 3dfx's Glide language, it would become the de facto standard in 3-D gaming and 3dfx would become the "architectural standard setter."*

STRATEGY AT NVIDIA

Nvidia was formed in 1993, by Jen-Hsun (pronounced Jen-Sun) Huang, Curtis Priem, and Chris Malachowsky. Huang had been an engineer-manager at LSI Logic. Priem and Malachowsky had been chief technology officer and vice president for hardware engineering, respectively, at Sun Microsystems.

At that time the industry was alive with talk about the coming multimedia revolution. However, at that moment existing audio cards worked with some software and not others. There was no standard way to compress or display video. CD-ROM drives were not fully standardized and there was no standard at all for 3-D graphics. Microsoft's Windows 95 and the wide use of Internet browsers were several years in the future.

Nvidia executive vice president of sales Jeff Fisher recalled that "the original dream was to be the Sound Blaster of multimedia." The company's first product, the NV1, introduced in 1995, was intended to establish a new multimedia standard. But its considerable audio capabilities were no better than the fast-moving competition's, and its quirky 3-D graphics approach did not catch on. The NV1 was a commercial flop.

Faced with the failure of the company's first product and the sudden rise of 3dfx, Jen-Hsun Huang reformulated the company's strategy. Key inputs came from a temporary technical advisory board made up of both insiders and expert outsiders.[2]

The new strategy was a sharp change in direction. Instead of multimedia, the company would focus on 3-D graphics for desktop PCs. Instead of its initial proprietary approach to graphics, the company would embrace the SGI-based triangle method. About the only thing that stayed unchanged was Nvidia's commitment to being a "fabless" chip company, focusing on design and outsourcing fabrication.

Progress in the semiconductor industry was based on reducing the size of a transistor. Smaller transistors meant more transistors per chip. Plus, smaller transistors were faster and consumed less power. The whole semiconductor industry coordinated around achieving a higher level of integration, based on smaller transistors, about every eighteen months. This rate of progress was called Moore's law. No one could jump much ahead of this pace because all the technologies, from photolithography to optical design to metal deposition to testing, had to advance in lockstep. The industry called this pattern of collective advance the "road map."

Nvidia's top management and its technology board sketched out a different road map, one that would push 3-D graphics performance at a much faster rate than Moore's law predicted. There were two factors crucial to making this happen. First, they anticipated a large jump in performance from putting more and more of the graphics pipeline onto a single chip. Second, most manufacturers, such as Intel, didn't keep cramming the maximum number of transistors possible onto a chip—they took advantage of increases in density to make more chips per wafer, thereby cutting the cost of a chip. Nvidia, by contrast, planned to use that extra density to add more parallel processors, boosting performance—a consequence of using the Utah-SGI "triangle bus" idea.

On the demand side, management judged that the market would buy virtually all the graphics processing power that could be provided. There was no sharp call for word processors or spreadsheets that ran one hundred times faster, but there was a very sharp demand for faster and more realistic graphics. Chief scientist David Kirk put it this way: "There is a virtually limitless demand for computational power in 3-D graphics. Given the architecture of the PC, there is only so much you can do with a more powerful CPU. But it is easy to use up one teraflop of graphics computing power. The GPU [graphics processing unit] is going to be the center of technology and value added in consumer computing."

With regard to a graphics language, Nvidia's management judged that it would be self-defeating to work with 3dfx's Glide. Therefore, they bet that Microsoft's new but unproven DirectX would become a workable high-performance graphics standard. They made this assessment after meeting with the DirectX team and finding them to be graphics enthusiasts who wanted to push the frontier as fast as possible.

Finally, CEO Jen-Hsun Huang believed that Nvidia could construct an advantage by breaking out of the industry's eighteen-month cycle. He reasoned that since it looked possible to advance graphics power three times faster than CPU power, Nvidia could deliver a substantial upgrade in graphics power every six months instead of every eighteen months.

This is the point where a bad strategist would have wrapped the concept of a faster development cycle in slogans about speed, power, and growth, and then sought to cash in by taking the company public. Instead, the Nvidia team designed a set of cohesive policies and actions to turn their guiding policy into reality.

The first step in executing the guiding policy was the establishment of three separate development teams. Each would work to an eighteen-month start-to-market cycle. With overlapping schedules, the three teams would deliver a new product every six months.

A two-month delay in a six-month cycle was much more serious than the same delay in an eighteen-month cycle. Accordingly, the second set of policies were meant to substantially reduce the delays and uncertainty in the development process.

A serious source of possible delays was a design error. After designing a chip, the company passed the design to a fabricator. After about one month, engineers received back the first samples of actual chips. If bugs were found in these chips, the design would have to be changed, new masks would have to be created, and a new fabrication run initiated. To address this source of possible delays, Nvidia invested heavily in simulation and emulation techniques and organized its chip design process around these methods.

Such tools were the forte of founder Chris Malachowsky, and he pushed the use of these tools for the formal verification of a chip's logic. Still, even if the logical design was correct, problems might arise in the physical functioning of the chip—issues related to time lags in the flow of electrons and to signal degradation. To protect against these kinds of problems, the company also invested in the more difficult task of simulating the electrical characteristics of the chip.

Another area of delay and concern was the creation of software drivers. Traditionally, drivers were written by the board makers, who could start driver development only *after* receiving working chips from the chip maker. In addition to the problem of delay, the new 3-D graphics methods demanded much more sophisticated drivers. Plus, board makers had mixed incentives about communicating driver problems back to the chip maker. For example, if Nvidia were selling chips to two board makers, each would tend to keep its learning and bug fixes to itself, so as not to benefit the other board maker. Finally, the current practice generated different drivers for identical chips on different boards, greatly complicating the tasks of keeping drivers current and of helping users update older drivers.

To address these problems, Nvidia took control of the creation and management of drivers for its chips, developing a unified driver architecture (UDA). All Nvidia chips would use the same driver software, easily downloaded over the Internet. The driver software would adapt itself to each chip by querying the chip about the actions it supported, and then the driver would tailor its commands to that chip. This approach would greatly simplify things for users because they would not have to be concerned with matching drivers to chips. It also meant that driver construction and distribution would be proprietary to Nvidia and taken out of the hands of the board makers.

To speed up driver development, the company made a significant investment in emulation facilities.[3] These were complex hardware "mock-ups" of new chips that allowed driver development to begin four to six months before the first true chips appeared.

The benefit of a faster cycle is that the product will be best in class more often. Compared to a competitor working on an eighteen-month cycle, Nvidia's six-month cycle would mean that its chip would be the better product about 83 percent of the time. Plus, there is the constant buzz surrounding new product introductions, a substitute for expensive advertising. As a further plus, the faster company's engineers will get more experience and, perhaps, learn more about the tricks of turning the technology into product.

Implementing the new strategy, Nvidia invested its remaining cash in emulation equipment and in engineering a new chip. Released in August 1997 as the RIVA 128, it received high marks from reviewers for its speed and resolution, but many judged that rival 3dfx's Voodoo had smoother images. The chip was a moderate success, keeping the company alive and providing funds to pay for more development.

With the next new chip, the RIVA TNT, released in 1998, Nvidia began to hit its stride. Appearing in coordination with Microsoft's new DirectX 6, it was the first chip to use the new unified driver architecture. The TNT and its "spring refresh," the TNT2, matched or surpassed the competition on most measures. Seven months after the TNT2, Nvidia released the GeForce 256, moving the 3-D graphics industry into new territory. GeForce 256 had nearly twenty-three million transistors, twice the complexity of Intel's Pentium II CPU. Its floating point calculation capacity was 50 gigaflops, the equivalent of the Cray T3D supercomputer. Chief scientist David Kirk told me: "At Nvidia, our technical path has been to crawl up the graphics pipeline. At each stage we put more operations onto specialized silicon, where performance improved by a factor of ten compared to the CPU. . . . With GeForce we got all of Silicon Graphics' pipeline steps on one $100 chip, running faster than the Reality Engine, which had cost $100,000 dollars in 1992."

As Nvidia gained leadership in performance, it began to focus even more intensely on the problems of the delays, driver problems, and extra costs created by its board makers. First, management tried to negotiate a new arrangement with Diamond Multimedia but were rebuffed because Diamond did not want to see a decrease in its margins.

A senior team then traveled to Dell and made a presentation. They described the obstacles created by current industry practices, showed the economic benefits of the unified driver architecture, and pointed out the lower prices contract board manufacturers could deliver. Dell reacted positively and agreed to offer boards with Nvidia chips, manufactured by Celestica Hong Kong Ltd. In the months and years to come, Nvidia increasingly relied on contract electronics manufacturers for board production and distribution. The contract manufacturers were free to brand the board as they chose; most chose to emphasize the Nvidia name.

Over the next five years, Nvidia continued its pattern of rapid releases, pushing the envelope in 3-D graphics capabilities. During the 1997–2001 period, Nvidia obtained extraordinary gains from integrating the graphics pipeline onto a single chip, achieving a 157 percent average annual gain in performance.* From 2002 to 2007, it achieved an annual performance gain averaging 62 percent per year, about as much as was possible, given the general movement of semiconductor technology. Intel CPUs, for example, increased their processing power (millions of operations per second) at about the same rate per year during that period. The difference is that the effects of Intel's performance increases have been substantially dulled by hardware and software bottlenecks it cannot control. On the other hand, as Nvidia's leaders envisioned, the performance of graphics chips is experienced directly and immediately by users. Enthusiasts continued to wait anxiously for each new improvement.

A change in technology will often set in motion a change in industry structure. In this case, the relationship between the chip maker and the board maker altered. Interestingly, few foresaw the importance of this shift. A standard approach to such a problem in established industries would be to have certain board makers work directly with Nvidia's emulators early in the development cycle. This, however, would increase a board maker's bargaining power and the leakage of proprietary knowledge to rivals.

With regard to Diamond Multimedia, Nvidia management believed that the shift from 2-D to 3-D graphics had eliminated most of Diamond's traditional value added. Yet companies do not slide quietly into the darkness. Diamond should have made the deal with Nvidia, but it elected to try to maintain its high margins (about 25 percent).

Standard industry analysis would classify powerful buyers such as Dell as a negative for Nvidia. But without powerful PC makers such as Dell and HP, Diamond might have maintained its hold on retail channels. It was the power of these concentrated buyers that allowed Nvidia to skate around Diamond's established brand. Note that, in general, if you have a "me-too" product, you prefer fragmented retail buyers. On the other hand, if you have a better product, a powerful buyer such as Dell can help it see the light of day.

---

* Here, performance is measured as "fillrate," the number of pixels output per second.

THE COMPETITION

For Nvidia's strategy in 3-D graphics to work, other firms would have to fall by the wayside, not being able to keep up. To a large extent, that is exactly what happened. Whenever a company succeeds greatly there is a complementary story of impeded competitive response. Sometimes the impediment is the innovator's patent or similar protection, but more often it is an unwillingness or inability to replicate the innovator's policies. Nvidia bet that it could rapidly charge up the graphics pipeline, but it also bet that key rivals would not be able to replicate its fast-release cycle.

Rival 3dfx followed spurious advice from Wall Street and the marketing instincts of a new CEO, setting out after the mass market. Instead of capitalizing on its leadership with enthusiasts, it allocated engineers away from the cutting edge to work on lower-tech boards, ramped up advertising in imitation of the "Intel Inside" campaign, and bought board maker STB Systems. Spreading its resources too thin, it attempted to compensate by stretching the goals for its next high-performance chip beyond the competencies of its development process. In the last months of 2000, 3dfx closed its doors, selling its patents, brands, and inventory to Nvidia, where many of its talented engineers wound up working. A surface reading of history makes it look like 3dfx did itself in with too many changes of direction. The deeper reality was that Nvidia's carefully crafted fast-release cycle induced 3dfx's less coordinated responses. As Hannibal did to Rome at Cannae, Nvidia enticed its rival into overreaching.

Rival Intel was unable to compete in the high-performance 3-D graphics market. One of the world's great companies, a technological powerhouse, Intel was, nevertheless, not infinitely flexible. According to industry analyst Jon Peddie, "Intel developed the i740 with the same processes and same approach that it used to develop its CPUs. This didn't work in the extremely competitive 3-D graphics industry. Intel's development cycle was 18–24 months, not 6–12 months. It didn't adapt to this quick development cycle. It wasn't about to redesign its whole development and fabrication process just for a sideline business."[4]

Intel did, however, succeed in dominating the standard 2-D graphics business by incorporating its offerings in its motherboard chipsets. In 2007, Intel announced a second plan to enter the high-performance 3-D graphics business but then canceled the project in December 2009.

At rival Silicon Graphics, founder Jim Clark left the company in 1994. The new CEO, Ed McCracken, aimed the firm at selling large workstations and servers to corporate America, instructing his lieutenants to "think out of the box and figure out how to grow 50 percent."[5] They attempted to engineer growth through the acquisition of a raft of workstation firms.

The challenge for SGI and its acquired firms was that Windows-Intel-based workstations were gaining in power and surpassing those based on their proprietary processors and operating systems. The strategy of agglomeration did nothing to meet that challenge. Silicon Graphics, the fount of so many of the ideas and personnel that sparked 3-D graphics, never entered PC-based 3-D graphics. Once having a market capitalization of more than $7 billion, it declared bankruptcy in 2006.

McCracken's "grow by 50 percent" is classic bad strategy. It is the kind of nonsense that passes for strategy in too many companies. First, he was setting a goal, not designing a way to deal with his company's challenge. Second, growth is the outcome of a successful strategy, and attempts to engineer growth are exercises in magical thinking. In this case, the growth SGI engineered was accomplished by rolling up a number of other firms whose workstation strategies had also run out of steam.

Nvidia's one serious competitor was, and remains, ATI Technologies. At first, ATI seemed to be left in the dust by Nvidia's six-month release cycle. Then, in 2000, it bought ArtX, a company formed by still another cadre of ex–Silicon Graphics engineers. The new blood made an immediate difference. ATI moved to a six-month release cycle and began to introduce chips that matched Nvidia's in performance. In 2006, CPU maker Advanced Micro Devices (AMD), Intel's archrival, orchestrated a merger with ATI.

Passing on ArtX was a strategic blunder by Nvidia. The network of human capital in this industry was sparse and well understood. Had there been many pockets of talent like ArtX, acquiring it would make no sense. But even though Nvidia did not need the extra expertise, acquiring it would deny these scarce competencies to a competitor.

WHAT NEXT?

Nvidia's chosen field is one of the fastest moving and most competitive on the planet. Its successful strategy of 1998–2008 does not ensure enduring success. In particular, by 2009 the waves of change Nvidia had exploited in its rise were waning. The SGI pipeline was fully realized. Most gamers are no longer waiting breathlessly for the next graphics chip. DirectX had become so complex that few game companies can master all of its features.

Strategically, Nvidia is presently engaged in a two-pronged pincer movement. One initiative has been opening up access to the computing power of its graphics chips. Each graphics processor contains hundreds of separate floating-point processors. Its new hardware supporting this concept is called Tesla and delivers desktop supercomputing. In November 2010, Chinese researchers announced the world's fastest supercomputer—powered by Nvidia's Tesla graphics chips.

The second arm of the pincer is Tegra—a complete system on a chip. This tactic is called "disruption from below" and aims to upset the Intel-AMD-Windows hegemony by building on a much simpler, more efficient platform. The chip is aimed at the makers of smart phones, netbooks, and game consoles. In a demonstration, Nvidia showed a lightweight Tegra-based device capable of playing a high-definition movie for ten hours on a single battery charge.

This pincer movement offers two ways to succeed and makes trouble for competitors. But there are many difficulties on both paths, and both are far from sure things.

◆

PART III

THINKING LIKE A STRATEGIST

In creating strategy, it is often important to take on the viewpoints of others, seeing how the situation looks to a rival or to a customer. Advice to do this is both often given and taken. Yet this advice skips over what is possibly the most useful shift in viewpoint: thinking about your own thinking.

Our intentions do not fully control our thoughts. We become acutely aware of this when we are unable to suppress undesired ruminations about risk, disease, and death.* A great deal of human thought is not intentional—it just happens. One consequence is that leaders often generate ideas and strategies without paying attention to their internal process of creation and testing.

This section of the book presents a number of ways of thinking about thinking that can help you create better strategies. Chapter 16, "The Science of Strategy," explores the analogy between a strategy

* See, for instance, James S. Uleman and John A. Bargh, eds., *Unintended Thought* (New York: Guilford Press, 1989).

and a scientific hypothesis. Each is an inductive leap that must be subjected to both logical and empirical tests before its validity can be ascertained. Chapter 17, "Using Your Head," presents some specific techniques that can be helpful in expanding the scope of your thinking about strategy and in subjecting your ideas to deeper criticism. Chapter 18, "Keeping Your Head," is designed to sharpen your sensitivity to the need to form an independent judgment about important issues. It tells the stories of the Global Crossing debacle and the financial crisis of 2008 to illustrate the ways in which many leaders and analysts abandoned their judgment to the excitements of the crowd.

◆

CHAPTER SIXTEEN

THE SCIENCE OF STRATEGY

Good strategy is built on functional knowledge about what works, what doesn't, and why. Generally available functional knowledge is essential, but because it is available to all, it can rarely be decisive. The most precious functional knowledge is proprietary, available only to your organization.

An organization creates pools of proprietary functional knowledge by actively exploring its chosen arena in a process called *scientific empiricism*. Good strategy rests on a hard-won base of such knowledge, and any new strategy presents the opportunity to generate it. A new strategy is, in the language of science, a hypothesis, and its implementation is an experiment. As results appear, good leaders learn more about what does and doesn't work and adjust their strategies accordingly.

STRATEGY IS A HYPOTHESIS

Standing in the hangar-sized Hughes Electronics fabrication facility, I marvel at the huge communications satellite. It gleams and sparkles like a jewel, each part fashioned with exquisite precision. A modern cathedral, the eighteen-thousand-pound device embodies the highest skills and knowledge of my civilization. In it, the technologies of orbital mechanics, solar power, three-axis orientation, and sophisticated computation, as well as the reception, amplification, and beaming of electromagnetic waves over entire continents, are woven together into a working harmony that will last decades unattended in stationary orbit, 22,500 miles above Earth's surface.

I am working with Hughes Electronics to help managers develop strategies for their businesses: communications satellites, spy satellites, missile systems, and various other aerospace activities. My clients are engineers who have risen to management positions by ability at performing, organizing, and directing technical work.

I had started by having them look at various examples of competitive strategy. A month later we did a short study of the communications satellite business. Today we are digging into the problem of creating strategies for the various business units. As we try to make progress, there is a growing sense of frustration. Partway into the session, Barry, an experienced engineering manager, speaks for several others, saying: "This strategy stuff is nonsense. Give me a break! There is no clear theory. Look, what we need is a way of knowing what will happen if we do A, versus what will happen if we do B. Then we can work out what will be the best strategy. We are actually very good at planning here. You can't build a major aerospace system without meticulous planning. But this strategy stuff seems vacuous."

Barry's attack hits home. I had once been an engineer, and I know an engineer doesn't design a bridge that *might* hold its load. An engineer starts with complexity and crafts certainty. I knew what it was like to be careful, to balance literally thousands of considerations in making a system work. I knew how maddening it was to move from that world to business, where an executive can choose an action based on gut feel and, even a year later, no one will know whether it was a good choice.

I search my mind for a response. Struggling for an answer, I make a connection between business strategy and the process of science:

> Where does scientific knowledge come from? You know the process. A good scientist pushes to the edge of knowledge and then reaches beyond, forming a conjecture—a hypothesis—about how things work in that unknown territory. If the scientist avoids the

edge, working with what is already well known and established, life will be comfortable, but there will be neither fame nor honor.

In the same way, a good business strategy deals with the edge between the known and the unknown. Again, it is competition with others that pushes us to edges of knowledge. Only there are found the opportunities to keep ahead of rivals. There is no avoiding it. That uneasy sense of ambiguity you feel is real. It is the scent of opportunity.

In science, you first test a new conjecture against known laws and experience. Is the new hypothesis contradicted by basic principles or by the results of past experiments? If the hypothesis survives that test, the scientist has to devise a real-world test—an experiment—to see how well the hypothesis stands up.

Similarly, we test a new strategic insight against well-established principles and against our accumulated knowledge about the business. If it passes those hurdles, we are faced with trying it out and seeing what happens.

Given that we are working on the edge, asking for a strategy that is guaranteed to work is like asking a scientist for a hypothesis that is guaranteed to be true—it is a dumb request. The problem of coming up with a good strategy has the same logical structure as the problem of coming up with a good scientific hypothesis. The key differences are that most scientific knowledge is broadly shared, whereas you are working with accumulated wisdom about your business and your industry that is unlike anyone else's.

A good strategy is, in the end, a hypothesis about what will work. Not a wild theory, but an educated judgment. And there isn't anyone more educated about your businesses than the group in this room.

This concept breaks the impasse. After some discussion, the group begins to work with the notion that a strategy is a hypothesis—an educated guess—about what will work. After a while, Barry starts to articulate his own judgments, saying "I think in my business we can . . ."

When engineers use a nice clean deductive system to solve a problem, they call it *winding the crank.* By this they mean that it may be hard work, but that the nature and quality of the output depends on the machine (the chosen system of deduction), not on the skill of the crank winder. Later, looking back, I realize the group had expected strategy to be an exercise in crank winding. They had expected that I would give them a "logical machine" that they could use to deduce business plans—a system for generating forecasts and actions.

ENLIGHTENMENT AND SCIENCE

If new insights or ideas are not needed, deduction is sufficient. There can be times when results are fine, when no new opportunities seem to have developed and no new risks have appeared. Then, the logical answer to the strategy question is simply "Keep it up, do more of the same." But in a world of change and flux, "more of the same" is rarely the right answer. In a changing world, a good strategy must have an *entrepreneurial* component. That is, it must embody some ideas or insights into new combinations of resources for dealing with new risks and opportunities.

The problem with treating strategy as a crank-winding exercise is that systems of deduction and computation do not produce new interesting ideas, no matter how hard one winds the crank. Even in pure mathematics, the ultimate deductive system, stating and proving an interesting new theorem is a profoundly creative act.

Treating strategy like a problem in deduction *assumes that anything worth knowing is already known*—that only computation is required. Like computation, deduction applies a fixed set of logical rules to a fixed set of known facts. For example, *given* Newton's law of gravity, one can deduce (calculate) the period of Mars's orbit around the sun. Or *given* the costs and capacities of tankers, pipelines, and refineries, one can optimize the flow of oil and refined product within an integrated oil company. If everything worth knowing is already known, the problem of action reduces to crank winding.

The presumption that all important knowledge is already known, or available through consultation with authorities, deadens innovation. It is this presumption that stifles change in traditional societies and blocks improvement in organizations and societies that come to believe that their way is the best way. To generate a strategy, one must put aside the comfort and security of pure deduction and launch into the murkier waters of induction, analogy, judgment, and insight.

■ ■ ■

Today we find it hard to comprehend that reason slumbered in the Western world for more than a thousand years. After the fall of Rome, inquiry was blocked by the omnipresent assumption that all important knowledge had already been revealed. Intellectual energy was channeled toward faith, art, battle, and self-discipline. Then, in the seventeenth century, something truly remarkable happened: Western Europe came alive with argument and debate. Men searched for first principles in science, politics, and philosophy, purposefully pushing aside the authority of power, faith, and custom. The period has become known as the *Enlightenment* (1630–1789). The leaders of the Enlightenment—Descartes, Hobbes, Hume, Jefferson, Leibniz, Locke, Newton, Paine, Smith, and Voltaire, to name a few—were the first to surpass the high point of rational inquiry achieved two thousand years earlier, in the era of Plato and Aristotle.

The intellectual trigger for the Enlightenment was Galileo Galilei's heresy trial. Born in Pisa, Italy, Galileo held a position in mathematics in Venice. In 1609, word of a spyglass invented by the Dutch reached him. He thought through the optics of such a device and ground lenses to build his own, better than anything the Dutch had. Looking at the night sky, he made astounding discoveries within a matter of weeks—he was the first to see and report mountains on the moon, the individual stars of the Milky Way, the phases of Venus, and the four largest moons of Jupiter.

At that time two distinct theories of celestial motion competed for acceptance: The Ptolemaic (sometimes called Aristotelian) held that Earth was the still center and that the heavens revolved about it. By contrast, the Copernican view held that the sun was the center, the stars immobile, and that Earth and the other planets revolved about the sun. Most practicing astronomers were Copernicans because the system gave more accurate predictions. Although the heliocentric model contradicted a number of biblical passages, the church in Rome had treated the astronomers' use of the theory as a set of procedures for calculation rather than as a worldview.

With the spreading fame of Galileo's discoveries, European dinner chatter turned to astronomy and to the Copernican theory. To Galileo, the phases and motion of Venus showed that it orbited the sun, not Earth, and his careful measurements of the periods of Jupiter's moons suggested that Earth did as well. In 1616, Galileo wrote "Letter to the Grand Duchess Christina," attacking the Ptolemaic system. The cardinals of the Inquisition ruled that Galileo's position was forbidden but took no action. In 1630, Galileo again wrote on the subject. This time the Inquisition sentenced him to arrest for the rest of his life. He was ordered not to believe in the Copernican system or to write about it.

The story of Galileo sped through Europe. Galileo's name became a rallying cry for those seeking to break the manacles on thought imposed by church and state. He died under house arrest in 1642. At that moment, John Locke, the towering philosopher of the Enlightenment, was ten and, not quite one year later, Isaac Newton was born.* Newton would invent calculus and show that the planets' orbits about the sun obeyed a natural law more precise and less forgiving than the commands of any cardinal, pope, or king. Locke would extend the concept of such natural laws to society and proclaim, "The natural liberty of man is to be free from any superior power on earth, and not to be under the will or legislative authority of man, but to have only the law of Nature for his rule."[1] It was Locke's natural liberty that, a century later, Thomas Jefferson penned into American history when he wrote "We hold these truths to be self-evident, that all men are created equal, that they are endowed by their Creator with certain unalienable rights, that among these are life, liberty and the pursuit of happiness."

If thought is freed from the bonds of human authority, how do people know what to believe? The Enlightenment's answer was *scientific*

* The standard date for Newton's birth is December 25, 1642. However, England's calendar at that time was Julian and the Vatican's was Gregorian. In the Gregorian calendar, Galileo died on January 8, 1642, and Newton was born on January 4, 1643, not quite one year later.

empiricism—we believe our senses and the data our instruments report to our senses. A scientist tests a belief by experiment or by the analysis of real-world data. With false beliefs thrown aside, we shall be left with the truth. This is the centerpiece of scientific thinking—the idea of *refutation*. Unless an idea can possibly be proved false by observable fact, it is not scientific. Other kinds of knowledge, such as self-knowledge and spiritual insight, are not ruled out, but such knowings are not scientific.

In science, a new idea or theory is called a *hypothesis,* a fancy word for a testable explanation for something that happens. (Of course, better scientists have better hypotheses.) The new theory cannot have been deduced from existing knowledge, else it wouldn't be new! It arises as an insight or creative judgment. The heart of the scientific method is that the *worth* of a hypothesis is determined by empirical data drawn from the physical world, not by the author's popularity, caste, or wealth. That is the radical revolution wrought by the Enlightenment.

A strategy is, like a scientific hypothesis, an educated prediction of how the world works. The ultimate worth of a strategy is determined by its success, not its acceptability to a council of philosophers or a board of editors. Good strategy work is necessarily empirical and pragmatic. Especially in business, whatever grand notions a person may have about the products or services the world might need, or about human behavior, or about how organizations should be managed, what does not actually "work" cannot long survive.

In science one seeks explanations for broad classes of events and phenomena; in business one seeks to understand and predict a more particular situation. But the lack of universality does not make business unscientific. Science is a method, not an outcome, and the basic method of good businesspeople is intense attention to data and to what works.

ANOMALIES

An anomaly is a fact that doesn't fit received wisdom. To a certain kind of mind, an anomaly is an annoying blemish on the perfect skin of explanation. But to others, an anomaly marks an opportunity to learn something, perhaps something very valuable. In science, anomalies are the frontier, where the action is.

When I was a graduate student living on a tight budget, an enlarged photograph of M31, the Great Nebula in Andromeda, served as my living room decoration. This familiar image shows a flattish disklike spiral, tilted up on the right by about 30 degrees, with a bright bulbous central core. M31 is a galaxy—a collection of stars, gas, and dust slowly rotating in space. The typical galaxy contains billions of stars, and the visible universe contains about 125 million galaxies.

From a great distance, our own Milky Way galaxy would probably look something like M31. In the Milky Way, our sun, Sol, lies about one-third of the way out from the center, in what is called the Orion Arm. Sol and her planets orbit the core of the galaxy once every 240 million years, traveling at a speed of 137 miles per second. Stars farther out from the center take longer than Sol to complete a revolution; those closer to the center complete their orbits about the core more quickly.

Since my days in graduate school, a major anomaly has been discovered with regard to galaxies like ours and M31. Because most of the mass of a galaxy lies in its dense bright core, the theory of gravity predicts that stars farther out from the core should not only take longer to orbit the core, they should also travel more slowly through space in their longer orbits around the core. More precisely, a star's speed in its swing about the core should be proportional to the inverse square root of its distance from the center. A star one-half as far out from the core as Sol should speed through space at *four times* Sol's speed. But measurements of many galaxies began to appear in the early 1980s showing that almost all of the stars in the spiral orbit at about the *same* speed, regardless of their distance from the core! Galactic "rotation curves" were flat. This is truly a huge anomaly. Something very basic about our worldview seems wrong.

This puzzle of galactic rotation drives a great deal of modern research in astronomy. Two hypotheses are presently under investigation. The favorite is that the glowing star matter we photograph is only about 10 percent of the physical universe—the rest is "dark matter"—not simply unlighted matter, but a special kind of matter that doesn't interact with light. By imagining galaxies as embedded in an invisible blob of dark matter, the anomaly is resolved by the gravity of this hidden dark mass. But, of course, this leaves open a great many other questions about the hypothesized dark matter. The other theory, less popular, is that received theories of gravity—Newton's and Einstein's—are wrong. Thus, the simple facts of galactic structure lead in amazing directions—either most of the universe is invisible dark matter, or gravitation theory is incorrect.

An anomaly like this appears through comparison. Merely looking at M31 does not suggest puzzles other than the overall mystery of creation. But as Sherlock Holmes said to Watson, "You see, but you do not observe." The anomalies are not in nature but in the mind of the acute observer, revealed by a comparison between the facts and refined expectations.

ESPRESSO ANOMALY

In 1983, Howard Schultz noticed an anomaly and from that insight a fascinating new business was eventually born. At that time, Schultz was the marketing and retail operations manager for a tiny chain of Seattle stores selling dark-roasted coffee beans. On a visit to Italy, Schultz discovered the Italian espresso experience. He recalled his first visit to an espresso bar in Milan:

> A tall thin man greeted me cheerfully, "*Buon giorno!*" as he pressed down on a metal bar and a huge hiss of steam escaped. He handed a tiny porcelain demitasse of espresso to one of the three people who were standing elbow to elbow at the counter. Next came a handcrafted cappuccino, topped with a head of perfect white foam. The barista moved so gracefully that it looked as though he were grinding coffee beans, pulling shots of espresso, and steaming milk at the same time, all while conversing merrily with his customers. It was great theater. . . .
>
> It was on that day I discovered the ritual and romance of coffee bars in Italy. I saw how popular they were, and how vibrant. Each one had its own unique character, but there was one com-

> mon thread: the camaraderie between the customers, who knew each other well, and the barista, who was performing with flair. At that time, there were 200,000 coffee bars in Italy, and 1,500 alone in the city of Milan, a city the size of Philadelphia.[2]

With a retailer's eye, Schultz also noticed the rapid customer turnover at the espresso bars and the relatively high prices being paid for coffee.

For Schultz, the experience in Milan was an anomaly. In Seattle, the market for dark-roasted arabica beans was a niche, populated by a small but growing group of especially discerning buyers. But the vast majority of people in Seattle, and in America—even the well-to-do—drank cheap, bland coffee. In Milan, expensive high-quality coffee was not a niche product but the mass-market product. And there was a further anomaly: in the United States, fast food meant cheap food and plastic surroundings. In Milan he saw "fast coffee" that was expensive and served in a lively social atmosphere, so different from that of an American Main Street diner or coffee shop. Americans, especially those in the Northwest, were at least as wealthy as Italians. Why should they drink "bad" coffee and not enjoy the pleasures of an espresso latte in a social setting?

Schultz formed a strategic hypothesis—*the Italian espresso experience could be re-created in America and the public would embrace it*. He returned to Seattle and explained his idea to the two owners of the company he worked for—the Starbucks Coffee Company. They listened and gave him a small space to try to brew up espresso drinks, but they did not share his belief in the project. They thought that Starbucks' strengths and purpose were in buying, roasting, and retailing fine arabica coffees, not in running an espresso bar. In addition, they thought that espresso coffee restaurants were nothing new, being a niche business frequented by bohemians, beatniks, hippies, and Gen X nocturnals, depending on the era.

COFFEE DIVERGENCE

When Howard Schultz pitched his proposal to the owners of Starbucks, the coffee shop was hardly a new idea. Arabs began to brew coffee six hundred years ago, and the first European coffee shop opened its doors in Oxford, England, in 1652 when Isaac Newton was ten years old. The cause of the Enlightenment may have been the Copernican revolution and the Protestant Reformation, but coffee was its daily fuel.

In England, coffeehouses developed a unique culture, far different from that of taverns. In coffeehouses, a penny would buy a table for the day, with entrance permitted to anyone with good clothes. Instead of inebriated revelry, or morose self-reflection, coffeehouses stimulated energetic talk and debate. Books and newspapers were available there, and many people used coffeehouses as their postal addresses. Newton frequented the Grecian (where he was seen to dissect a dolphin); John Dryden held forth at Will's. Much later, Adam Smith finished *The Wealth of Nations* at the British Coffee House (Cockspur Street) that was a London hangout for Scottish thinkers. Joseph Addison, Alexander Pope, and Jonathan Swift held forth at Buttons.

In England, tea eventually replaced coffee as the daytime beverage of choice. London coffeehouses gradually disappeared, morphing into private clubs, restaurants, and businesses. Edward Lloyd's coffeehouse became Lloyds of London and Jonathan's coffeehouse in "Change Alley" became the London Stock Exchange, where runners are still called "waiters."

In the United States, history took a different course. The Boston Tea Party, the Revolution, and the War of 1812 interrupted trade in tea, reviving interest in coffee. Americans found in coffee an inexpensive tea substitute that could be drunk in quantity. By 1820, the transition was complete, and the United States became the largest market for coffee in the world.

In the early twentieth century, an alternative to the original Ethiopian coffee tree (arabica) was found in the Congo—the robusta coffee plant. The robusta plant grew faster, was more disease resistant, was easier to harvest, and contained more caffeine. It also had a harsher, less mellow taste. But mixing robusta with arabica took off much of the harsh edge, especially if you added sugar and cream. The new inexpensive bean was the key to supercharging the growing American coffee habit. Instant coffee was the final step in the path that took American coffee-drinking practices a great distance from their European origins.

While Americans were developing robusta and instant coffee, Italian Luigi Bezzera invented the espresso machine (1901). This device made a cup of coffee by passing hot steam through a charge of ground-roasted coffee beans. The reaction of the steam and the coffee produced a rich, almost syrupy, beverage. The theory was that the quick brewing time prevented the extraction of bitter coffee oils and reduced the amount of caffeine. A small porcelain cup of Italian espresso has a brown foamy *crema* on its surface, which fades within a minute. The *crema* layer traps aromatics and volatile flavors. The drink could not be easily prepared at home as it needed high-pressure steam and expensive equipment and was quite labor intensive. Italian espresso bars became popular places for a quick pick-me-up and urban social interaction.

TESTING THE HYPOTHESIS

A deep problem Schultz faced was that his vision required a radical change in consumer tastes and habits. What he observed in Milan was not just a different business model but the result of several hundred years of divergent social history. In the United States, coffee had emerged as a bland tea substitute to be drunk both at meals and at breaks throughout the day. In southern Europe, coffee was an alcohol substitute, taken in small strong doses at lively "bars." Whether he knew it or not, Schultz wanted to do more than just open a coffee shop; he wanted to change American tastes and habits.

Schultz's second problem was that there seemed nothing new about coffee, espresso, coffee bars, or espresso shops. Millions of other Americans had traveled to Italy and experienced Italian espresso bars. Knowledge about these businesses was hardly privileged. To expect to make money from a new business, the entrepreneur should know something that others do not, or have control of a scarce and valuable resource. The delicacy in the situation was that Schultz's proprietary information was only a glimmer in his mind, a mood, a feeling. Others, exposed to exactly the same information and experiences, did not have this insight or feeling. The privacy of his insight was both blessing and curse. Were it easily shared with others, Schultz himself would have been irrelevant. But because it could not be fully shared, it was difficult to convince others to back the project. Luckily for Schultz, his hypothesis could be tested without a vast investment. Opening a single espresso bar would cost several hundred thousand dollars, but not the hundreds of millions or billions that some ventures require.

After some time, Schultz left Starbucks to start his own shop (Il Giornale). The new shop was a direct copy of an Italian espresso bar. In it, he "didn't want anything to dilute the integrity of the espresso and the Italian coffee experience."[3] The seven-hundred-square-foot space had Italian decor and no chairs—it was a stand-up bar just like the bars in Milan. Shots of espresso were served in small porcelain cups. Opera music played in the background, the waiters wore formal shirts and bow ties, and the menu was peppered with Italian.

Had Schultz stuck to this initial concept, Il Giornale would have remained a single small espresso bar. But, like a good scientist who carefully studies the results of experiments, Schultz and his team were alert to customer response. Il Giornale, once started, became a living experiment.

One of the most important resources a business can have is valuable *privileged* information—that is, knowing something that others do not. There is nothing arcane or illicit about such information—it is generated every day in every operating business. All alert businesspeople can know more about their own customers, their own products, and their own production technology than anyone else in the world. Thus, *once Schultz initiated business operations, he began to accumulate privileged information*.

As knowledge accumulated, he altered policies. He took the Italian off the menu, then eliminated the opera music. He knew the baristas were central, but he did away with their vests and bow ties. He departed from the Milanese model and put in chairs for the sit-down trade. Over more time, Schultz discovered that Americans wanted takeout coffee so he introduced paper cups. Americans wanted nonfat milk in their lattes, so, after a great deal of soul searching, he allowed nonfat milk. In the technical jargon of international business, he gradually "localized" the Italian espresso bar to American tastes.

In 1987, his company bought out Starbucks' retail operations and adopted the Starbucks name. The new firm combined the old Starbucks business of selling dark-roasted arabica coffee beans with the new one of operating espresso bars. By 1990, the company was profitable. In 1992, it went public with 125 stores and two thousand employees.

By 2001, Starbucks had become an American icon, with 4,700 worldwide outlets and $2.6 billion in revenue. The bulk of its revenues came from selling coffee drinks—the company called them *handcrafted beverages*. The rest came from the sale of coffee beans, some other food items in its coffee bars, and licensing agreements with food-service firms. Only a few years before, "coffee" had been seventy-five cents and came in a plastic foam cup. Now the urban landscape is peppered with Starbucks outlets, and the sight of young professionals sipping pint-sized three-dollar takeout lattes has become commonplace.

Howard Schultz envisioned an Italian espresso bar in Seattle. He tested this hypothesis and found it wanting. But the test produced additional information, so he modified his hypothesis and retested. After hundreds of iterations, the original hypothesis has long since vanished, replaced by a myriad of new hypotheses, each covering some aspect of the growing, evolving business. This process of learning—hypothesis, data, anomaly, new hypothesis, data, and so on—is called *scientific induction* and is a critical element of every successful business.

CAPTURING PROPRIETARY INFORMATION

One element of Starbucks' success was that many people were willing to pay premium prices for its "handcrafted" beverages served in urban oasis settings. But you should always consider the competition. What kept the competition at bay for so many years? In the spring of 2001, seeking an answer to this question, I traveled to Paris and talked to Joe Santos. Joe was then a strategy instructor at INSEAD, the international school of management in France. But before he joined the academy, Joe Santos had been the CEO of Segafredo Zanetti, a major Italian coffee company and an important European supplier of espresso roasts to restaurants and espresso bars.

"Joe," I asked, "espresso coffee was your specialty and the specialty of a number of big European companies. Why did Starbucks pick up this opportunity rather than one of the big espresso roasters? Surely you saw what was happening by the late 1980s?"

In response, Joe explained that it was difficult to react because the European industry had difficulty understanding Starbucks:

> We were aware of Starbucks, but you must understand the issue of scale. Segafredo supplies over fifty thousand different cafés and restaurants each week. That is a huge volume, and Starbucks was quite small. And the large American roasters, Kraft, Sara Lee, and P&G, were all focused on the mass market.*
>
> It was also difficult, from a European perspective, to understand exactly what Starbucks was. In Europe, coffee roasters are distinct from restaurants. Although Starbucks was known as a coffee company, it was really a retailer. McDonald's is a retailer, but it is never confused with a "beef" company! Yet Starbucks was called a "coffee company," and Americans seemed to think that its coffee was special.
>
> Europeans see Starbucks as "American coffee." Americans think Starbucks is an Italian espresso bar. But at an Italian espresso bar, everyone drinks standing up at the bar; almost everyone takes a small cup of pure espresso in a tiny porcelain cup. Café-latte is for breakfast only, or for children. There is no takeout; there are no tables. The coffee is not a restaurant brand but is supplied by one of the major coffee companies, like Segafredo. Finally, Italian espresso bars are small family businesses, not parts of a giant chain.

* Kraft's main brand was Maxwell House. Sara Lee's (MJB, Hills Bros., Chase & Sanborn) were acquired in 1998 from Nestlé and Café Pilão. P&G's main brand was Folgers, sold to Smucker's in 2008. P&G began to make and market Dunkin' Donuts brand coffee in 2007.

By contrast, at Starbucks people drink coffee at tables or take it out. They drink from paper cups and there is a very long, complex menu of drinks Europeans have never heard of or wanted. The coffee is all Starbucks' own brand and the store is company owned. And almost all of the drinks are milk based. In fact, viewed from Europe, Starbucks is more of a milk company than a coffee company and most of its drinks are simply coffee-flavored milk.

And then, Starbucks married together not only coffee and restaurants, but also the American penchant for chains and public financing. It expanded much faster than European companies. By the time we began to understand Starbucks, it was well established. But you should also understand that Starbucks is still a small player in the overall world coffee business.

Joe Santos's comments imply that incumbents had difficulty understanding Starbucks because it was vertically integrated—because it roasted, branded, and served its own coffee in its own company restaurants. Starbucks did not vertically integrate to purposefully confuse the competition. It did so in order to be able to mutually adjust multiple elements of its business and to capture the information generated by each element of its business operations.

Integration is not always a good idea. When a company can buy perfectly good products and services from outside suppliers, it is usually wasteful to go through the expense and trouble of mastering a new set of business operations. However, when the core of a business strategy requires the mutual adjustment of multiple elements, and especially when there is important learning to be captured about interactions across business elements, then it may be vital to own and control these elements of the business mix.

CHAPTER SEVENTEEN

USING YOUR HEAD

I am twenty-five and nervous. Each doctoral student at the Harvard Business School is expected to write cases based on field interviews. So, in the summer of 1967, I am in Los Angeles, assigned to write a strategy case. Sitting across from a senior manager's desk, I hold a yellow legal pad and a ballpoint pen, but I have no idea how to proceed. No one has coached me on interviewing senior executives about strategy.

Fred Fletcher, the general manager of Fansteel Inc.'s Advanced Structures division, shows no sign that he has noticed my youth or inexperience. He simply asks me how we should begin. I have to say something, so I say, "Let's start with what you are trying to accomplish here. What is the purpose of the Advanced Structures division?"

Fletcher tells me that the division is charged with integrating the activities of six recently acquired firms, each a specialist in making things out of a high-tech material (for example, titanium, columbium, tungsten, fiber-epoxy composites, and specialty ceramics). The idea is to bring more of a science base to these essentially craft-based enterprises and act like a general contractor with respect to aerospace prime contractors.

I am surprised that these high-tech businesses are small entrepreneurial job shops. Fletcher explains that they have grown up in the Los Angeles area in support of the aerospace industry. Universities don't teach about real fabrication issues, and neither do trade schools. The large established firms have skills in design but little knowledge about actually forming objects out of exotic materials. Basically, each of these businesses is run by someone who has a special knack with a particular material, like making high-precision castings out of tungsten, or body armor out of ceramics, or cladding a fuel tank in columbium.

I ask about his experiences in trying to combine these skills or to jointly sell these capabilities. I ask about the competition. I ask about his division's competitive strengths and its weaknesses. I ask him to describe the most difficult management issues he faces.

All in all, I ask about six or seven questions and fill fifteen pages of yellow legal pad with notes. The whole interview lasts about three hours. When it is done, Fletcher stands and shakes my hand. "I didn't know what to expect," he says. "But that was the most useful conversation I've had all year."

For weeks after, I held that baffling comment up and examined it, turning it over in my mind like an odd-shaped stone. There had been no real conversation. All I had done was ask the obvious questions about strategy and write down his answers. How could that have been the most valuable conversation of the year? Perhaps, I thought, Fletcher was glad to have someone to talk to who wasn't his boss, his subordinate, or a customer—someone who had a simple agenda and who was happy just to listen.

MAKE A LIST

It was fifteen years before I genuinely understood Fletcher's comment. The occasion was a lunch in Pittsburgh, in Republic Steel's executive dining room. During the morning, I had made a presentation to the board of directors of Republic Steel's insurance business, a joint venture with UK-based Hogg Robinson. At lunch, our conversation turned to the glory days of Pittsburgh and to Andrew Carnegie, the man who was once the richest American, the creator of U.S. Steel. "Since you are a consultant," my host remarked, "you will appreciate this story:"

It was 1890, and there was a cocktail party here in Pittsburgh. All the movers and shakers were there, including Carnegie. He held court in a corner of the room, smoking a cigar. He was introduced to Frederick Taylor, the man who was becoming famous as an expert on organizing work.

"Young man," said Carnegie, squinting dubiously at the consultant, "if you can tell me something about management that is worth hearing, I will send you a check for ten thousand dollars."

Now, ten thousand dollars was a great deal of money in 1890. Conversation stopped as the people nearby turned to hear what Taylor would say.

"Mr. Carnegie," Taylor said, "I would advise you to make a list of the ten most important things you can do. And then, start doing number one."

And, the story goes, a week later Taylor received a check for ten thousand dollars.

My immediate reaction to the story was puzzlement. Was this a joke? Why would Carnegie pay ten thousand dollars for this advice? Making a list is baby-steps management. Pick up any book on self-help, on organizing yourself, or on the nuts and bolts of running an office or organization, and it will proffer this advice: "Make a list." How could that be of any real use to an experienced businessperson? It was just too simple. Yes, we all make shopping lists, but did Andrew Carnegie, a titan of industry, really benefit from making a list of the ten most important things to do?

Later that night, I saw that there was a deeper truth in the story. Carnegie's benefit was not from the list itself. It came from actually constructing the list. The idea that people have goals and automatically chase after them like some kind of homing missile is plain wrong. The human mind is finite, its cognitive resources limited. Attention, like a flashlight beam, illuminates one subject only to darken another. When we attend to one set of issues, we lose sight of another. People can forget to call someone. You may forget to buy milk on the way home because you have attended to driving instead of shopping. And, more important, people can forget their larger purposes, distracted by the pull of immediate events. A busy professional, caught up in career building, may pay scant attention to marriage and children, regaining a sense of priorities only after damage has been done. A CEO, locked in competition with another bidder for a company, can lose track of the broader reasons for the acquisition.

Given Frederick Taylor's assignment, some people might have listed the bills they had to pay or the people they needed to see. One can only guess at Carnegie's list, but the ten-thousand-dollar payment suggests that it wasn't just a list of errands.

Taken seriously, Taylor's injunction was not simply to make a list of important issues. It was not simply to make a list of things to do. And it wasn't to make a list of what might be important. Taylor's assignment was to think through the *intersection* between what was important and what was actionable. Carnegie paid because Taylor's list-making exercise forced him to reflect upon his more fundamental purposes and, in turn, to devise ways of advancing them.

Fletcher's comment, made fifteen years before, suddenly made more sense. When I asked about his division's purpose, its competitive strengths and weaknesses, and the management issues he faced, he had to reflect and bring these issues to the forefront. The interview reminded him about his broader situation and the things he had to do to move forward. He was essentially reminded of his "list" and various priorities during our conversation.

Making a list is a basic tool for overcoming our own cognitive limitations. The list itself counters forgetfulness. The act of making a list forces us to reflect on the relative urgency and importance of issues. And making a list of "things to do, *now*" rather than "things to worry about" forces us to resolve concerns into actions.

Today, we are offered a bewildering variety of tools and concepts to aid in analysis and the construction of strategies. Each of these tools envisions the challenge slightly differently. For some it is recognizing advantage; for others it is understanding industry structure. For some it is identifying important trends; for others it is erecting barriers to imitation. Yet, there is a more fundamental challenge common to all contexts. That is the challenge of working around one's own cognitive limitations and biases—one's own myopia. Our own myopia is the obstacle common to all strategic situations.

Being strategic is being less myopic—less shortsighted—than others. You must perceive and take into account what others do not, be they colleagues or rivals. Being less myopic is not the same as pretending you can see the future. You must work with the facts on the ground, not the vague outlines of the distant future. Whether it is insight into industry structures and trends, anticipating the actions and reactions of competitors, insight into your own competencies and resources, or stretching your own thinking to cover more of the bases and resist your own biases, being "strategic" largely means being less myopic than your undeliberative self.

TIVO

At eight a.m. the group of seventeen managers settles into the room. It is a rainy fall day in 2005, the second day of a three-day program. I am working with the group each morning on strategy. The most senior executive is sitting in the center of the front row, a good sign. When the senior person sits in the back, and to the side, I have learned that it generally signals an early exit rather than engagement.

Today, we are studying TiVo, a much more complicated situation than yesterday's case. I start the session by joking that I saw some late-night partying and am worried that no one has prepared the materials. I ask, "Did everyone do the assignment?"

They all nod affirmatively or say, "Yes."

The assignment was to write one paragraph describing a recommended strategy for TiVo. The responses are now stacked neatly on the podium in the front of the room. I point to the stack and say, "Well, then you must have all seen the quick and easy solution to TiVo's problems!"

They laugh because they all appreciate that the situation facing TiVo is thorny. There are issues of technology, competition, intellectual property, manufacturing efficiency, standards, bargaining with cable and satellite TV providers, privacy, and the role of television in marketing.

I have glanced briefly at their recommendations, having planned to compare these pre-discussion commitments to their post-discussion views, a way of measuring the contribution of the discussion. But looking at these short one-paragraph recommendations, I was struck anew by the variety of judgment within even a homogeneous group like this one. Yesterday, this group had proven to be unusually open and frank, less self-protective than most. I decided to work with them on thinking and judgment.

"Before we get into TiVo's situation," I say, "I want to back up a step and ask you a question that was not on the assignment for today. I want to ask you *how* you arrived at your recommendations. How did you come up with your response to this assignment?"

It isn't the question they have been expecting, and there is a long moment of quiet. People shift in their seats and look at one another. I glance pointedly at the most senior executive. He speaks up, saying that he had "read the case and made some marginal notes."

"While you were reading the case," I ask, "what did you think about?"

"He was thinking about getting a beer!" a colleague jokes.

We all laugh. "Besides the need for a Sam Adams," I press, "what did you think about?"

"Well, it's actually hard to remember. I guess I was mainly thinking that this is a great product, a real innovation, yet the company is losing money because of the cost of manufacturing the boxes."

"Fine. You began to focus on manufacturing."

"Yes, I think they need to stop subsidizing the manufacture of these units. I think—"

"Good," I say. "Let's not get into the specifics of your recommendation just yet. I want to stay with *how* you arrived at that insight."

He looks down at his copy of the case. It has some notes in the right-side margins. I want to see if we can actually talk about where his ideas came from. I called his advice an "insight" to suggest that he need not make up some grandiose story about his analytical prowess.

"It's really just experience, or at least, my experience. I saw these large losses. And they seem to be due to manufacturing. . . . Well, no. To be honest, the first thing I thought of was that most customers are paying for a giant hard disk that they don't need. If you only want to time-shift two programs, you don't need to store a whole season. So, I thought, why not use smaller disks and make only the more intensive users pay for hardware upgrades?"

"So, your initial idea was . . . an intuition . . . about an action. Unbundle the disk capacity, maybe price discriminate?"

"Yeah. That's it."

"Fantastic. Very interesting. Did you go down any other avenues?"

"No. . . . Hey, you only wanted one paragraph!"

I am pleased with his contribution. Honest and interesting. Of course, just because I had asked for only one recommendation didn't mean he was constrained to consider only one approach. But I don't want to point that out just yet.

I turn to another member of the group who has a hand halfway up. She says, "I just thought about the situation and came up with a recommendation. It just sort of emerged as I was thinking about the problem. I realized that if other firms come to dominate the cable TV segment, while TiVo holds the satellite TV segment, it will lose the battle for scale."

"Where did that idea come from?" I ask.

"Well, I don't really remember."

"That's how good ideas come to us," I say. "There are lots of sausage-making tools being hawked for strategy work, but good ideas don't come out of mechanical tools. Conceptual tools may help us get oriented, but, in the end, good ideas basically just pop into our heads. It's called 'insight.'"

She likes this feedback but tries to look modest.

"Did any other approaches to the problem pop into your head, or just that one?" I ask.

"Well, I don't remember any. . . . It was just that one."

"Great—it is important to be honest with ourselves about this." I had started with the most senior people to give the more junior associates a chance to be honest.

Another participant wants to contribute. He says, "Reading the TiVo case, I had the immediate sense that the company is trying too hard to get into bed with the TV industry. But it is not a natural alliance. TiVo helps move shows around in time, helps skip commercials, and cuts into loyalty to channels. It provides a consumer benefit, not a TV broadcaster or network benefit. Its problem is that it is an outsider—not illegal like Napster, but similarly loved by the consumer and hated by the industry."

Once again, I have to remind them that we are trying to get at how these points of view developed. "What led you to that view?" I ask.

"I don't know," he says. "I was thinking, I guess, about FCC commissioner Michael Powell's comment that TiVo is 'God's machine.' So many people love it yet it is having so much commercial trouble."

His one-paragraph recommendation repeats this description of the problem but has little in the way of any recommendations. That lack is a different issue, and I defer it to later.

As I go around the room, only one person reports having given anything more than the briefest consideration to more than one course of action. Most of them had first identified a problem area—manufacturing, cable companies, software rivalry, and so on—and then created a recommendation aimed at that area. No one using this two-step approach had gone back and considered rethinking the initial identification of a key problem area. Nor had any of them investigated more than one response to that problem.

I perch on the stool in front of the class and try to talk about what we have just learned:

> When you prepared for this class, each of you read the same material. But some focused on one issue and others on another. Some focused on manufacturing, some on software, some on cable TV provider relationships, and so on. When it came to recommending a course of action, almost everyone chose the first one they thought of.
>
> This is predictable. Most people, most of the time, solve problems by grabbing the first solution that pops into their heads—the first insight. In a large number of situations this is reasonable. It is the efficient way to get through life. We simply don't have the time, energy, or mental space to do a full and complete analysis of every issue we face.

My comments make people uncomfortable. A participant pushes up a hand up and says: "According to *Blink*, a first judgment may be best.[1] Gladwell says that people make complex judgments without knowing how they do it. Trying to analyze everything may lead to poorer decisions."

It is a good point. Malcolm Gladwell's *Blink* is a great read, a fascinating book. He argues that we all have the ability to process certain kinds of complex information quickly and come up with a judgment and yet not know how we got there. We all know this is true, especially with regard to making decisions about other people and social settings, and about matching patterns—seeing that one thing has characteristics that remind us of another. These are lightning-quick computations. Gladwell makes the case that we should trust these judgments made in the blink of an eye, especially when they are made by people with good experience.

Our instincts can often produce amazingly good judgments. But our instincts also tell us, incorrectly, that our instincts are always right. You should recognize which situations require deeper reflection. Are competitors or nature leading us into a trap? Can we can set a trap for less-wary adversaries?

I explain that *Blink* judgments may work for people situations and certain kinds of pattern matching. Unfortunately, there is also a good deal of research revealing that most people are poor at making many kinds of judgments, whether done in a blink or in a month. Of special concern are judgments about the likelihoods of events, about one's own competence relative to others', and about cause-and-effect relationships. In estimating the likelihood of an event, even experienced professionals exhibit predictable biases. For example, people tend to place more weight on vivid examples than on broad statistical evidence.[2] My MBA students will each predict that they will get a grade putting them in the top half of the class, even after this information is fed back to them.[3] In reasoning about natural data, people tend to see patterns where there is only randomness, tend to see causes rather than associations, and tend to ignore information that conflicts with a maintained theory.

Turning back to the participant who brought up *Blink*, I ask, "Would you want the president of the United States to make a decision to go to war in the blink of an eye? Do you think it is appropriate for a CEO to decide on a merger without carefully thinking through the costs and benefits?" These are rhetorical questions, and he nods that he accepts that some issues seem to be too important and too complex to concede to instant intuition.

"So," I continue, "in strategy work this quick closure can get us into trouble. Almost by definition, strategy is about very difficult yet very important issues. Because they are important situations, they may deserve more than a quick closure around our first hunch. You *know* that. And because you know that, we have a puzzle. *Why would experienced executives, like yourselves, go with quick closure in a strategy situation?*"

After a few moments, a participant says, "There wasn't enough time."

"Always a problem," I agree. But I keep scanning the room.

"It's a judgment call," another blurts out. "There is no 'answer' to this kind of thing; there is only someone's judgment about what makes the most sense. There are too many moving parts. . . ."

It is an acute observation. We are all aware of the basic formal approach to making a decision. List the alternatives, figure out the cost or value associated with each, and choose the best. But in a situation such as TiVo's, you cannot perform this kind of clean "decision" analysis. It is too complex, too ill-structured. Thus, the most experienced executives are actually the quickest to sense that a real strategic situation is impervious to so-called decision analysis. They know that dealing with a strategy situation is, in the end, all about making good judgments. So, they make a judgment call.

"That's right," I say. "It *is* a judgment. In the end, what we recommend will be a best judgment, based on what we know. Still, why not revisit that judgment and generate alternative views? And, why not then evaluate them in light of one another? Why the overly quick closure on the first?"

I don't probe for an answer to this question. I stand up and start pacing in the front of the room. I tell them that I have observed and thought about this for many years and that I have a view about what happens to us:

> Facing a complex situation like this makes most people uncomfortable. The more seriously you take it, the more you will see it as a real and difficult challenge that requires a coherent response. And that realization will, in turn, make you even more uncomfortable. It is so ill-structured. There are too many variables, so many factors, too many unknowns, no clear list of potential actions and

no way to make clear links between actions and outcomes. You are not even sure what the problem is. Like a swimmer dropped into very choppy waters, it is hard to get your bearings. Under pressure to develop a way out of the difficulty, that first idea is a welcome relief. Thank goodness, here is something to hang on to! It feels much better to get oriented.

The problem is that there might be better ideas out there, just beyond the edge of our vision. But we accept early closure because letting go of a judgment is painful and disconcerting. To search for a new insight, one would have to put aside the comfort of being oriented and once again cast around in choppy waters for a new source of stability. There is the fear of coming up empty-handed. Plus, it is unnatural, even painful, to question our own ideas.

Thus, when we do come up with an idea, we tend to spend most of our effort justifying it rather than questioning it. That seems to be human nature, even in experienced executives. To put it simply, our minds dodge the painful work of questioning and letting go of our first early judgments, and we are not conscious of the dodge.

Willing them to understand, I say, "But, you do not have to be a captive to that unconscious dodge. You can *choose* how you will approach a problem; you can guide your own thinking about it." I want them to see that this is the heart of the matter. This personal skill is more important than any one so-called strategy concept, tool, matrix, or analytical framework. It is the ability to think about your own thinking, to make judgments about your own judgments.

SOME TECHNIQUES

To create strategy in any arena requires a great deal of knowledge about the specifics. There is no substitute for on-the-ground experience. This experience accumulates in the form of associations between situations and "what works" or "what can happen" in those situations. Just as doctors prescribed aspirin for headache and fever without knowing how it worked, just as the ancient Romans dealt in life insurance without any theory of probability, so you must normally work with patterns and analogies. Of course, in some cases, our knowledge is even stronger, and we have theories about the causal structure of the situation—about what causes what.

In strategy work, knowledge is necessary but not sufficient. There are many people with deep knowledge or experience who are poor at strategy. To guide your own thinking in strategy work, you must cultivate three essential skills or habits. First, you must have a variety of tools for fighting your own myopia and for guiding your own attention. Second, you must develop the ability to question your own judgment. If your reasoning cannot withstand a vigorous attack, your strategy cannot be expected to stand in the face of real competition. Third, you must cultivate the habit of making and recording judgments so that you can improve.

What follows are a few techniques that I have found useful in jogging minds loose from their ruts, for helping to check that strategies have some coherence, and for improving your ability to make judgments as well as critique them. There are, of course, other ways to guide your own thinking. As I describe these techniques, you will recognize some that you have used or come across. Rather than let those recognitions glimmer and fade, it might be useful to make a list.

The Kernel

The kernel is a list reminding us that a good strategy has, at a minimum, three essential components: a *diagnosis* of the situation, the choice of an overall *guiding policy,* and the design of *coherent action.* The concept of the kernel defines the logic of a strategy—the bare-bones minimum. For a strategy to have any bite, it must chart a direction based on a diagnosis of the situation. Absent a diagnosis, one cannot judge one's own choice of an overall guiding policy, much less someone else's choice. A strategy must also translate the overall directive into coordinated action focused on key points of leverage in the situation. (The concept of the kernel and its elements is explored in greater depth in chapter 5.)

When one has an initial insight into what to do about a challenging situation, it never occurs in the form of a full-blown strategy. Rather, the lightning of insight strikes in one of the three elements of the kernel. It may be an insight into action, as in the case of the participant who wanted to put smaller disk drives in TiVo machines. It may be an insight into a general directive, as it was for the participant who wanted to shift focus to the cable TV segment. Or insight may arrive in the form of a diagnosis, as in the case of the participant who saw TiVo as the consumer's friend but also as a Napster-like thorn in the side of the industry.

There is nothing wrong with a localized insight. We have no real control over the process of insight and should be glad when it works at all. What the kernel does, however, is remind us that a strategy is more than a localized insight. It is an internally consistent argument that leads from facts on the ground to diagnosis, thence to an overall directive, thence to action. The kernel reminds us to expand the scope of our thinking to include all three elements.

There are those who prefer to begin their approach to strategy with action. My own insights, however, normally don't start with action. I tend to use a problem-first structure. I am better at starting with a frame or diagnosis of the situation and then working through the guiding policy and action elements of the kernel. At the start of most consulting engagements, the client wants an appraisal of a particular course of action or wants advice on what to do. I almost always back up and try to create a better diagnosis of the situation before getting into recommendations.

Problem-Solution

Many attempts at strategy lack a good diagnosis. Hence, it is useful to have mental tools for working backward from a guiding policy to the realm of diagnosis and fact. There is nothing deep about this process other than realizing that it can and should be done.

People normally think of strategy in terms of action—a strategy is what an organization does. But strategy also embodies an approach to overcoming some difficulty. Identifying the difficulties and obstacles will give you a much clearer picture of the pattern of existing and possible strategies. Even more important, you will gain access to how changes in some factors may radically alter the mix of efficacious strategies. To gain this change in perspective, shift your attention from *what* is being done to *why* it is being done, from the directions chosen to the problems that these choices address.

Applying the problem-solution methodology to TiVo's situation means identifying the obstacles it is attempting to overcome. A simple engineering view would be that it tries to let consumers time-shift television viewing and, perhaps, skip commercials. Other ways of addressing this problem—solutions that compete with the TiVo solution—are VCRs, video-on-demand services, and DVD rental and sales, especially of entire commercial-free seasons of TV shows.

A slightly different perspective is gained by defining the problem as the content-aggregator's control of the set-top box. Companies such as Comcast, Time Warner, DirecTV, and EchoStar bundle set-top boxes with their television services. These boxes provide, at a minimum, access to the regular and premium channels and any video-on-demand or other interactive services offered. They may also include, usually for a higher price, digital video recorder (DVR) features of various levels of sophistication. For a TiVo box to be an economical solution for the average consumer, it must access regular and premium channels as well as download scheduling information over the cable or satellite link.[4] It can do this only under a contractual agreement with the cable or satellite company. These companies' ability to bundle set-box rentals with service contracts, and the cable companies' monopoly positions, allow them to extract most of TiVo's possible profits.

Monopolies that use bundling to restrict competition are an old story in antitrust, as illustrated by the cases of IBM, the regional telephone companies, and Microsoft. As long as monopoly cable companies can bundle, it will always be extremely difficult for outside companies to add value to the television experience. This perspective suggests that TiVo spend less on marketing and more on a legal attack on the industry's structure. In such an attack, it would have many important, and larger, allies.

Create-Destroy

Overcoming quick closure is simple in principle: you look for additional insights and strategies. But, most of the time, when asked to generate more alternatives, people simply add one or two shallow alternatives to their initial insight. Consciously or unconsciously, they seem to resist developing several robust strategies. Instead, most people take their initial insight and tweak it slightly, adding a straw-man alternative, or including options such as "walk away," or "more study," that are generic to any situation rather than being responsive to the special circumstances at hand.

A new alternative should flow from a reconsideration of the facts of the situation, and it should also address the weaknesses of any already developed alternatives. The creation of new higher-quality alternatives requires that one try hard to "destroy" any existing alternatives, exposing their fault lines and internal contradictions. I call this discipline *create-destroy*.

Trying to destroy your own ideas is not easy or pleasant. It takes mental toughness to pick apart one's own insights. In my own case, I rely on outside help—I invoke a virtual *panel of experts* that I carry around in my mind. This panel of experts is a collection of people whose judgments I value. I use an internal mental dialogue with them to both critique my own ideas and stimulate new ones. I try to do this before putting my ideas before others.

The panel of experts trick works because we are adept at recognizing and comprehending well-integrated human personalities. Thinking through how a particular well-remembered expert might respond to a problem can be a richer source of criticism and advice than abstract theories or frameworks.

My own personal virtual panel of experts contains respected executives I have known and worked with, people who educated and trained me, colleagues I have worked with over the years, and certain people whose points of view emerge clearly from their own written work or from biography. When I face a problem, or have generated a first hunch, I turn to this panel and ask, "What is wrong with this approach to the situation? What would you do in this case?"

Professor Bruce Scott, who chaired my dissertation committee long ago in 1971, sits on my panel of experts. In my imagination, I can see him, leaning back in his chair and asking me to explain why anyone should listen to me and to tell him what the action implication is . . . and there had better be one. Also present is Professor Alfred D. Chandler Jr., who passed away in 2007 but who lives on in my panel. Unimpressed by strategies of quick profit and narrow focus, Chandler speaks in terms of broad historical trends and the power of scale and scope to build enduring enterprises.

For advice on technology strategy, as in the case of TiVo, I might turn to panel of experts members David Teece and Steve Jobs. David Teece is a longtime friend and colleague and a master in strategy, economics, the law, and business. I have never spoken to him about TiVo, but in my imagination his eyes crinkle and he says, "They don't have a lock on DVR technology, so there will be other companies offering similar software and hardware. The cable and satellite companies are in much stronger positions, controlling key complementary assets. They probably should be licensing the software rather than trying to build equipment. They are trying to make money on advertising, but if there were real money there, the cable and satellite players would take it away from them."

Steve Jobs, cofounder of Apple, founder of NeXT, and CEO of Pixar until it was acquired by the Walt Disney Company, is the world's best-known Silicon Valley entrepreneur. Since guiding the development of the Macintosh computer, Jobs's basic operating principles have become the stuff of legend: (1) imagine a product that is "insanely great," (2) assemble a small team of the very best engineers and designers in the world, (3) make the product visually stunning and easy to use, pouring innovation into the user interface, (4) tell the world how cool and trendy the product is with innovative advertising.

Steve Jobs is great at criticism. Arrogant and smart, he cuts to the heart of an issue with no wasted effort. In 1997, we used Apple as the "living case" in the UCLA Anderson MBA strategy course. I and several other faculty members met with Jobs to discuss Apple's future prospects. "I know Stanford," he said, "but I am not all that familiar with UCLA Anderson."

My colleague and department chair, Jack McDonough, responded by offering the school's party line: "We like to think that we are the entrepreneurial school."

"That's interesting," said Jobs. "Which Silicon Valley entrepreneurs have come out of your program that I would recognize?"

Jack grimaced, then answered truthfully, "There aren't any."

"Well, then, you've failed," Jobs said with finality. That day, he became part of my mental panel of experts.

What would Jobs think of TiVo? What you get from a person is not a conceptual framework or theory, but a viewpoint integrated into a personality. Jobs, I think, would dislike the TiVo business—the company does not control enough of the variables to deliver a truly "cool" experience. Even if you put the world's best design team at work on making a better TiVo, much of the functionality would depend on how the machine interacts with the cable or satellite provider. If you could vertically integrate with DirecTV or Comcast, then, perhaps, you could really deliver something interesting. Not just movies, but music on demand. Not just a TV box, but an integrated wireless Internet delivery system. Just as he did with the iPod and iPhone, Jobs would want to integrate the machine, the user experience, and the delivery of product into something fairly seamless.

Listening to Teece's and Jobs's imaginary counsel, I am reminded that good strategies are usually "corner solutions." That is, they emphasize focus over compromise. They focus on one aspect of the situation, not trying to be all things to all people. As Jobs might argue, TiVo could be a much more interesting proposition were it merged with a major platform, providing something more integrated than current DVR offerings. And as Teece might observe, they are already trying to do too many conflicting things, things that put them in competition with their platform customers.

Learning from others can be more than simply listening to them, watching them, or reading what they write. When you build your own panel of experts you go one step farther, trying to shape your understanding of their teachings into a virtual personality. When it works, it does so because we humans have built-in software for understanding other humans, software that is more expert at recognizing and recalling personalities than at almost anything else.

PRACTICING JUDGMENT

A sailor has to judge the wind and a ski racer must judge the texture of the snow. In business and politics, and in many aspects of military strategy, most of the important judgments are about people, especially anticipating their actions and reactions. Judgment begins with knowing yourself, your abilities and biases. Then it extends to knowing other individuals. Much more complex is judgment about small groups and how they will react in response to information or challenges—the domain of many managers, trial lawyers, and platoon leaders. Finally, there is judgment about large groups of people and markets—the domain of marketing and advertising experts, corporate management, and political leadership.

Good judgment is hard to define and harder still to acquire. Certainly some part of good judgment seems to be innate, connected with having a balanced character and an understanding of other people. Still, I am convinced that judgment can be improved with practice. For that practice to be effective, you should first commit your judgments to writing.

One way to see the need for pre-commitment is to imagine an MBA student who has studied and prepared a business case for class. Reading and thinking about the case, many different issues have crossed her mind. She will have tried to think of a number of ways to handle the case situation, and there will be some she prefers to others. Then, in a one-hour case discussion, it is probable that every issue she identified will have been mentioned and every action she considered will also have been put forward. As these issues and actions are examined and evaluated, she thinks, "I thought of that." When the class finally narrows down the defensible interpretations of the situation and the range of useful action, she will probably think, "Yes, I had considered all that."

What this student has missed is the opportunity to pre-commit to a position and thereby subsequently evaluate her own judgment. To commit to a judgment is to choose an interpretation of which issues are critical and which are not and then to choose an implied action. By committing to a judgment—especially a diagnosis—you increase the probability that you will disagree with some of the assessments of others, and thereby increase the chance of learning something.

The same principle applies to any meeting you attend. What issues do you expect to arise in the meeting? Who will take which position? Privately commit yourself in advance to some judgments about these issues, and you will have daily opportunities to learn, improve, and recalibrate your judgment.

CHAPTER EIGHTEEN

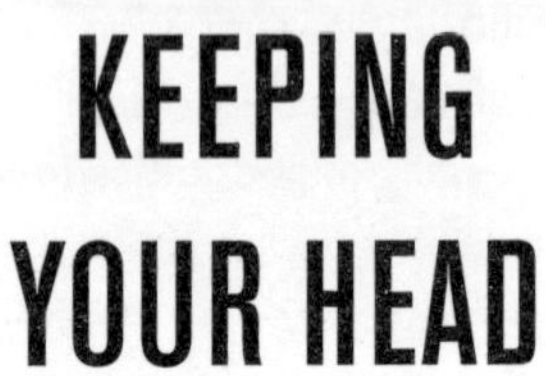

KEEPING YOUR HEAD

If you can keep your head when all about you
Are losing theirs . . .
—"If," Rudyard Kipling

Good strategy grows out of an independent and careful assessment of the situation, harnessing individual insight to carefully crafted purpose. Bad strategy follows the crowd, substituting popular slogans for insights.

Being independent without being eccentric and doubting without being a curmudgeon are some of the most difficult things a person can do. I will not pretend that I have the formula for achieving this subtle balance, but I will tell you two stories that may help. They should alert you to being swept along in the strong current of the crowd. The first story is about Global Crossing and the cardinal lesson is about assessing the fundamentals. The stock market was wrong about Global Crossing, and it did not take inside information to see this. The second story is about the financial crisis of 2008 and the strong roles played by social herding and a bias called the *inside view*.

GLOBAL CROSSING

After a decade of attempts, the first successful Atlantic cable was laid in 1866, thanks to the entrepreneurial zeal of Cyrus Field of the United States and, in Britain, Charles Bright and the Brett brothers. The event was greeted with huge parades and joyous celebrations on both sides of the Atlantic. Before then, messages between the old and new worlds were carried by sail and steam, a two-to-three-week passage at sea. Wars could be won or lost and kingdoms fall in two weeks. With Cyrus Field's cable, suddenly, through the miracle of electricity, the press of a telegraph key in England made a "click" in America. The Atlantic community was suddenly knit together by a slim copper wire.

Ninety years later, in 1956, the first transatlantic *telephone* cable was laid. At a cost of $250 million, it provided thirty voice circuits between the United States and the United Kingdom. During the next forty years, over a dozen new and increasingly sophisticated telephone cables were laid across the Atlantic. Each new cable project was carried out by a consortium of national telephone companies. At the completion of each project, the cable's capacity was split among consortium members. Neither the cables nor the national telephone companies competed with one another. All prices were fixed by either regulators or international agreements, and there were no alternatives to the national operators for handling international traffic.

In 1997, two former AT&T managers (William Carter and Wallace Dawson) were seeking funding for a privately owned cable project they called Atlantic Crossing. To this venture they brought their personal expertise and a turnkey contract with AT&T to do the work of building and maintaining the cable. Carter and Dawson had talked to GE Capital about funding, but small Los Angeles–based Pacific Capital Group worked faster. Gary Winnick and his three partners at Pacific Capital put together a deal: $75 million in equity and $660 million in debt would finance construction and initial operations. A new corporation, Global Crossing, was formed to carry out the project, with Winnick as its chairman.

Atlantic Crossing-1 (AC-1) was an 8,886-mile loop of optical fibers connecting the United States to the United Kingdom and Germany. The new cable more than doubled the total capacity under the Atlantic. The telephone industry measured capacity in STM-1, one STM-1 being a data rate high enough to carry the information contained in 2,016 voice circuits. AC-1 had an initial capacity of 256 STM-1, and it was expected that advancing technology would soon double that to 512 STM-1: about 80 gigabits per second or about 1 million voice circuits.

The cost of a submarine cable depended more on its length and the ocean's depth than on its data capacity. The total cost of the AC-1 was $750 million, about $1.5 million per STM-1. It took fifteen months to complete, and operations began in the summer of 1998.

Global Crossing offered the 256 STM-1s for sale at a cut-rate price of $8 million each.* This was considerably less than the $18 to $20 million price charged by the most recent telephone company consortium project. By the end of 1998, 35 percent of the AC-1's capacity had been sold for an aggregate amount of $950 million, more than paying back the $750 million cost of construction. After six months of operations, Global Crossing offered stock to the public, and the resulting price valued the firm at an astounding $19 billion. Six months later it was valued at $38 billion, more than the Ford Motor Company.

Much of the enthusiasm for Global Crossing arose from the burgeoning traffic on the Internet. Undersea cables were digital, carrying voice traffic by converting it to data and carrying data traffic directly. Internet traffic was said to be doubling each year, and forecasters saw no end in sight. George Gilder, a high-tech guru, wrote this in Global Crossing's 1998 annual report:

> With growth in the number of international Internet users rapidly outpacing U.S. growth, undersea traffic will grow several times faster than terrestrial traffic. Take my word for it. Over the next five years, the submarine portions of the Internet will prove to be an agonizing choke point. Thus Global Crossing has a truly cosmic position as the supplier of the missing element that completes the global system.

* The sale was technically for a twenty-five-year right to the capacity.

Looking to the future, Global Crossing planned a second Atlantic cable (AC-2), projected to again cost $750 million but this time delivering 2,048 STM-1 of capacity, a unit cost of only one-fourth that of the AC-1. This staggering reduction in unit cost derived from the advances in optical multiplexing technology—more colors of light per fiber and more base capacity per fiber. These technologies were not proprietary to Global Crossing, being available to any cable builder. In fact, a new consortium of national operators was planning a cable with a capacity of 4,096 STM-1, and the private 360atlantic project planned a cable that would add another 4,096 STM-1 over four years. Indeed, engineers expected that by simply changing the electronics at each end of the present AC-1, the cable's capacity could be again almost doubled to 1,000 STM-1. Furthermore, engineers forecasted that by 2001, a wholly new four-fiber cable (like the AC-1) would have a capacity of 20,480 STM-1.

■ ■ ■

I became interested in Global Crossing in 1998, as I examined the overall surge in telecommunications industry investment. I wondered how new players like Global Crossing and others could be valued so highly by the stock market. Seeking insight, I visited David Cleevely, the managing director of Analysys, in Cambridge, England. Cleevely was a well-regarded observer of the new telecommunications economics.

"The key thing to understand," Cleevely told me, "is the huge advantage of the fat pipe." By "fat pipe," he meant very high-capacity fiber optic channels. He moved to the small whiteboard in his office and drew two circles, one small and one large. Cleevely wrote "300 M£" beneath each, and continued. "The cost of laying fiber is mainly the cost of right-of-way and digging. Or of laying it under the ocean. Recent advances let us install enormous capacity at no more cost than building a narrow pipe. The economies of scale of the fat pipe are decisive. The fat pipe wins."

Economies of scale have always played a central role in strategy thinking. The logic seems simple—the fat pipes of the new-wave telecom builders and operators gave them much lower average unit costs.

As my taxi struggled back to London in the afternoon traffic, I thought about fat pipes, scale economies, and telephone calls. What was the "cost" of moving one telephone call, or one megabyte of data, under the Atlantic Ocean?

The concept of cost is tricky. People talk as if products have costs, but that is shorthand easily leading to confusion. Choices, not products, have costs. The cost of choosing to make one more unit of a product is sometimes called *marginal, or variable, cost*. The cost (per unit) of choosing to produce at a fixed rate for a year is called *average cost*. The cost per unit of choosing to build a plant and produce at a fixed rate is called *long-run average cost*. The cost of filling a rush or special order has no particular name, but it clearly exists. There really is no such thing as the single correct "cost" of a product. It all depends on the decision—on what is being compared to what.

The cost of "deciding" to carry one more telephone call was only that of the electrical power required—essentially zero. The cost of deciding to carry one more call every day for a year was still very close to zero. The cost of deciding to turn on the cable and carry thousands of calls every day for a year began to include maintenance and overhead expenses, but not the capital cost of the equipment. I began to realize that the "cost" of moving data over all of these cables was essentially zero, whether they were fat or narrow. And, with the advent of competition in a formerly monopolized industry, there was nothing keeping prices from falling to cost.

The introductory topic taught in any modern course on business strategy is the connection between industry structure and profit. This topic is usually called the "Five Forces," following Michael Porter's pioneering analysis of industry structure, published in 1980. A quick summary is that a terrible industry looks like this: the product is an undifferentiated commodity; everyone has the same costs and access to the same technology; and buyers are price sensitive, knowledgeable, and willing to switch suppliers at a moment's notice to get a better deal.

In early 1999 I asked a class of UCLA MBA students to analyze Global Crossing's entry into the transatlantic cable business. Step by step the students looked at each aspect of the industry:

- One STM-1 on a transatlantic cable is as close to a perfect commodity as the human mind has been able to create. *Not good.*

- One operator's capacity is essentially indistinguishable from another's. *Not good.*

- Global Crossing has introduced competition into the business, and three other private companies have announced plans to enter. *Not good.*

- The technology is not proprietary. *Not good.*

- Technology is making it ever cheaper to add huge chunks of new capacity: overcapacity is a near certainty. *Not good.*

- The capital costs of transatlantic cables are very literally "sunk." If prices don't cover capital costs, old cables will nevertheless continue to operate. *Not good at all.*

One struggles to imagine a worse industry structure.

"But the Internet is doubling in size every year," a student said.

"True," I said. "But capacity is growing even faster, and the cost of capacity is falling even faster than that. Look, given your analysis, the endgame is clear. There will be overcapacity, prices will fall to cost, which is close to zero, and no one will make a profit."

"That is not what the stock market is saying," another student said dismissively. Playing what passed for a trump card in 1999, he said, "I don't care what this industry analysis says, the market is saying that this is one of the biggest profit opportunities of all time."

■ ■ ■

It has always been understood that stock prices reflect expectations about future profits. But the doctrine that stock prices are trustworthy, accurate estimators of future profits arose in the 1970s and was in full bloom by 1999.

Here is an example of how that logic shaped analysis. In 1998, a Lehman Brothers report estimated that total capacity of 1998 U.S. terrestrial fiber systems was seventy times the 1998 working capacity, which was, in turn, quite a bit larger than current demand. In a normal industry, the holders of excess capacity compete with one another, trying to earn a little revenue, and this drives down prices. Was there a glut of installed capacity in the fiber-optic industry? The Lehman analyst wrote:

> In order to begin to fill the potential capacity, bandwidth needs per user, number of users, and usage/month have to increase. If every phone line in the country were upgraded to a T1 [1.5 megabits per second], then network capacity would have to increase just 24 times (at constant usage levels). Therefore, in order arrive at 70 times increases even higher speeds and greater usage is required [*sic*].[1]

At this point a good analyst should conclude that there seems to be too much capacity. But the stock market was saying otherwise. So the next paragraph in the Lehman report offers an almost psychotic break in reasoning, expressing a sublime faith in the voice of the stock market:

> We believe that electronic commerce will grow exponentially helping to drive demand for higher bandwidth for Internet and data services. PC industry pundits see the day when every person has electronic agents constantly in the network pulling down data to the PC that is customized to the individual user. In addition, there is potential for connecting virtually every appliance with a chip to the Internet to increase the usefulness of the appliance and communicate information to users and manufacturers.

At a late 1999 conference I discussed this issue over lunch with a group of strategy consultants. They brushed aside the immediate problem of price competition. "The new players like Qwest and Global Crossing have years to gain market share against the high-priced old-line national operators," opined a Boston Consulting Group consultant. In easy conversation, all referred to the enormous stock market performance of Qwest, WorldCom, Global Crossing, and other new-wave telecommunications players. Their huge valuations were taken as strong proof of sound, even brilliant, business strategies.

At that time many consultants' presentations were simply comparisons between the stock performances of companies following one approach versus another. Why bother to do the hard work of evaluating the logic of a business strategy if the all-knowing stock market does a better job? If WorldCom's stock appreciated faster than Sprint's and MCI's, then rolling up fiber loops *must* be better than being a broadline network operator. Like the voice of a deity, the "market" had spoken.

■ ■ ■

In the spring of 2001, I began to write a case on Global Crossing.[2] I was particularly fascinated with the situation facing Gary Winnick. He had made a huge profit on the AC-1, but that venture had the structure of a onetime real estate deal. He had constructed the "building" for $750 million and sold the "condos" for more than $2 billion, and, amazingly, wound up with a company valued at $30 billion. Why were his sophisticated telecom customers, I wondered, so willing to overpay? Why pay Global Crossing $8 million for an STM-1 when the cost of creating a new STM-1 was less than $1.5 million? Did investors really think he could keep doing it again and again? What do you do, I wondered, when your stock seems outrageously overvalued?

Finishing the Global Crossing case became a race against time. My final scheduled interview with Winnick was canceled because the company declared bankruptcy on that day in December 2001. Today, years after the telecommunications meltdown, newspapers and business magazines have reduced that era to a list of rogue CEOs, with Winnick in the middle of the list. But that analysis is just as foolish as were the extravagant expectations of 1999. What happened to Global Crossing was a microcosm of what happened to the whole set of new-age telecom carriers: trillions of dollars in expected revenues never materialized.

The telecom companies built too much fiber capacity. How much is too much? The combined plans in place for the Atlantic in 2001 amounted to 16,384 STM-1s. That would be enough capacity to allow thirty-five million people, half in Europe and half in America, to broadcast continuous real-time video coverage of their lives to one another, twenty-four hours a day seven days a week.

Critically, as capacity surged on the transatlantic route, a secondary market soon developed. Stuck with mountains of unused capacity, the original customers, mostly national operators, tried to make a little money by offering their unused capacity for resale or on short-term leases. Fierce price competition quickly became the norm. In late 1999, the price of an STM-1 collapsed from $6.5 million to $2 million. By early 2002, one could buy a transatlantic STM-1 for $325,000, only 4 percent of Global Crossing's original asking price!

What happened to the fantastically high and growing revenues expected from the Internet? Two things went wrong. First, contrary to George Gilder's forecast, Internet traffic over undersea cables grew much more slowly than did terrestial traffic. Most Internet traffic was local, not international. Furthermore, the need for rapid response times pressed many high-usage websites to duplicate their servers city by city, obviating the need for huge intercontinental bandwidth.

Second, despite its rate of growth, Internet traffic did not earn high revenue. The telecom industry was used to charging high prices for handling "corporate data" and failed to think through the obvious: The rapid growth of Internet traffic was largely a result of its near-zero price. It was exploding because of individual Web browsing, pornography, and music (now video) piracy. The absurd idea that major corporations would be the driver of growth, or that consumers would pay high fees to companies who moved Internet traffic, met a messy death. Costs and prices fell even faster than traffic grew.[3]

The collapse of prices could have been foreseen by anyone doing a simple Five Forces analysis. Why was this analysis ignored? Because the stock market promised something better. Consultants, investors, analysts, and strategists were beguiled by the market values of the new network operators. "Yes, their products look like perfect commodities," one told me, "but something new is happening. The market is giving them a vote of confidence." Thus, judgment fled.

■ ■ ■

For centuries, mathematicians believed that within any axiomatic system—such as geometry, arithmetic, or algebra—every statement was either true or false. In 1931, Viennese mathematician Kurt Gödel proved that this intuition was wrong. He showed that sufficiently complex logical systems are "incomplete." That is, they contain statements and propositions that cannot be judged true or false within the logic of the system. To judge their truth one most look beyond the system to outside knowledge.[4]

I believe this idea applies, metaphorically, to human systems. Specifically, when executives and experts invest and manage solely based on recent stock market signals, the flow of information from corporate investment decisions to traders to stock prices and then back to corporate decisions becomes a closed circle. The "axiom" of market accuracy anchors the circle's center. In the fiber-optic business, this closure was sealed because analysts measured "growth" by looking at increases in installed capacity. Within that closed system, a question such as "Are transatlantic cables an overcapacity commodity business?" became what Kurt Gödel would call an *un-decidable proposition*. To answer this question one would have to look outside the closed system and make an independent estimate of the situation.

Similar closed circles occur when political leaders create public policy based on opinion polls. "Is it wise to have large government agencies committed to making a rapidly growing number of high-leverage mortgage loans?" The question is un-decidable within the logic of popular opinion and election campaigns. Only by looking carefully at the past and at the experiences of other nations can the question be answered.

Another closed circle occurs when schools design curricula based on student ratings, and students apply to schools based on past ratings. In modern business schools, for example, the question "Should graduate students be required to read a book?" has become un-decidable. To break the circular logic one must look at knowledge and principles that are more deeply rooted than current popular opinion.

SOCIAL HERDING AND THE INSIDE VIEW

The financial and economic crisis of 2008 was the bursting of an immense credit bubble, the largest in history. In a credit bubble, lending standards become less and less stringent. Easy credit, in turn, helps drive up prices within a class of assets, usually real estate or equities. These newly risen asset values then form the collateral for further borrowing. The recent credit bubble had a large real estate component but extended to a wide variety of deals—leveraged buyouts, major mergers, industry roll-ups, certain hedge funds, and so on.

There can be asset bubbles without easy credit. In the late 1990s, rising prices of dot-coms drew in more and more buyers for their stocks, pushing up prices even faster. But with little leverage, the 2000 crash in dot-com prices had only a minor impact on the larger economy. It is too-easy credit, showing up as overleveraged borrowers, that transmits shocks from company to company, from person to person, from sector to sector, and from nation to nation, turning what would otherwise be individual losses into a collective calamity.[5]

When Bear Stearns collapsed in 2008, its reported leverage was 32 to 1. That is, it had $1 of equity for each $32 of debt. (Bear Stearns' typical leverage was actually more like 50 to 1, but the company followed a policy of reducing its leverage at the end of each month for reporting purposes.) Some of its hedge funds were leveraged 85 to 1. Lehman Brothers was about as leveraged as Bear Stearns. Citigroup, Merrill Lynch, and the rest of Wall Street were not far behind.

The first homeowners to walk away from their mortgages in late 2006 had taken out 90 percent first mortgages as well as second "piggyback" loans to cover the 10 percent down payments. What is more, they had taken out home-equity loans to pay for new furniture and other consumption goods. By 2007, overleveraged positions had become epidemic on Wall Street and among a good chunk of homeowners.

As in other credit bubbles in other times and other places, things seem fine as long as the value of assets put up as collateral continue their bubbly rise in value. On the way up, as asset values inflate, deal makers, companies, homeowners, and banks all feel that borrowings are "secured" by asset values—stocks, homes, and companies. They feel that there is ground under their feet.

In the Road Runner cartoons there is the moment when Wile E. Coyote mistakenly runs off the top of a cliff but continues to hang in the air, his feet churning. Not until he looks down and sees that there is nothing under his feet does he begin to fall. In credit bubbles, that moment comes when asset prices first begin to decline. It takes only a gentle deflation of the asset bubble to trigger the collapse. As asset prices begin to drift downward, investors who have recently bought inflated assets using high leverage suddenly realize there is no ground under their feet. The more nimble rush to sell before their equity is wiped out. And those sales, in turn, drive down prices faster. This new downward lurch in prices panics still more overleveraged owners and they, too, rush to sell. This process is called "unwinding" or "deleveraging." *As large numbers of people try to unwind at the same time, the selling pressure makes asset prices fall even more sharply*. Bankers, suddenly regaining their sanity, also start deleveraging, which reduces the amount of credit available in the economy. The slowing economy causes even more defaults and distressed sales of assets. This feedback from debt to asset sales, to falling asset prices, back to more defaults and yet more asset sales, is called "debt deflation." It was first explained by Irving Fisher in the midst of the Great Depression. Easy credit quickens the boom, and its consequences accelerate the bust.

Look at the following chart and you can see the rising tide of household debt relative to income. Here, household debt includes mortgages, automobile loans, and consumer credit. In 1984, the average household owed 60 percent of its annual after-tax income in debt. By 2007, that had grown to 130 percent of after-tax income.

Although standard media coverage during most of the 1980s and 1990s focused on government debt, it is striking that, relative to the economy as a whole, it was not the government that was going on a borrowing spree. It was the debt held by households and financial institutions that exploded. Household debt began its upward surge in 1984. By 1988, household debt exceeded all government debt and it continued to grow rapidly until the recession of 2008.

One can heap blame on foolish citizens and venal mortgage brokers,

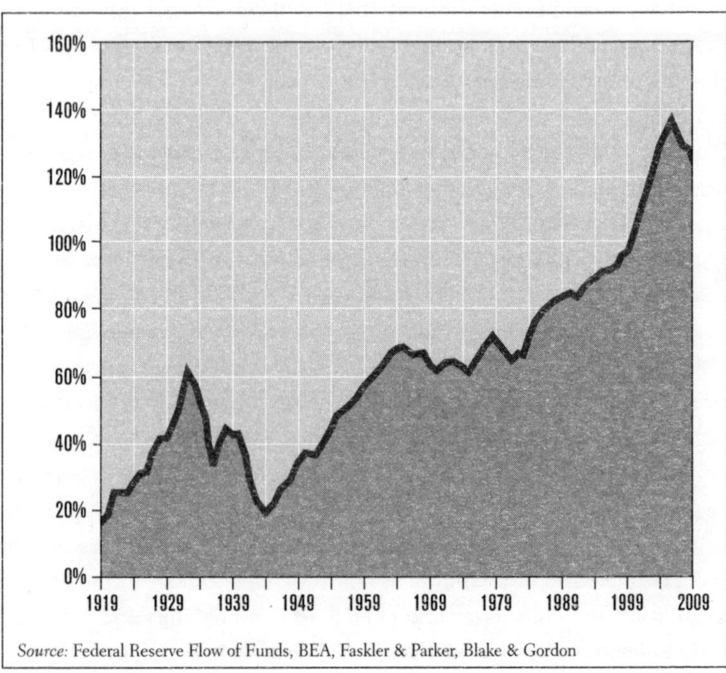

but this crisis was a product of the decisions made in Washington and on Wall Street. Washington is supposed to oversee the overall stability and health of the economy and especially the financial sector. Wall Street is supposed to be expert at pricing and packaging risk. In this case, both failed miserably. How did this happen? What were they thinking?

This disaster—like the Johnstown Flood, the burning of the *Hindenburg,* the aftermath of Katrina* in New Orleans, the BP gulf oil spill, and many other man-made disasters—was the result of five intertwined errors in human judgment and behavior.

* The flood of New Orleans was caused by storm surge, which would have been held back by natural wetlands had they not been "developed" over the years. Plus, the system of dykes engineered to protect against storm surge were improperly designed and constructed.

1. There was *engineering overreach,* where designers built systems whose failure modes and failure consequences exceeded their ability to comprehend or analyze. The new financial instruments created in the decade leading up to the 2008 crisis had failure modes no one understood or predicted.

2. There was what I call the *smooth-sailing fallacy,* where people assume that a lack of recent tremors and storms means that there is no risk. This fallacy was institutionalized by the financial industry's doctrine of measuring risk by analyzing past vibrations in prices. A system with a critical design flaw—such as the *Hindenburg,* the New Orleans levees, or the building of a mountain of securities on the premise that home prices never decline—does not necessarily display the flaw until it collapses. The collapse is virtually certain, but it is not signaled by a history of shakiness or vibration. Importantly, the collapse is not due to totally unforseeable or almost impossible events—things the financial community tends to call "black swans"[6] or "tail-risks." Given the design flaws in the system, a collapse was inevitable.

3. There are many organizations and individuals working under *risk-seeking incentives*. Whenever you profit greatly if things go well and other people take the loss when things go poorly, you become a risk seeker. The core of the malincentives have been the federal government's willingness to bail out large entities with unpayable debts—New York City in 1975, Continental Illinois in 1984, and especially Long-Term Capital Management in 1998. Such bailouts encourage future excess risk taking. In addition, the financial services industry floats in a sea of top-executive compensation arrangements and middle-man fee structures that are all upside and no downside. And since these movers and shakers are not just passive actors, the incentives work to actually increase the amount of riskiness in the economy.

4. There is *social herding*. When we don't know about something, it may be sensible to look at the behavior of others, assuming that

at least some of them know things that we do not. But if everyone else is doing the same, then this process of mutual calibration can result in all the members of a group undertaking uninformed actions or believing that the "other guy" is paying attention to fundamentals.

5. Finally, there is the *inside view,* a label given by Nobel laureate Daniel Kahneman and coauthor Dan Lovallo to the tendency to ignore related pertinent data—to believe that "this case is different."[7]

The fourth and fifth problems—social herding and the inside view—deserve special attention, especially with regard to the 2008 financial crisis. An important virtue of a good leader is putting the situation in perspective and having cool-minded judgment. Both virtues help mitigate the bias inherent in social herding and the inside view.

The inside view describes the fact that people tend to see themselves, their group, their project, their company, or their nation as special and different. Thus, for example, many people are aware of today's outside-view statistic that talking on a cell phone while driving increases your accident risk by a factor of five—about the same as being drunk. But the inside view of the situation is "I am a good driver; those statistics don't apply to me." Similarly, we know that although most new restaurants fail, each entrepreneur thinks his or her new restaurant is different.

In the 2008 financial and economic crisis, such inside-view premises were widely held and expressed, rising above mere assertion and becoming doctrines—principles that, though unprovable, serve as the basis for argument, policy, and action. In particular, the belief that the economic histories of other nations and other times had little relevance to modern America played a key role. Secondly, there was the belief that the Federal Reserve's expertise at managing interest rates had eliminated the risk of major economic swings—that times had changed. There was a belief in the power of America's "deep and liquid" financial markets to withstand and absorb shocks. And there was a belief in the efficacy of Wall Street's new tools for managing, pricing, and parceling risk. All of these doctrines blocked the simple realization that what had happened to others, and what had happened here a number of times before, was happening again. Real estate prices were soaring and too much easy credit was being extended on all fronts.

The outside view of the situation was hardly complex. The international evidence is clear—sharp economic problems following credit booms, especially credit booms connected with real estate booms, are frequent and very damaging. In fact, during the past fifty years there have been twenty-eight severe house-price boom-bust cycles and twenty-eight credit crunches in twenty-one advanced Organization for Economic Co-operation and Development (OECD) economies.[8] As Richard Herring and Susan Wachter of the Wharton School at the University of Pennsylvania observed, "Real estate cycles may occur without banking crises. And banking crises may occur without real estate cycles. But the two phenomena are correlated in a remarkable number of instances ranging over a wide variety of institutional arrangements, in both advanced nations and emerging economies."[9]

Looking back in U.S. history, one finds that the dangerous mixture of easy credit and real estate booms has repeatedly appeared because of the country's deepest political and cultural roots. For almost two centuries, the U.S. federal government has pursued a broad agenda of settling open lands, promoting the ownership of small farms, and now pushing the individual ownership of homes. It is a program that unites populists with those who see a nation of freeholders as a bulwark against the tyrannies of oligarchy and collectivism. It unites Democrats and Republicans, rich and poor, Wall Street and Main Street.

The ordinary working people and immigrants who are the objects of this program rarely have the wealth to buy property outright, often lacking even the funds for a down payment. Therefore, there have been constant political and financial "innovations" in methods for extending credit to settlers, farmers, and prospective homeowners. When times turn bad, these loans default and, for a time, the whole economy is damaged.

America's first depression, in 1819, was a direct result of the government selling large tracts of public land on easy credit. These sales were especially concentrated in Tennessee, Mississippi, and Alabama. Attracted by high prices for crops, especially cotton, settlers borrowed heavily from highly leveraged state banks to purchase land and supplies. The consequent massive increase in production, coupled with the gradual recovery of European agriculture from the devastation of the Napoleonic wars, triggered a collapse in prices in 1819. In 1818, cotton was 31 cents a pound; in 1819 it was half that, and by 1831 it had fallen to 8 cents a pound. Land prices followed suit and massive defaults ensued. The crisis was exacerbated by the Second Bank of the United States' policy of calling in loans and demanding payment in specie.* The crisis spread to the cities and, in Philadelphia, real estate prices fell by 75 percent. Thousands languished in debtors prisons.

Eighteen years later, the Panic of 1837 was rooted in the federal government's sale of thirty million acres of public land—a chunk of real estate constituting a large part of what is now the Midwest. Financing for these land sales came from the new legions of state and local banks and was mostly in the form of private banknotes. States such as Indiana and Illinois began to anticipate future tax revenue from this new land and borrowed against this hoped-for revenue to finance development projects, especially canals. When confidence in all of these banknotes faltered, the ensuing collapse took down almost one-half of the banks in the nation, devastated land values, and started a six-year depression.

After the end of the Civil War, the United States began constructing railroads on a transcontinental scale. Wanting to settle and develop the West, the federal government gave away vast tracts of land to companies that were to build railroads connecting the two coasts. The Northern Pacific, for example, received land grants equal in area to New England, spread along a route from Chicago to the Pacific Ocean. These railroad companies issued bonds that were sold at a discount by networks of brokers, dealers, and salespeople all over North America and Europe.

The business concept was incredibly bold—the Northern Pacific would sell large parcels of their land-grant empires to American settlers and poor immigrants. This would populate the West, and the new

* That is, gold or currency fully backed by gold reserves.

settlers' demand for commercial rail transport would, in the end, make these massive investments pay off. By 1870, over $1 billion in U.S. railroad bonds had been sold in Europe. Northern Pacific agents scoured northern Europe, seeking immigrants accustomed to harsh winters—the ancestors of Garrison Keillor's Lake Wobegon residents. As people settled these lands, more credit was extended to finance their purchases of land, their seed and cattle, and the construction of their homes and towns.

When this giant credit bubble burst, it was devastating. In September 1873, the New York Stock Exchange closed for ten days and a chain reaction of bank failures and corporate collapses followed. About eighteen thousand businesses failed, including one-quarter of the United States' railroads. Unemployment reached 14 percent and the U.S. labor movement began in earnest.

Twenty years later, the Panic of 1893 was triggered by the failure of railroad bonds and by farm bankruptcies. Newly leveraged farms failed in large numbers as crop prices collapsed. The dive in prices was not a fluctuation, but the inevitable outcome of rising farm productivity and the soaring amount of western land coming under cultivation. Unemployment climbed to over 12 percent, and the national economy did not recover for seven years.

In the same era, a phenomenal land boom and bust occurred during the late nineteenth century in Melbourne, Australia. Beginning in 1880, the government borrowed to invest in railways, the harbor, water systems, and urban transport. Although there was no shortage of land, and although Melbourne was, by 1886, one of the geographically largest cities in the world, a speculative boom pushed prices to levels far beyond those in London or New York. Michael Cannon's wonderful book *The Land Boomers* says this (page 18):

> The land mania of the 1880s took two main forms. The first was based on a plethora of building societies, whose optimistic officials believed that every family in the colony could simultaneously build their own house, keep up the payments through good times and bad, and support an army of investors who were being paid

> high rates of interest for the use of their money. The second form of mania was the deeply held belief that it was impossible to lose money by investing in land, a belief that persists to the present day.

The bust, in 1891, was devastating. Melbourne land became almost fully illiquid, there being no cash buyers at any price. Stock prices collapsed—the share price of the city's Tramway company falling by 90 percent.[10] Banks and businesses failed in large numbers, and the economy fell into a depression. A strident union movement began, and Melbourne's growth and confidence were stopped in their tracks for at least a generation.

In America, the nineteenth-century credit crises grew out of initiatives aimed at settling western lands and at the concomitant extension of the railroads. During most of the twentieth century, the focus switched to home ownership. In housing, a myriad of government policies, tax breaks, regulations, oversight organizations, and other instruments have, over generations, promoted an ever-increasing rate of home ownership. The original Jeffersonian ideal was a nation of citizen farmers, each owning the means of his or her own support. Today, this vision has morphed into one of a nation of homeowners, each working 100 days a year to pay their taxes and another 125 days a year to pay their mortgages.

The opening salvo in the home ownership campaigns was fired by Herbert Hoover's 1922 "Own Your Own Home" program. The battle was joined in earnest when Franklin D. Roosevelt created the Federal Housing Administration and Fannie Mae. It accelerated when Harry Truman pushed through the GI Bill. The modern emphasis on home ownership among minorities was begun by Bill Clinton. In 1995 he promised to push home ownership from 65 percent to 67.5 percent of families by 2000, an increase of several million. His National Homeownership Strategy aimed to "cut transaction costs . . . reduce down-payment requirements . . . [and] increase the availability of alternative financing products in housing markets throughout the country."[11] Under the leadership of Housing and Urban Development secretary Henry Cisneros, the government reduced the standards required for a mortgage to qualify for federal insurance. Instead of five years of stable income, three were now enough. Instead of face-to-face interviews with borrowers, now paperwork was enough. Instead of physical branch offices, lenders now only needed a telephone. When George W. Bush came into office, he stepped on the accelerator even harder, unveiling a plan to increase the number of black and Hispanic homeowners by 5.5 million.

Despite the large amount of historical and international evidence that easy-credit real estate booms have sad and costly endings, policy makers, economists, and financial industry leaders defended the status quo with a variety of inside-view arguments and doctrines. For instance, even as the mortgage crisis began to unfold in late 2007, Treasury secretary Henry Paulson continued to extol America's "deep and liquid" financial markets and preach the advantages of our system to China:

> The U.S. economy also faces challenges from our housing market and in our capital markets as risk is being reassessed and repriced. As we work through this period, deep and liquid U.S. capital markets are playing a vital role in maintaining stability, just as they have in providing the financing which allowed 69 percent of U.S. families to own homes. Similarly, China needs to further open its financial sector, to develop capital markets that can provide access to the capital it needs for continued inclusive economic growth.[12]

Paulson's confidence was strengthened by social herding among Wall Street barons, academic economists, and political leaders. In praising America's "deep and liquid" financial markets, the herd conveniently skipped over the giant bag of flammable gas keeping those markets buzzing—easy credit, overleveraging, a vast expanse of unpriceable derivative securities, long-term assets financed with overnight borrowing from trigger-happy counterparties, and huge top management bonuses for taking on hidden risks.

In parallel with this trust in "deep and liquid" financial markets was a belief in the competence of the Federal Reserve. Indeed, many experts shrugged off the mounting leverage because they believed that the Federal Reserve's monetary policies had reduced the overall risk in the economy. Here, for example, is Ben Bernanke, currently the chair of the board of governors of the U.S. Federal Reserve, speaking in 2004 to the Eastern Economic Association:

> One of the most striking features of the economic landscape over the past twenty years or so has been a substantial decline in macroeconomic volatility. . . . The variability of quarterly growth in real output (as measured by its standard deviation) has declined by half since the mid-1980s, while the variability of quarterly inflation has declined by about two-thirds. Several writers on the topic have dubbed this remarkable decline in the variability of both output and inflation the "Great Moderation."[13]

As he spoke in 2004, the Federal Reserve's short-term target rate was a very low 2.25 percent, mortgage lending was soaring, and home prices were accelerating into the blue. Why weren't alarm bells ringing? Because the government doesn't include home prices in its inflation index—the index includes only the rental rate of homes. And as owners expect larger future capital gains, rental rates don't inflate. In addition, a flood of imported low-priced clothing, electronics, furniture, and other goods, especially from China, was keeping U.S. consumer prices low. And the rapidly growing number of poor immigrants from Mexico and Central America helped cap working peoples' wages outside of the public sector. So, to those at the Fed, it was a wonderful new world where they could constantly "juice" the economy with low interest rates without producing any upward jolts in consumer goods prices or wages.

In addition to believing that the Fed had things under control, policy makers and financial leaders placed a great deal of trust in the value of the recent explosion in mathematical financial engineering and the creation of derivative securities (securities based on other securities). Although there were some voices cautioning that these new financial vehicles were new and untested, the dominant position was that the economy was growing and the finance industry was prospering, hence these new financial innovations *must* be doing something beneficial. Here is Alan Greenspan, then chair of the Federal Reserve Board, speaking in 2005:

> Conceptual advances in pricing options and other complex financial products . . . have significantly lowered the costs of, and expanded the opportunities for, hedging risks that were not readily deflected in earlier decades. . . . After the bursting of the stock market bubble in 2000, unlike previous periods following large financial shocks, no major financial institution defaulted, and the economy held up far better than many had anticipated.[14]

Singing out of the same hymnal, Timothy Geithner, then president of the Federal Bank of New York and today secretary of the Treasury, said this in 2006:

> [W]e are now in the midst of another wave of innovation in finance. The changes now under way are most dramatic in the rapid growth in instruments for risk transfer and risk management, the increased role played by nonbank financial institutions in capital markets around the world, and the much greater integration of national financial systems.
>
> These developments provide substantial benefits to the financial system. Financial institutions are able to measure and manage risk much more effectively. Risks are spread more widely, across a more diverse group of financial intermediaries, within and across countries.[15]

The Old Testament instructs "Pride goes before destruction, a haughty spirit before a fall."[16] In retrospect, we can hear the hubris in Bernanke's and Greenspan's and Geithner's statements. The benefits of the U.S. financial system's innovative new tools were claimed without sufficient evidence. Just because there were a lot of clever swaps and new securities, and just because they had not yet crashed and burned, did not mean they could not or would not. It takes long-term real-world stress testing in a wide variety of conditions—through up and down real estate markets, up and down economic cycles, low and high interest rates, low and high inflation, and other conditions—together with various combinations of all of these, to warrant the kind of confidence these financial luminaries exuded.

■ ■ ■

Social herding presses us to think that everything is OK (or not OK) because everyone else is saying so. The inside view presses us to ignore the lessons of other times and other places, believing that our company, our nation, our new venture, or our era is different. It is important to push back against these biases. You can do this by paying attention to real-world data that refutes the echo-chamber chanting of the crowd—and by learning the lessons taught by history and by other people in other places.

NOTES

INTRODUCTION: OVERWHELMING OBSTACLES

1. I use the term "inspirational leadership" to demark the aspect of leadership concerned with motivation and linking people to shared values. I use the more general "leadership" to include any and all of the functions of leaders, including planning, strategy, and so on.

CHAPTER 1: GOOD STRATEGY IS UNEXPECTED

1. Bruce W. Nelan, "Strategy: Saddam's Deadly Trap," *Time,* February 11, 1991. Available at www.time.com/time/magazine/article/0,9171,972312,00.html.
2. "As the History of Warfare Makes Clear, Potential for Catastrophe Remains," *Los Angeles Times,* February 23, 1991, 20.
3. During Desert Storm, the United States destroyed bunkers of Iraqi chemical weapons at Tallil. By 1998, UNSCOM had eliminated or overseen the destruction of more than eighty thousand chemical munitions and tons of bulk chemical agents.
4. A great deal of controversy erupted over whether the war was ended too early in that two Republican Guard divisions escaped to Basra. This debate generally ignored the fact that Iraq had maintained more than twenty army divisions (770,000 soldiers) in Iraq, safely positioned far from the theater of operations.
5. The current equivalent publication is FM 3-0. It can be found online at http://www.globalsecurity.org/.

CHAPTER 2: DISCOVERING POWER

1. Pankaj Ghemawat, "Wal-Mart Stores' Discount Operations," Harvard Business School case study 9-387-018, 1986.
2. Andrew Marshall and James G. Roche, "Strategy for Competing with the Soviets in the Military Sector of the Continuing Political-Military Competition," typed manuscript, 1976. Now declassified, this document can be viewed at www.goodstrategybadstrategy.com/.

CHAPTER 3: BAD STRATEGY

1. Also present were David M. Abshire, CEO of the Center for the Study of the Presidency, former U.S. ambassador to NATO, and special counsel to President Reagan; Lieutenant General David W. Barno, former commander, Combined Forces Command in Afghanistan; Andrew Krepinevich, president of the CSBA, author of *The Army and Vietnam,* an analysis of U.S. strategy in Vietnam, and former member of the National Defense Panel and the Joint Forces Command's Transformation Advisory Board; Andrew Marshall, director of the Department of Defense's Office of Net Assessment; Captain Jan van Tol, CSBA senior fellow and former special assistant to the vice president and commander of the USS *Essex;* and Barry Watts, CSBA senior fellow, former air force officer, director of Northrop Grumman's Analysis Center, and head of the DOD's Office of Program Analysis and Evaluation.
2. Michele A. Flournoy and Shawn W. Brimley, "Strategic Planning for U.S. National Security: A Project Solarium for the 21st Century," Princeton Project on National Security, 2005, 1, http://www.princeton.edu/~ppns/papers/interagencyQNSR.pdf.
3. Barry D. Watts, "Why Strategy? The Case for Taking It Seriously and Doing It Well," Center for Strategic and Budgetary Assessments, 2007. Barry Watts is a senior fellow at the CSBA. See also the updated version, "Regaining Strategic Competence," CSBA, 2009, by Andrew F. Krepinevich and Barry D. Watts, available at http://www.csbaonline.org/.
4. The White House, "The National Security Strategy of the United States of America," 2002 and 2006; and the Department of Defense, "The National Defense Strategy of the United States of America," 2005. These documents were printed by the White House and delivered to Congress, but not officially published by the government. They are available at georgewbush-whitehouse.archives.gov/nsc/nss/2002 and georgewbush-whitehouse.archives.gov/nsc/nss/2006.
5. Lutz Schubert, Keith Jeffrey, and Burkhard Neidecker-Lutz, "The Future of Cloud Computing," European Commission on Information Society and Media, 2010. Available at cordis.europa.eu/fp7/ict/ssai/docs/cloud-report-final.pdf.
6. Ciara Ryan, "Strategies of the Movers and Shakers," Arthur Andersen, Risk Consulting, August 15, 2000. Available at www.goodstrategybadstrategy.com/.
7. "Bridging the Gap," Defense Advanced Research Projects Agency, February 2007. Available at www.darpa.mil/Docs/DARPA2007StrategicPlanfinalMarch14.pdf.

8. LAUSD's official figure is $11,000 per student. This, however, omits spending on transportation, capital improvements, construction, and interest on school bond debt.

CHAPTER 4: WHY SO MUCH BAD STRATEGY?

1. Nicolas de Condorcet, a French philosopher and mathematician, was the first to mathematically analyze democratic voting rules. He died in prison following the French Revolution.
2. Kenneth Arrow, *Social Choice and Individual Values* (New York: John Wiley and Sons, 1951).
3. NSC 162/2, "Basic National Security Policy," October 30, 1953. Available at www.fas.org/irp/offdocs/nsc-hst/nsc-162-2.pdf.
4. This conversation is reported in Andrew S. Grove, *Only the Paranoid Survive: How to Exploit the Crisis Points That Challenge Every Company and Career* (New York: Doubleday, 1996), 89.
5. Max Weber, "The Sociology of Charismatic Authority," in *Max Weber: Essays in Sociology,* eds. and trans. H. Gerth and C. W. Mills (London: Routledge and Kegan Paul, 1948).
6. Dow Chemical Company, 2009 Annual Report to Shareholders, 24.
7. Strategic Planning Council, "Strategic Plan," California State University, Sacramento, 2007, 2.
8. "CIA Vision, Mission & Values," last reviewed April 12, 2007, https://www.cia.gov/about-cia/cia-vision-mission-values.
9. Prentice Mulford, *Thoughts Are Things* (London: G. Bell and Sons, Ltd., 1908), 96. Reprinted by Kessinger Publishing (Whitefish, MT), 1996. Emphasis added.
10. Wallace D. Wattles, *The Science of Getting Rich* (Radford, VA: Wilder Publications, 2007), 14. Originally published in 1910, this work is now in the public domain.
11. Ernest Holmes, *Creative Mind and Success* (New York: G. Putnam's, 1997), 17. First published by R. M. McBride, 1919.
12. Peter M. Senge, *The Fifth Discipline: The Art and Practice of the Learning Organization* (New York: Doubleday, 1990), 207.
13. Steven Wozniak, cofounder of Apple Computer, attributed much of his company's rise to VisiCalc: "VisiCalc and the floppy disk sent this company into the number one position. . . . After VisiCalc, it was perceived that 90 percent of all Apple IIs sold were going to small businesses. . . . Originally we were a home hobby computer. Now, suddenly, small businesses were buying Apple IIs." Quoted in Gregg Williams and Rob Moore, "The Apple Story," *Byte,* January 1985, 173–74.

14. Ford's newspaper, the *Dearborn Independent*, published a long series of articles critical of Jewish influence in American life. These articles were gathered into a book titled *The International Jew: The World's Foremost Problem*. In his autobiography, Ford explains his critique of Jews as defending against an "Orientalism which has insidiously affected every channel of expression." See Henry Ford, *My Life and Work* (Garden City, NY: Doubleday, 1922), 251–52. See also Anne Jardin, *The First Henry Ford: A Study in Personality and Business Leadership* (Cambridge, MA: MIT Press, 1970).
15. Mark Lipton, *Guiding Growth: How Vision Keeps Companies on Course* (Boston: Harvard Business School Press, 2003), 81.
16. Peter Senge, C. Otto Scharmer, Joseph Jaworski, and Betty Sue Flowers, *Presence: Exploring Profound Change in People, Organizations, and Society* (New York: Doubleday, 2005), 134–35.

CHAPTER 5: THE KERNEL OF GOOD STRATEGY

1. "Castles in the Sand," Deutsche Bank, Global Markets Research, July 30, 2008, 3.
2. "Starbucks Corporation: Slower Growth De-levers Margins, but Greater EPS Visibility Ahead," Oppenheimer Equity Research, July 31, 2008, 4. Available at www.goodstrategybadstrategy.com.
3. William G. Ouchi and Lydia G. Segal, *Making Schools Work: A Revolutionary Plan to Get Your Children the Education They Need* (New York: Simon and Schuster, 2003).
4. X [George Kennan], "The Sources of Soviet Conduct," *Foreign Affairs*, July 1947, 566–82.
5. "The Vision and Values of Wells Fargo," Wells Fargo, 2007. Available at www.goodstrategybadstrategy.com.
6. Private conversation, 1995.

CHAPTER 6: USING LEVERAGE

1. The ancient Greeks had accurately measured the diameter of the earth. They also measured the distance to the moon, but got that wrong because their method was extremely sensitive to errors in the measurement of the angle between the sun and the half-lit moon.
2. Donald Wright, et al. *On Point II: Transition to the New Campaign* (Fort Leavenworth, KS: Combat Studies Institute Press, 2008), 568.
3. Bob Woodward, *State of Denial* (New York: Simon and Schuster, 2006), 122.
4. These predictions were described in Pierre Wack, "Scenarios: Uncharted Waters Ahead," *Harvard Business Review,* September–October 1985, 73–89.

5. It is difficult to observe this effect in data because few firms are foolish enough to advertise below the threshold. For a very cunning research design that observes a threshold effect in advertising, see Jean-Pierre Dubé, Günter Hitsch, and Puneet Manchanda, "An Empirical Model of Advertising Dynamics," *Quantitative Marketing and Economics* 3, no. 2 (2005): 107–44.

CHAPTER 7: PROXIMATE OBJECTIVES

1. Wernher von Braun to the Vice President of the United States, 20 April 1961, NASA Historical Reference Collection, NASA Headquarters, Washington, DC.
2. The first better photograph of the surface was taken by *Ranger* 7 in 1964, snapped at an altitude of about one thousand feet before it smashed into the surface. The photo did little to settle the hard-soft-sharp debate, and it showed only objects that were larger than about three feet.
3. "Tentative Model for the Lunar Environment," JPL Document 61-263, 1961.
4. Oran W. Nicks, *Far Travelers: The Exploring Machines* (Washington, DC: Scientific and Technical Information Branch, National Aeronautics and Space Administration, 1985), 3.
5. Herbert Goldhamer, "The Soviet Union in a Period of Strategic Parity," RAND R-889-PR, November 1971, 7, quoted by Watts, "Why Strategy?" 5.
6. The obvious drawback to this process of elaboration is that the people in the offices on the fiftieth floor may have unrealistic ideas about what can actually be done on the ground. The first best cure for this is for some people on the fiftieth floor to have had ground-level experience. The second best solution is lots of communication up and down the tower as the strategy is put together. The third best solution is to change the objective once there is very strong evidence that it can't be achieved. That, however, rarely happens without a turnover in leadership. Some of the reason is ego, but a lot of it is common sense. Not everyone likes or agrees with every strategic path, and there are always those within the organization who would prefer or benefit from a change in direction. If you have a policy of changing direction whenever you hit a snag, such people will be happy to create the necessary snags.

CHAPTER 8: CHAIN-LINK SYSTEMS

1. The logic of quality matching is not obvious at first glance, but it is by such deductions that scholars earn their keep. See Michael Kremer, "The O-Ring Theory of Economic Development," *Quarterly Journal of Economics,* 108, 1993: 551–575.

CHAPTER 9: USING DESIGN

1. The Roman Republic elected members of the senate and two consuls, who were joint executives and magistrates of the government, each able to veto the other. In times of war, at least one consul was normally a general and led the army. In times of extreme emergency, the senate asked the consuls to appoint a dictator, who ruled with absolute authority for a six-month term.
2. What happened next is equally fascinating. Hannibal sent ambassadors to talk with Rome, expecting a peace treaty that would acknowledge his territorial gains. Rome refused to talk. Any nascent peace movement was stopped in its tracks when the senate outlawed the word "peace." Every male citizen was mobilized, and Rome returned to a policy of harassing Hannibal but avoiding major battles in Italy. After some time, a skilled Roman commander, Publius Cornelius Scipio, was given a free hand to conquer Spain and he did, denying Hannibal a key source of supplies and manpower. Scipio then took his armies across the Mediterranean, attacked Carthage itself, and conquered it. Hannibal never lost a battle in Italy, but Carthage lost the war. After defeating Carthage, Rome went on to subdue Macedon, Syracuse, and the Seleucid Empire.
3. Theodore Ayrault Dodge, *Hannibal: A History of the Art of War Among the Carthaginians and Romans Down to the Battle of Pydna, 168 B.C., with a Detailed Account of the Second Punic War* (New York: Da Capo Press, 1995), 633. First published in 1891.
4. Alexander of Macedon had achieved stunning victories using tactics, formations, and weapons developed by his father, Philip. His victory over Darius at Gaugamela a century earlier was strategically as brilliant as Cannae, as well as being bolder, but was less orchestrated and relied less on multiple coordinated actions.
5. The technical word for these gains to various combinations of parts or resources is "complementarities."
6. Technically, the better metric to work with is surplus—the difference between what the buyer is willing to pay for the car and the cost to produce and deliver it. Willingness to pay is higher for wealthier buyers and higher for those who especially value the product's differentiating characteristics.
7. Steve Postrel makes this same point with regard to knowledge. To do design work, he argues, teams need both specialized knowledge and knowledge of how the specialties fit together. But, he argues, you can achieve the same performance by having more of one and less of the other. See his article, "Islands of Shared Knowledge: Specialization and Mutual Understanding in Problem-Solving Teams," *Organizational Science* 13, no. 3 (May–June

2002): 303–20. At a more basic level, the idea of factors being partial substitutes arose in classical economics. David Ricardo argued that one could increase the amount of crops grown by applying more labor to existing land or by having the existing number of farmers work more land. See David Ricardo, "On the principles of political economy and taxation," *The Works and Correspondence of David Ricardo,* 3rd ed., ed. P. Sraffa (Cambridge: Cambridge University Press, 1821). Reprinted in 1951.

CHAPTER 10: FOCUS

1. James S. Garrison, "Crown Cork and Seal Company, Inc.," rev. Stephen Bradley and Sheila M. Cavanaugh, Harvard Business School case study 378-024, 1987.
2. This statement was in an earlier version of the case. I provided this and other information in a supplement I handed out.

CHAPTER 11: GROWTH

1. Meena Panchapakasen, "Indecent Expansion," *Financial World,* July 6, 1993.
2. Mark Tran and Mark Milner, "Americans Plan to Wrap Up World in Pounds 3.3 Bn Deal," *Guardian,* May 24, 1995.
3. Michael Porter, *Competitive Strategy* (New York: Free Press, 1980).
4. For this chart I have measured return on capital as the ratio of after-tax EBIT (sometimes called NOPAT) to lagged invested capital plus goodwill. Thus, the numerator is the profit that would have been earned were debt replaced by equity, and the denominator is assets less nondebt current liabilities.
5. "An In-House M&A Team Reshapes a Company," *Global Finance,* March 1997.

CHAPTER 12: USING ADVANTAGE

1. "Tora Bora Revisited: How We Failed to Get Bin Laden and Why It Matters Today," Report to Members of the Committee on Foreign Relations, United States Senate, November 30, 2009. According to this analysis, U.S. Commander General Tommy Franks did not use the full forces available because he "feared alienating Afghan allies."
2. The phrase comes from biology where it describes any barrier to interbreeding. See Richard Rumelt, "Towards a Strategic Theory of the Firm," in *Competitive Strategic Management,* ed. R. Lamb (Englewood Cliffs, NJ: Prentice-Hall, 1984), 556–70. Reprinted in *Resources, Firms, and Strategies: A Reader in the Resource-Based Perspective,* ed. N. J. Foss (New York: Oxford University Press, 1998).

3. An equivalent argument was that the "advantage" didn't make the new owner any better off because he could, at any time (in our imaginary setting), sell the machine for $100 million, invest the proceeds, and earn $10 million in interest.
4. The machine's opportunity cost, properly defined, is zero because it has no value in use outside the silver industry. Return on invested capital is only "above average" when key resources have not been recently marked to market.
5. Frank B. Gilbreth, *Bricklaying System* (New York: Myron C. Clark Publishing, 1909). Gilbreth, along with Frederick Taylor, are considered the fathers of scientific management.
6. The idea is so general and widespread that it resists precise attribution. In 1951, Edith Penrose introduced economists to the idea that firms grew and expanded because of underutilized skills and resources. In my 1972 dissertation I called the knowledge underlying linkages among businesses *core skills*. Eighteen years later, writing with much greater persuasiveness and using better examples, Gary Hamel and C. K. Prahalad catapulted their phrase "core competence" right out of specialist circles and into common usage.
7. Steven N. Wiggins and Gary D. Libecap, "Oil Field Unitization: Contractual Failure in the Presence of Imperfect Information," *American Economic Review,* 75, 1985: 368–85.

CHAPTER 13: USING DYNAMICS

1. Quoted in Michael Kanellos, "Intel's Accidental Revolution," CNET News.com, November 14, 2001.
2. Grove, *Only the Paranoid Survive,* 45.
3. Ibid., 44–45.
4. Bechtolsheim designed the hardware and Yeaker wrote the software. While at Stanford, Bechtolsheim also did his initial design for the Sun 1 workstation, before he left to cofound Sun Microsystems. Yeager joined him there.
5. John Sutton, *Technology and Market Structure* (Cambridge, MA: MIT Press, 1999), ch. 5.
6. Boston Consulting Group, "The Transition to a New Environment Has Begun," 1997. At that time, AT&T's network was more than ten times larger than WorldCom's and was mostly older technology. The difference in average cost per unit had nothing to do with AT&T's ability to build modern capacity similar to WorldCom's.

CHAPTER 14: INERTIA AND ENTROPY

1. "Strategic Plan for the Consumer Computer Market," AT&T Consumer Products, Strategic Planning and Consumer Information Products Section, July 1983. Company confidential.
2. The very popular economic valued added (EVA) measure, trademarked by Stern, Stewart & Co., has the same problem since it is also based on "invested capital" measured at historical cost.
3. "Gain to operating" was defined as current cash operating profit (after taxes) less the annualized cash flow that could be obtained by closing the outlet, selling off the inventory, and leasing (or subleasing) the property at market rates. In computing current cash profit, I eliminated the various interest and mortgage interest expenses the company charged against each outlet. In addition, I stopped the allocation of "overhead" that was actually the owners' salaries and benefits and allocated the remaining corporate expenses based on cost of goods sold instead of square feet. I also added incentive payments to the wage bill for each location.
4. The formal term for this is "corruption"—the decay of an original form. But this word has lost its original meaning and now connotes moral perversion.
5. Alfred Sloan, *My Years with General Motors* (New York: Doubleday, 1990), 67.

CHAPTER 15: PUTTING IT TOGETHER

1. "Vidia" is an amalgam of "video" and "via," from Latin words meaning "to see" and "the way" or "the road." The letter "N" is an abbreviation of the Latin *natus,* meaning "to come into existence."
2. Ed Catmull (Pixar), John Carmack (id Software), Doug Kay (Mondo Media, Web graphics), and Pat Hanrahan (Stanford Computer Graphics Lab). David Kirk (Crystal Dynamics) was hired to be chief scientist.
3. Whereas simulation was accomplished by software programs running on general-purpose computers, emulation was done by configuring special chips to behave like the target chip. Slower than the actual chip would be, emulation was much faster than simulation.
4. Jon Peddie Research is a technically oriented marketing and management consulting firm specializing in graphics and multimedia.
5. Quoted by Way Ting, former vice president at SGI, in Robert Hof, Ira Sager, and Linda Himelstein, "The Sad Saga of Silicon Graphics," *BusinessWeek,* August 4, 1997.

CHAPTER 16: THE SCIENCE OF STRATEGY

1. John Locke, *Second Treatise on Government,* 1690, ch. 4, available at http://www.constitution.org/.
2. Howard Schultz and Dori Jones Yang, *Pour Your Heart into It: How Starbucks Built a Company One Cup at a Time* (New York: Hyperion, 1997), 50–51.
3. Ibid., 87.

CHAPTER 17: USING YOUR HEAD

1. Malcolm Gladwell, *Blink: The Power of Thinking Without Thinking* (New York: Little, Brown, 2005).
2. This is called *base-rate neglect*. It may be explained by the representativeness heuristic. See Daniel Kahneman and Amos Tversky, "On the Psychology of Prediction," *Psychological Review* 80, no. 4 (July 1973): 237–51.
3. This is probably an example of the inside-view bias applied to competitive settings. See Daniel Kahneman and Dan Lovallo, "Timid Choices and Bold Forecasts: A Cognitive Perspective on Risk Taking, *Management Science* 39, no. 1 (January 1993): 17–31, as well as Colin Camerer and Dan Lovallo, "Overconfidence and Excess Entry: An Experimental Approach, *American Economic Review* 89, no. 1(March 1999): 306–18.
4. A stand-alone TiVo box duplicates functions already provided in the bundled set-top box and must download scheduling information over the telephone line or an Internet connection rather than directly over the cable TV link. These added costs and complications keep it from being a mass-market solution.

CHAPTER 18: KEEPING YOUR HEAD

1. Garrahan, Bath, and Stricker, "Emerging Network Companies: Exploiting Industry Paradigm Shifts," Lehman Brothers, October 27, 1998.
2. R. P. Rumelt, "Global Crossing (A) and (B)," Anderson School at UCLA case study, 2002, www.goodstrategybadstrategy.com.
3. For a detailed and nuanced exploration of the fiber optic capacity bubble, see Andrew Odlyzko, "Bubbles, Gullibility, and Other Challenges for Economics, Psychology, Sociology, and Information Sciences," University of Minnesota School of Mathematics, 2010, http://www.dtc.unm.edu/~odlyzko.
4. See Torkel Franzén, *Gödel's Theorem: An Incomplete Guide to Its Use and Abuse* (Wellesley, MA: A K Peters, Ltd., 2005). Gödel showed that logical systems at least as complex as arithmetic were incomplete.

5. For one analysis, see Nobuhiro Kiyotaki and John Moore, "Credit Cycles," *Journal of Political Economy* 105, no. 2 (April 1997): 211–48. They say, "The dynamic interaction between credit limits and asset prices turns out to be a powerful transmission mechanism by which the effects of shocks persist, amplify, and spill over to other sectors."
6. This term was popularized by Nassim Taleb in his book *The Black Swan: The Impact of the Highly Improbable* (Random House, 2007). However, as Taleb argued on his blog, the financial crisis was not a "black swan," because it was not "highly improbable."
7. Daniel Kahneman and Dan Lovallo, "Timid Choices and Bold Forecasts: A Cognitive Perspective on Risk Taking," in *Fundamental Issues in Strategy: A Research Agenda,* eds. Richard Rumelt, Dan Schendel, and David Teece (Harvard Business School Press, 1994), 71–96.
8. The OECD, a descendant of the Marshall Plan, contains thirty-three advanced countries. Its purpose is to foster economic progress and trade.
9. Richard J. Herring and Susan Wachter, "Real Estate Booms and Banking Busts: An International Perspective," Wharton Financial Institutions Center working paper 99-27, 1999.
10. "Australia Frightened; the Results of an Abnormal Land Boom," *New York Times,* August 15, 1892.
11. U.S. Department of Housing and Urban Development, Urban Policy Brief, no. 2, August 1995.
12. Henry M. Paulson Jr., "Open Statement at the Meeting of the U.S.-China Strategic Economic Dialogue," U.S. Department of the Treasury press release hp727, December 12, 2007.
13. Ben Bernanke, "The Great Moderation," remarks to the Eastern Economic Association, February 20, 2004.
14. Alan Greenspan, "Economic Flexibility," remarks to the National Association for Business Economics, September 27, 2005.
15. Timothy F. Geithner, speech at the Global Association of Risk Professionals (GARP) Seventh Annual Risk Management Convention, New York, February 28, 2006.
16. Proverbs 16:18.

ACKNOWLEDGMENTS

I owe debts to everyone who taught me and worked with me over the years. They are, literally, too numerous to mention and I will limit most specific acknowledgments to those who read and commented on portions of this manuscript.

Dan Vivoli, senior vice president at Nvidia, helped me open doors at that company. He read my chapter on Nvidia at least twice, providing helpful feedback each time. Stewart Resnick (chairman of Roll International) was generous with his time and insights.

Allen Webb, with McKinsey & Company, read a number of the chapters and offered many useful insights, as did Lang Davison, when he was with McKinsey. Sid Barteau, formerly vice president of sales at American Can Company, helped me understand the more recent dynamics in the can industry and provided feedback on my treatment of Crown Cork & Seal. Francesco de Leo, presently executive chairman of Green Comm Challenge, has been a patient sounding board. Andy Marshall, the director of net assessment at the DOD, read and commented on several of these chapters. Barry Watts, senior fellow at the Center for Strategic and Budgetary Assessments, has been a careful reader of my work and offered wonderfully insightful feedback.

Dan Lovallo, at the University of Sydney, read several of my chapters and offered long evenings of discussion on these topics. I am deeply appreciative of his enthusiasm and interest in this project. Charles O'Reilly, at Stanford University, helped me sort out my opinions about leadership and vision. Among my colleagues at UCLA, Steve Lippman, John de Figueiredo, Steve Postrel, Craig Fox, and John Mamer all read various chapters and made wonderfully helpful comments.

I want to thank the Kunin family for the endowed chair I hold—the

Harry and Elsa Kunin Chair in Business & Society. The earnings on their endowment free me from the ritual of begging for research support and let me follow my interests. I also want to acknowledge the support of UCLA Anderson's dean, Judy Olian, who encouraged my work on this book.

My literary agent, Michael Carlisle (InkWell Management), skillfully cajoled me into performing the surgery on my manuscript that was necessary to make it saleable. My editor, John Mahaney, patiently directed the further operations needed to make it readable. My thanks to both of them.

I could not have written this book without the love and support of my wife, Kate. A former teacher and researcher in strategy, Kate read and reread these chapters, always with patience and always offering pointed criticisms while marking passages she especially liked with small happy faces.☺

Richard Rumelt
UCLA Anderson
richard.rumelt@anderson.ucla.edu

INDEX

Accenture, 40
action:
  coherent, 77, 87–94
  coordinated, 129–30
  moving to, 88
Addison, Joseph, 251
Advanced Micro Devices (AMD), 236
advantage, 9, 160–77
  competitive, 29, 85, 163–64
  and creating demand, 173–75
  deepening, 170–71
  extending, 171–73
  "interesting," 164–69
  and isolating mechanisms, 175–77
  and silver machine problem, 167–68
  value-creating changes, 169
  wrestling the gorilla, 160–61
advertising, threshold effect in, 103
Afghanistan, 161–62
Agnelli famly, 157
airlines:
  Continental, 204–8
  deregulation of, 197, 204–5, 206–8
Alcatel-Lucent, 208n, 210
Alexander of Macedon, 304n4
al Qaeda, 161–62
Alvarez, Luis, 193
Amazon, 163n
ambiguity, resolving, 108–11
ambition, 5
Amelio, Gil, 11
American Airlines, 207
American Can Company, 143
Andersen Consulting, 13, 40
Andropov, Yuri, 102
anomalies, 247–49
Ansco, 194
anticipation, 85, 98–100, 128–29
AOL (America Online), 197
Apple Inc., 11–15, 163, 191, 208
  and competition, 11, 14, 203
  success of, 74
Archimedes, 97
Aristotelian theory, 245–46
Aristotle, 245
Army, U.S.:
  envelopment maneuver by, 18–19
  field manual of, 3–4
ARPANET, 191
Arrow, Kenneth, 61
Arthur Andersen, 38, 40
ArtX, 235, 236
asset bubbles, 286
AT&T, 192, 197
  and competition, 270
  and deregulation, 196
  inertia of culture in, 208–10
  and transatlantic cable, 277
ATI Technologies, 235–36
Atlantic cable, 277–81
Atlantic Crossing, 277
attraction, law of, 72
attractor states, 198–201
Avaya Inc., 208n
Avery, William, 151–56

bad strategy, 32–57
  and avoiding hard work, 58
  bad objectives, 32, 51–57
  commonness of, 58
  detection of, 7
  failure to face the challenge, 32, 41–44
  fluff, 32, 37–40
  hallmarks of, 32
  inability to choose, 59–64
  mistaking goals for strategy, 32, 45–51
  nature of, 4–5, 7–8, 36–37
  and New Thought, 58, 71–76

bad strategy, (cont.)
origin of concept, 33–37
template-style, 58, 64–70
bar-code scanners, 25
Bass, Bernard, 65
battle of the titans, 196
Bear Stearns, 286
Bechtolsheim, Andy, 191
Bell Laboratories, 208n, 209–10
Bennis, Warren, 65
Berlin Airlift, 82
Berlin Wall, fall of, 29
Bernanke, Ben, 296, 297
Bezzera, Luigi, 252
biases, predictable, 195–97
bin Laden, Osama, 71, 162
black swans, 289
Blockbuster, 202
blue box (router), 191
BMW, 130
Boeing Fleet Planner, 205–6
Booz Allen Hamilton, 41
Bosack, Len, 191
BP Gulf oil spill, 288
brand-name protections, 175
Braniff International airlines, 205
Braun, Werner von, 107–8
Brett brothers, 277
Brewer, David, 54–55
Bright, Charles, 277
British Airways, 2
British Telecom, 197
Brown, Harold, 29
Brown, Richard, 157
Buffett, Warren, 163
bundling, 270
Bush, George H. W., 15, 20, 82
Bush, George W., 3–4, 33–34, 100, 295
Bushnell, Nolan, 224
business-process transformation, 170
Buwalda, Phyllis, 109–11
Byrne, Rhonda, 73–74

Cable & Wireless, 157
California State University at Sacramento, 69
Calle, Craig, 151, 155
Cambodia, Khmer Rouge in, 211
Cannae, 125–30
Cannon, Michael, *The Land Boomers*, 293–94
Canon, 137
Carmack, John, 226
Carnegie, Andrew, 258–59
Carter, William, 277
Catmull, Edwin, 224
Celestica Hong Kong Ltd., 232
centralized direction, 92–93
chain-link systems, 116–23
excellence, 122–23
getting stuck, 117–18
getting unstuck, 119–21
Challenger, O-rings, 116
challenges:
failure to face, 32, 41–44
ill-structured, 81
overcoming, 2, 4
Chambers, John, 191
Chandler, Alfred D. Jr., 272
change:
adjustments for, 66
main effects of, 180–81
as objective, 120
and perspective, 179
reengineering, 170
resistance to, 64
in technology, 233
value-creating, 169
waves of, *see* waves of change
charisma, 64–66, 67, 106
Chen Brothers, 52–53
Cheney, Dick, 20
Children's Crusade, 66–67
choice, 86–87
and decision theory, 129
inability to make, 59–64
strategy as, 62, 64
Chopra, Deepak, 73
Christian Science, 72, 73
Churchill, Winston, 48, 64
CIA (Central Intelligence Agency), 69–70, 100
Cisco Systems, 182–83, 184, 190–93, 198
Cisneros, Henry, 294
Citigroup, 286
Civil Aeronautics Board (CAB), 204, 206, 207
Clark, Jim, 224–25, 235
Cleevely, David, 279

Clinton, Bill, 294
cloud computing, 37
clusters, 119
Coca-Cola, 180
coherence, 77, 85, 87–94, 268
  loss of, 1
  of policies and actions, 9
Comcast, 273
Compaq, 137
competition, blocking, 236, 270
competitive advantage, 29, 85, 163–64
complexity, reducing, 85
computer industry, vertical disintegration of, 83
concentration, 102–5
Condorcet's paradox, 60–61
Connelly, John F., 142, 151, 154, 155
Conrad, Pete, 110
containment, 81–82
Continental Airlines, 204–8
Continental Can Company, 143
Continental Illinois bailout, 289
Conway, John, 153
Cook, Dick, 172
coordination, 92, 94, 115
Coors Brewing Co., 146
Copernican theory, 245–46, 251
copyrights, 175
core competence, 306n6
Cornell University, 68–69
corruption, 307n4
costs:
  average, 280
  buyer's, 170n
  fixed, 194
  long-run average cost, 280
  marginal (variable), 280
Coyote, Wile E., 287
create-destroy, 271–73
credit bubbles, 286, 293
Crown Cork & Seal, 142–50, 151–56
CSBA (Center for Strategic and Budgetary Assessments), 33
culture:
  inertia of, 208–12
  use of term, 211

Daimler AG, 138
dark matter, 248–49
DARPA (Defense Advanced Research Projects Agency), 43–44
David and Goliath, 21–22
Dawson, Wallace, 277
debt deflation, 287
DEC (Digital Equipment Corporation), 59–62, 63, 189, 191
decisions, formal theory of, 129
Defense Department, U.S., 28–31, 68
deleveraging, 287
Dell, 12, 137, 232, 233
Delta Airlines, 197, 207
demand, creating, 173–75
democracy, group irrationality in, 61
demonstration effect, 199
Denton, Carl and Mariah, 214–15, 217
Denton's Inc., 214–18, 222
depressions:
  (1819), 292
  financial crisis (2008), 290
  Panic of 1837, 292
  Panic of 1893, 293–94
deregulation:
  airlines, 197, 204–5, 206–8
  telecommunications, 194–95, 196, 204
Descartes, Rene, 245
Desert Storm, 15–20
design, 124
  anticipation, 128–29
  the arc of enterprise, 134–38
  and competition, 137
  of coordinated action, 129–30
  costs of, 186, 187
  and entropy, 220–21
  nature of, 134
  order out of chaos, 138–41, 220
  parts of a whole, 130–34
  premeditation, 128
  trade-offs in, 132, 133–34
  trial and error in, 187
determination, 5
diagnosis, 77, 79–84, 268
Diamond Multimedia, 233
DirecTV, 273
Disney Company, 172–73
Dodge, Theodore, 127
Doom (PC game), 225–26
Doriot, Georges F., 88

Dow Chemicals, 67–68
Drucker, Peter, 65
Dryden, John, 251
DuPont, 171–72
du Pont, Pierre, 218
dynamics, 178–201
  and high ground, 178–81
  see also waves of change

Eastern Airlines, 207
eBay, 168–69
economies of scale, 279
Eddy, Mary Baker, 72
Einstein, Albert, 249
Eisenhower, Dwight D., 62, 64, 65
Embraer (Brazil), 173
Emerson, Ralph Waldo, 71, 75
energy crisis, 99–100, 108
engineering overreach, 289
England, Battle of Trafalgar, 1
Enlightenment, 245–47, 251
Enron, 38–40, 67–68
enterprise, arc of, 134–38
Enterprise Rent-A-Car, 137
entropy, 214–22
  Denton's, 214–18
  GM, 218–22
  scientific definition of, 202
European Business Group, 88–90
Evans, David, 224
excellence, 122–23
experience, 267–68
experts, virtual panel of, 271–73

Facebook, 163n
Fahd, king of Saudi Arabia, 20
failure to face the challenge, 32, 41–44
Falkenhayn, Erich von, 48
Fansteel Inc., 257–58
Federal Reserve System, 295–97
FedEx, 137
Feldman, Al, 204, 208
Ferris, Dick, 205
fiber optic channels, 279, 283
Field, Cyrus, 277
Fisher, Irving, 287
Fisher, Jeff, 228
Five Forces framework, 153, 280, 284
Fletcher, Fred, 257–58, 260
Flowers, Betty Sue, 75
fluff, 32, 37–40
focus, 142–50, 155
Ford, Henry, 74–75, 218
Ford Motor Company, 91, 180
  Model T Ford, 218
forecasting, biases in, 195–97
fragmentation, 211
Franklin Mint, 164
Frontier Airlines, 207, 208
Fuji film, 194
Fuld, Richard, 3

gain to operating (GTO), 215–16
galactic rotation, 248–49
Galileo Galilei, 245–46
games, and 3-D graphics, 225–27, 236
Gandhi, Mahatma, 64, 67
Gates, Bill, 12, 98, 138
Geithner, Timothy F., 297
General Electric (GE), 180, 194
General Motors (GM):
  bankruptcy declared by, 222
  chain-linked issues in, 117–18, 123
  entropy in, 218–22
  models and prices, 219, 220, 221, 222
Gerstner, Lou, 83, 84
Getty, J. Paul, 104
Getty Foundation, 104–5
Getty Trust, 104–5
Gilbreth, Frank, 170
Gilder, George, 284
Gladwell, Malcolm, *Blink*, 264–65
Glide (language), 227, 229
Global Crossing, 276, 277–84
goals:
  mistaking for strategy, 32, 45–51
  objectives vs., 52
  setting, 6–7
Gödel, Kurt, 285
Goldhamer, Herbert, 111
good strategy:
  and competition, 11
  core of, 2
  kernel of, *see* kernel
  nature of, 6, 9, 11
  overcoming challenges in, 2, 4
  simplicity of, 1–2, 12, 85
Google, 100, 137, 200, 203

Gorbachev, Mikhail, 102
Gore-Tex, 160
Gorin, Ralph, 190–91
Graham, Bob, 16
graphics pipeline, 224–25, 229, 232, 236
gravity, theories of, 249
Greenspan, Alan, 296–97
group irrationality, 61
Grove, Andy, 63, 186
  Only the Paranoid Survive, 188–89
growth, 151–59
  by acquisition, 156
  healthy, 159
  reasons for, 156
  and strategy, 235
  value created in, 155–56
guiding policy, 77, 84–87, 268
Gulf War (1991), 15–20

Haig, Douglas, 48
Hannibal, 125–29, 234
Hay Associates, 41
heliocentric universe, 245–46
Herring, Richard J., 291
Hershey's, 180
high ground, 178–81
Hindenburg disaster, 288, 289
Hobbes, Thomas, 245
Hogg Robinson, 258
Holmes, Ernest, *Creative Mind and Success,* 73
Hoover, Herbert, 294
household debt, 286–88, 291–92, 294–95
HP (Hewlett-Packard), 12, 62, 137, 233
Huang, Jen-Hsun, 223, 227, 228, 229
Hughes Electronics, 241–44
Hume, David, 245
hump chart, 216–17
Hunt's products, 180
Hussein, Saddam, 15, 17, 36, 99
hypothesis:
  in science, 247
  strategy as, 241–44, 247

IBM, 83–84, 179
  and antitrust litigation, 192, 196, 270
  and change, 188–89, 190, 191, 192, 194
  and competition, 137, 138

id Software, 226
IKEA, 122–23
Iklé, Fred C., 33
Ilford, 194
inertia:
  business definition of, 202
  and competition, 202–3, 204
  of culture, 208–12
  by proxy, 212–14
  revelations of, 204
  of routine, 203–8
inflation index, 296
information:
  privileged, 253
  proprietary, 254–56
innovation, 5, 178
Inquisition, 246
INSEAD, 88
inside view, 276, 290–91, 298
insight, 263, 264
  game-changing, 10
  localized, 269
instinct, 265
Intel:
  choices in, 63
  and competition, 137, 188, 229, 232, 234–35
  first microprocessor from, 185–86, 189
  "Intel Inside" campaign, 234
  and Windows, 11, 14, 83, 235, 236
Intermedia Communications, 213
International Harvester, 41–43
Internet:
  PC games on, 226
  rise of, 192, 196, 197, 278, 281, 282, 284
Internet Protocol (IP) networking, 191–92, 198–99
Iran, and Iraq, 15, 17
Iraq:
  invasion of Kuwait, 15–17
  and Iran, 15, 17
  U.S. invasion of, 3–4, 98–99
  and weapons of mass destruction, 34
isolating mechanisms, 175–77

Jaworski, Joseph, 75
Jefferson, Thomas, 245, 246, 294

Jobs, Steve:
and Apple, 12–15
on author's expert panel, 272, 273
and next big thing, 14–15
Joffre, Joseph, 48
Johnson, Lyndon B., 107
Johnstown Flood, 288
judgment, 268, 274–75
Jurassic Park (movie), 225

Kahneman, Daniel, 290
Katrina, Hurricane, 288, 289
Kellogg's, 180
Kennan, George, 82–83
Kennedy, John F., 106–8
Kenworth trucks, 138–39
kernel, 77–79, 268–69
coherent action in, 77, 87–94, 268
diagnosis in, 77, 79–84, 268
elements of, 7, 77
guiding policy in, 77, 84–87, 268
Khalid, Prince (Saudi Arabia), 20
Khmer Rouge, 211
King, Martin Luther Jr., 64, 106
Kipling, Rudyard, 276
Kirk, David, 232
Kmart, 25, 27, 137
Knight Ridder, 209
knowledge, 268
already known, 244–45
Kobayashi, Koji, 196
Kodak Corporation, 180, 194
Korean War, 82
Kovacevich, Richard, 84
Kreider, Torsten, 151
Kuwait:
Iraqi invasion of, 15–17
weapons in, 36

law of attraction, 72
leadership:
charismatic, 64–66, 67, 106
inspirational, 5–6
responsibility of, 2
and strategy, 66
transformational, 56, 65
use of term, 299n1
Lehman Brothers, 2–3, 286
Leibniz, Gottfried Wilhelm, 245
Lerner, Sandy, 191
leverage, 85, 97–105
and anticipation, 98–100
and concentration, 102–5
and pivot points, 101–2
Lévy, Jean-Bernard, 181–83, 184, 188, 190
limiting factors, 117
Lippman, Steven, 167
Lipton, Mark, *Guiding Growth,* 75
lists, making, 53, 258–61
Lloyd, Edward, 251
Lloyds of London, 251
Locke, John, 245, 246
Logan, Chad, 45–47, 49–50, 71
London Stock Exchange, 251
Long-Term Capital Management, 289
Lorenzo, Frank, 207–8
Los Angeles Unified School District (LAUSD), 53, 54–57
Lovallo, Dan, 290
Lynch, Peter, 142

M31 galaxy, 248–49
Madison, James, 97
Malachowsky, Chris, 227, 230
Mamer, John, 79
Mao Tse-tung, 92
Marshall, Andy, 28–31
Marshall, George C., 65
Matra Communications, 181–84
McCardell, Archie, 41, 43
McCormick, Cyrus, 41
McCracken, Ed, 235
McDonald's, 80
McDonnell Douglas, 206
McDonough, Jack, 272–73
Merrill Lynch, 286
microprocessors:
first, 185–86, 189, 204
and smart computers, 189
and software, 191
and waves of change, 196
Microsoft:
and Apple, 12
and competition, 137, 138, 188, 203, 270
DirectX, 229, 232, 236
and Google, 100

and Justice Department, 12
Windows, 11, 14, 83, 176, 235, 236
mission, 67
Mogadishu, 99
momentum, 103
monopolies, 270
Moore, Geoffrey, *Crossing the Chasm,* 227
Moore, Gordon, 63, 186
Moore's law, 186, 228–29
Morgridge, John, 191
mortgages, 286–88, 289, 294–96
Moses, 64, 66
Mulford, Prentice, *Thoughts Are Things,* 72, 74
Murata, Noritoshi, 101
Myst (PC game), 225

NAFTA, 141
Nanus, Bert, 65
Napoléon Bonaparte, 1
Napster, 199, 263
NASA, Jet Propulsion Laboratory (JPL), 108–11, 131–34
Nasser, Jacques, 91
National Can Company, 143
national security, 33–36, 64
NATO, 33, 35, 82
natural laws, 246
Navistar, 138
NEC Corporation, 70, 196
Nelson, Horatio, Viscount, 1
Nestlé, 113
Netflix, 202
network, 26–27, 190
network effect, 163n
networking:
corporate, 191
IP, 191–92
proprietary protocols in, 192
New Age ideas, 74
Newland, Ted, 99
newspaper industry, 199–201
New Thought, 58, 71–76
Newton, Isaac, 245, 246, 249, 251
New York Air, 208
New York City bailout, 289
New York Times, 199–201
NeXT, 13, 15
Nicks, Oran W., 110
Northern Pacific, 292–93
Northern Telecom, 181
nuclear power, 199
Nucor, 138
Nvidia, 223–24
and competition, 137, 234–36
formation of, 227
strategy at, 227–33
Tesla graphics chips, 236
what next?, 236–37

objectives:
bad strategy, 32, 51–57
blue-sky, 54, 56
change itself as, 120
dog's dinner, 53
feasible, 112
goals vs., 52
hierarchies of, 113–15
long-term, 53
proximate, 92, 106–15
Ocean Spray, 174
oil:
energy crisis, 99–100, 108
price of, 204
and property rights, 175–76
Olsen, Ken, 61–62
OPEC, 99
opinion polls, closed circles of, 285
Organization for Economic Co-operation and Development (OECD), 291
Ouchi, Bill, *Making Schools Work,* 81

Paccar, 138–41
Pacific Capital Group, 277
Paine, Thomas, 245
Palmer, Robert, 62
patents, 175
Paulson, Henry M. Jr., 295
Peale, Norman Vincent, 73
Peddie, Jon, 234
Penrose, Edith, 306n6
People Express, 208
Perot, H. Ross, 48
personal mastery, 75
perspective, 179
Peterbilt trucks, 138–39

Petraeus, David, *Army/Marine Corps Counterinsurgency Field Manual,* 3–4
Philadelphia Savings Fund Society (PSFS), 212
pivot points, 101–2
Pixar, 172
PJ (pilot), 114–15
planning, 50–51
Plato, 245
Pol Pot, 211
POM Wonderful, 165, 166, 173–75
Pope, Alexander, 251
Porter, Michael, 153, 163, 280
positive thinking, 58, 73–74, 75, 76
Powell, Michael, 264
power:
  discovery of, 22
  and leverage, 97–105
  sources of, 95–96
Pratt & Whitney, 194
Priem, Curtis, 227
Princeton Project on National Security, 33–34
problem-solution, 269–70
profit:
  gain to operating (GTO), 215–16
  hump chart, 216–17
  streams of, 212
profitability, 169
Project Solarium, 62
property rights, 175–76
Protestant Reformation, 71, 251
proximate objectives, 92, 106–15
  creating options, 111–13
  hierarchies of, 113–15
  resolving ambiguity, 108–11
proxy, inertia by, 212–14
Ptolemaic theory, 245–46

Quake (PC game), 226
Qualcomm, 186–87
quality matching, 117, 120
Qwest, 282

Randolph, Edmund, 97
Rao, Srikumar S., 75–76
Reagan, Ronald, 30, 102
reason, and Enlightenment, 245–47
Reed, John, *Ten Days That Shook the World,* 30
reengineering, 170
Reformation, 71, 251
refutation, 247
Religious Science movement, 73
Republic Steel, 258
Resnick, Lynda, 164–65, 173–75
Resnick, Stewart, 164–68, 173–74
Ricardo, David, 305n7
risk-seeking incentives, 289
RIVA TNT chip, 231, 232
road map, use of term, 228
Roche, James, 29–31
Roll International Corporation, 164–67
Rolls-Royce, 187, 194
Roman Republic, 304n1
Romero, John, 226
Rommel, Erwin, 127
Roosevelt, Franklin D., 93, 294
Rossignolo, Gianmario, 157, 159
routine, inertia of, 203–8
Rowntree, 113
Rutherford, Alan, 151

salience effect, 103
Santos, Joe, 254–55, 256
Saudi Arabia, 36
Saul, king of Israel, 21
Scharmer, C. Otto, 75
Schlesinger, James R., 33
Schultz, Howard, 249–54
Schwarzkopf, Norman, 16–20
science, 241–56
  anomalies in, 248
  and Enlightenment, 245–47
  hypothesis in, 247
  as method, 247
  refutation in, 247
scientific empiricism, 241, 246–47
scientific induction, 254
Scipio, Publius Cornelius, 304n2
Scott, Bruce, 272
SEATO, 82
Segafredo Zanetti, 255
semiconductors, 228
Senge, Peter:
  The Fifth Discipline, 74, 75
  Presence, 75

September 11 attacks, 33–34, 161
Seven & i Holdings, 101
7-Eleven, 101
Shaw, George Bernard, 106
Shell International, 99
Silicon Graphics Inc. (SGI), 224–25
  and competition, 235
  and graphics pipeline, 232, 236
  and triangle bus, 228, 229
simplification, 211
skiing in the fog, 193
Sloan, Alfred, 218–20
Smith, Adam, 245, 251
smooth-sailing fallacy, 289
social herding, 289–90, 298
software:
  advantage of, 184–87
  development cycle of, 187
Sony, 216
Southwest Airlines, 207
Soviet Union, collapse of, 29–31
specie, 292
Sputnik (1957), 106
S. S. Kresge Corporation, 25
Stalin, Joseph, 92
Starbucks:
  anomaly and, 249–50
  capturing proprietary information, 254–56
  and competition, 254–55
  and divergence, 251–52
  formation of, 250
  ill-structured challenge of, 80–81
  testing the hypothesis, 252–54
  vertical integration, 256
stock market, as closed circle, 285
stock prices, and expectations, 281–82, 284
Strategic Defense Initiative, 30
strategic objectives, bad, 32, 51–57
strategic resources, 135–37
strategy:
  basic idea of, 9
  as choice, 62, 64
  coherence of, 9
  corner solution, 273
  create-destroy, 271–73
  entrepreneurial component of, 244
  and growth, 235
  as hypothesis, 241–44, 247
  and judgment, 274–75
  and leadership, 66
  mistaking goals for, 32, 45–51
  misuse of term, 5–7
  nature of, 6–7, 66
  problem-solution, 269–70
  science of, 241–56
  template-style, 58, 64–70
  thinking about, 239–40
  see also bad strategy; good strategy
strategy retreat, 2
supply-chain management, 28
surplus, 304n6
Surveyor moon landing, 108–11
sustainability, 163
Sutherland, Ivan, 224
Swift, Jonathan, 251

tail-risks, 289
Taliban, 161–62
Taylor, Frederick, 259, 260
Teece, David, 272, 273
Tegra system, 236–37
Telecom Italia, 13, 156–59
telecommunications:
  Atlantic cable, 277–81
  Cisco Systems, 182–83, 190–93, 198
  convergence of computing and, 196
  deregulation of, 194–95, 196, 204
  economics of, 279–80
  fat pipes, 279
  Global Crossing, 276, 277–84
  inertia by proxy in, 213–14
  inflection points in, 188–90
  and Internet, 191–92, 198–99
  Italia, 13, 156–59
  Matra, 181–84
Teleflora, 164–65
Texas Air, 207–8
Thatcher, Margaret, 157
thermodynamics, second law of, 202
thought:
  about thinking, 239–40
  anomalies of, 247–49
  hypothesis, 241–44, 247
  techniques, 267–73

3dfx Interactive, 226–27, 228, 229, 234
3-D graphics:
competition in, 234–36
and gamers, 225–27, 236
graphics pipeline, 224–25, 229, 232, 236
and triangle bus, 228, 229
threshold effect, 103
Tinelli, Marco, 119–21, 123
TiVo, 261–67, 269, 270, 273
Tomb Raider (PC game), 227
tools, 268
Toyota, 98–100, 221, 222
Trafalgar, Battle of, 1
transcendentalism, 71
transcontinental railroads, 292–93, 294
transformation, 170
triangle bus, 228, 229
Truman, Harry S., 64, 65, 82, 294
Tupper, Matt, 175
20/20 plan, 45–47, 49

underperformance, 55
United Airlines, 205, 207
United Nations, 35
University of Utah, 224, 229
Unix, 208–9
unwinding, 287
USAir, 207
U.S. Steel, 258

value-creating changes, 169
values, 67–68
vertical integration, 256
Vietnam War, 3, 82, 99
VisiCalc, 227
vision, 65, 67, 74
Voltaire, 245
Volvo, 138
Voodoo (graphics board), 227, 231
Voyager mission, 131, 133

Wachter, Susan, 291
Wack, Pierre, 99–100
Wal-Mart, 23–28
and competition, 24–25, 26, 27, 137
conventional wisdom broken by, 23, 26–27
integrated logistics in, 25
network of, 26–27
Walton, Sam, 23, 28, 31
Warnock, John, 224
War on Drugs, 108
Wattles, Wallace, *The Science of Getting Rich,* 72–73, 74
waves of change:
attractor states in, 198–201
and deregulation, 194–95
discerning the fundamentals of, 184–87
in early stages, 180
exogenous, 178–80
forecasting biases in, 195–97
guideposts for, 193
incumbent responses to, 198
main effects of, 180–81
rising fixed costs, 194
swell of, 181–84
in telecommunications, 188–93
Weber, Max, 65
Web 2.0 business, 4
Welch, Jack, 47, 71
Wells Fargo, 84
Western Electric, 208n, 210, 216
Whole Foods, 52
Williams, Harry, 104–5
winding the crank, 243–44
Winfrey, Oprah, 74
Winnick, Gary, 277, 283
Woodward, Bob, 99
WorldCom, 197, 213, 282, 283
World War I, Passchendaele, 47–49
World War II, centralized direction in, 93
Wozniak, Steve, 74
wrestling the gorilla, 160–61

Xerox, 135–37, 191

Yahoo!, 137, 197
Yeager, William, 191

Zoradi, Mark, 172–73